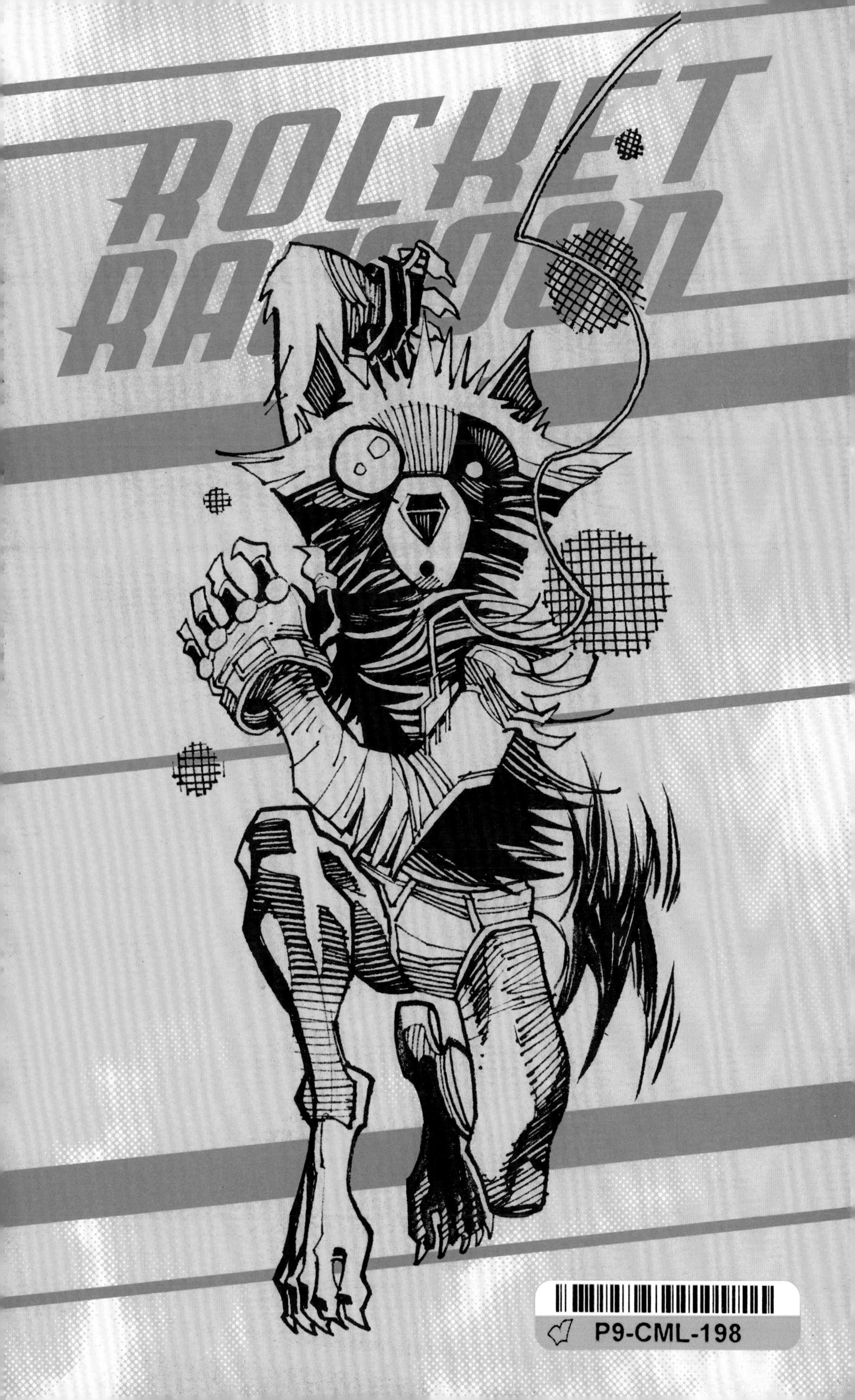
ROCKET

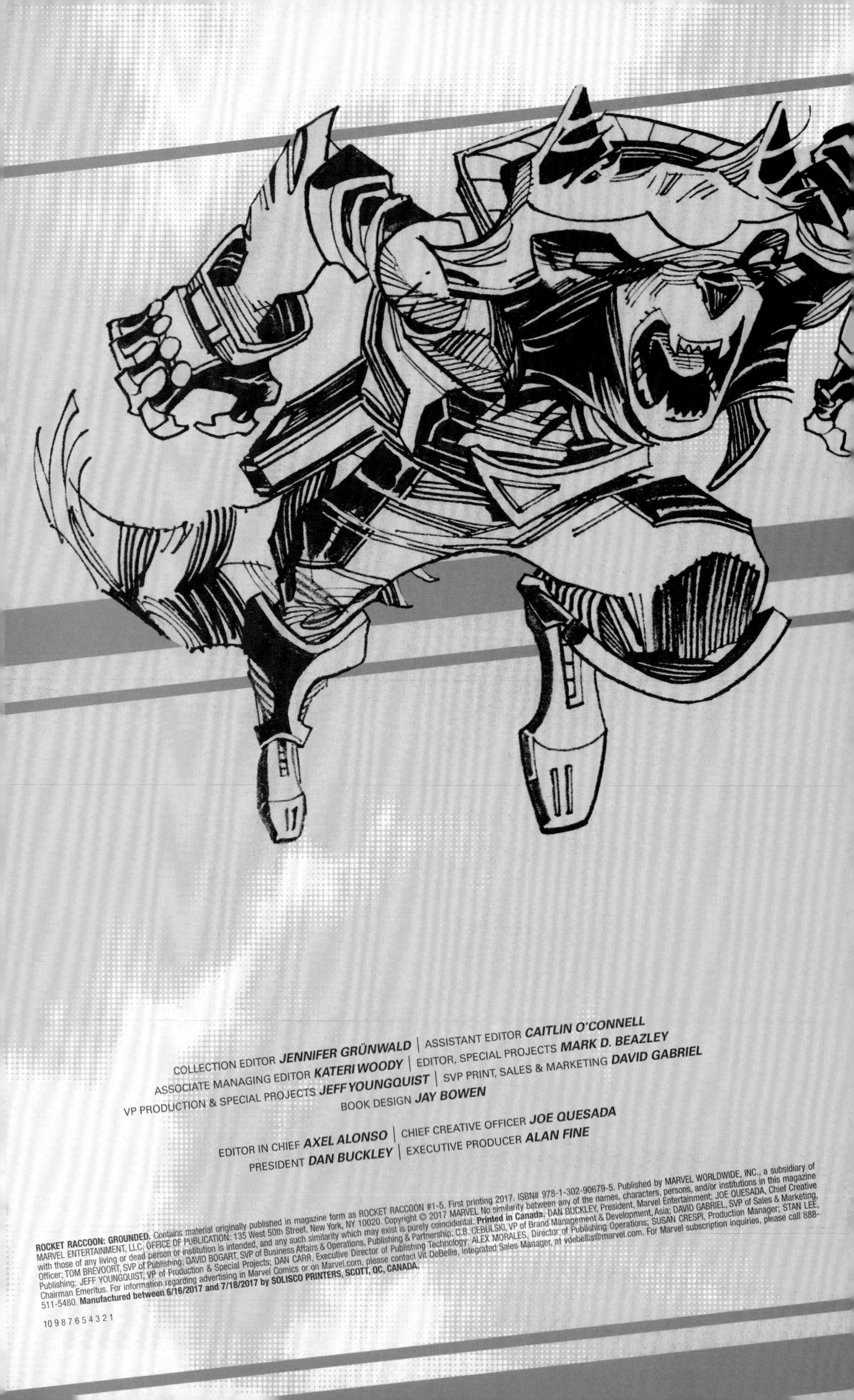

COLLECTION EDITOR **JENNIFER GRÜNWALD** | ASSISTANT EDITOR **CAITLIN O'CONNELL**
ASSOCIATE MANAGING EDITOR **KATERI WOODY** | EDITOR, SPECIAL PROJECTS **MARK D. BEAZLEY**
VP PRODUCTION & SPECIAL PROJECTS **JEFF YOUNGQUIST** | SVP PRINT, SALES & MARKETING **DAVID GABRIEL**
BOOK DESIGN **JAY BOWEN**

EDITOR IN CHIEF **AXEL ALONSO** | CHIEF CREATIVE OFFICER **JOE QUESADA**
PRESIDENT **DAN BUCKLEY** | EXECUTIVE PRODUCER **ALAN FINE**

ROCKET RACCOON: GROUNDED. Contains material originally published in magazine form as ROCKET RACCOON #1-5. First printing 2017. ISBN# 978-1-302-90679-5. Published by MARVEL WORLDWIDE, INC., a subsidiary of MARVEL ENTERTAINMENT, LLC. OFFICE OF PUBLICATION: 135 West 50th Street, New York, NY 10020. Copyright © 2017 MARVEL No similarity between any of the names, characters, persons, and/or institutions in this magazine with those of any living or dead person or institution is intended, and any such similarity which may exist is purely coincidental. **Printed in Canada.** DAN BUCKLEY, President, Marvel Entertainment; JOE QUESADA, Chief Creative Officer; TOM BREVOORT, SVP of Publishing; DAVID BOGART, SVP of Business Affairs & Operations, Publishing & Partnership; C.B. CEBULSKI, VP of Brand Management & Development, Asia; DAVID GABRIEL, SVP of Sales & Marketing, Publishing; JEFF YOUNGQUIST, VP of Production & Special Projects; DAN CARR, Executive Director of Publishing Technology; ALEX MORALES, Director of Publishing Operations; SUSAN CRESPI, Production Manager; STAN LEE, Chairman Emeritus. For information regarding advertising in Marvel Comics or on Marvel.com, please contact Vit DeBellis, Integrated Sales Manager, at vdebellis@marvel.com. For Marvel subscription inquiries, please call 888-511-5480. **Manufactured between 6/16/2017 and 7/18/2017 by SOLISCO PRINTERS, SCOTT, QC, CANADA.**

10 9 8 7 6 5 4 3 2 1

ROCKET RACCOON

GROUNDED

MATTHEW ROSENBERG
WRITER

JORGE COELHO
ARTIST

ANTONIO FABELA WITH
MARCIO MENYZ (#4) **& RAIN BEREDO** (#5)
COLOR ARTISTS

JEFF ECKLEBERRY
LETTERER

DAVID NAKAYAMA
COVER

KATHLEEN WISNESKI
ASSISTANT EDITOR

DARREN SHAN
EDITOR

JORDAN D. WHITE
CONSULTING EDITOR

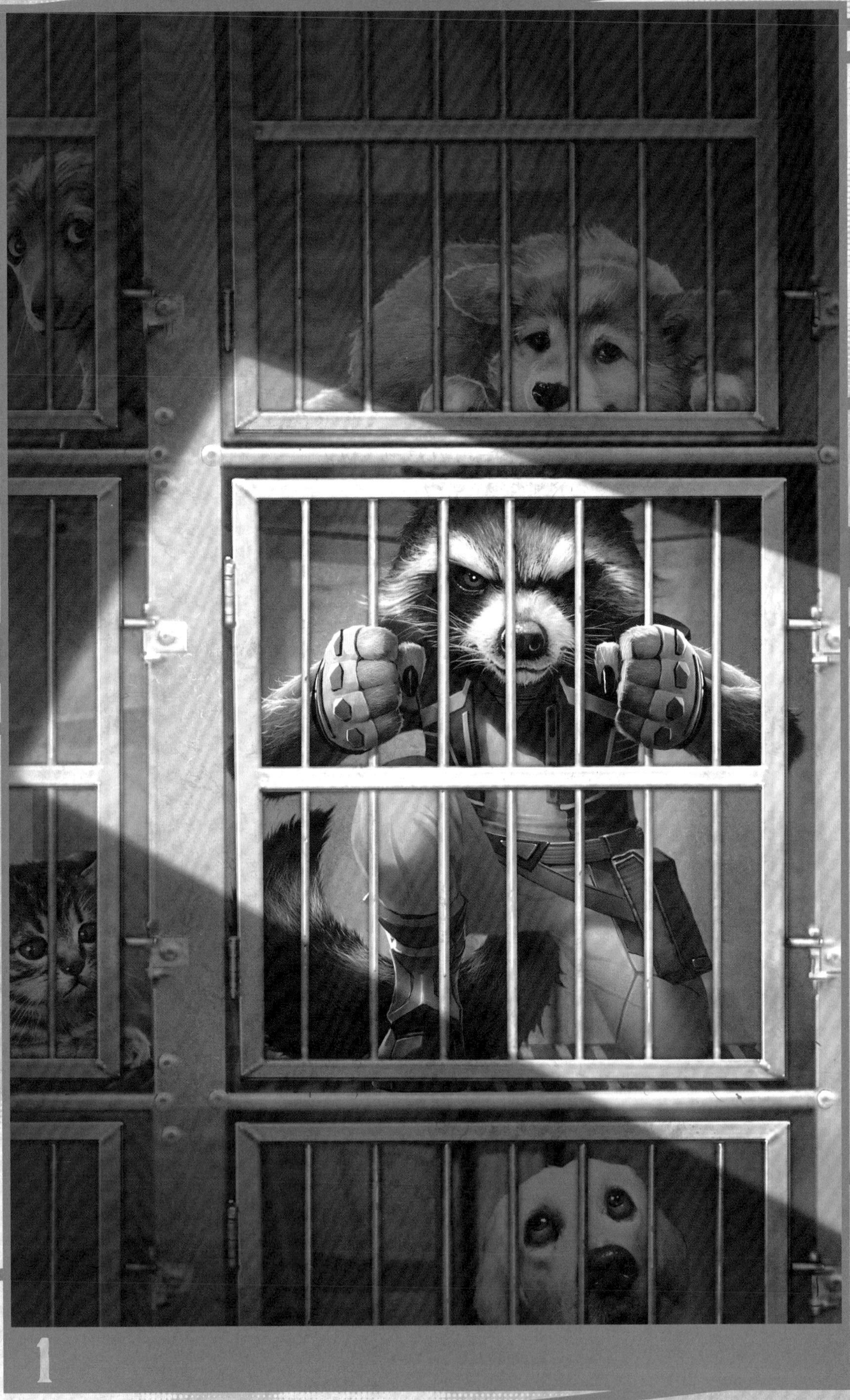
1

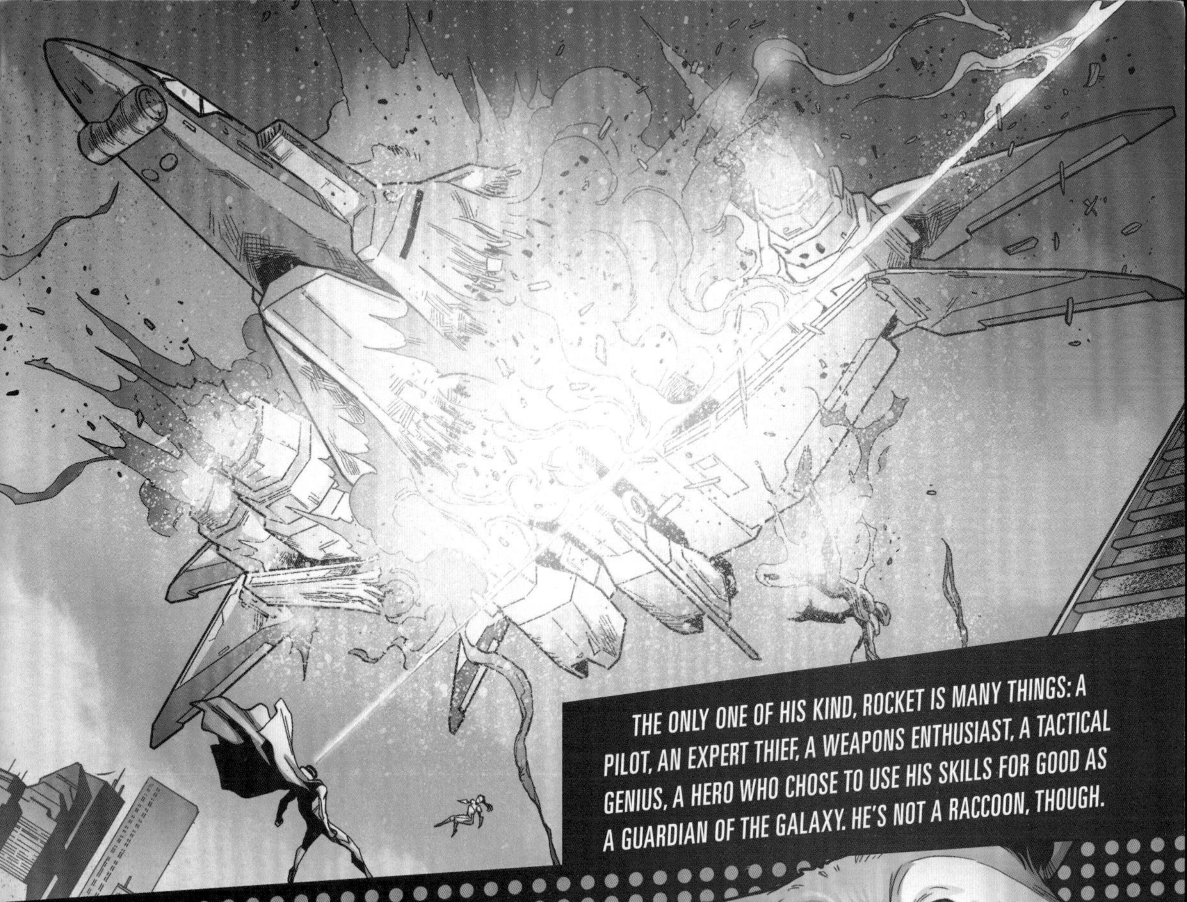

THE ONLY ONE OF HIS KIND, ROCKET IS MANY THINGS: A PILOT, AN EXPERT THIEF, A WEAPONS ENTHUSIAST, A TACTICAL GENIUS, A HERO WHO CHOSE TO USE HIS SKILLS FOR GOOD AS A GUARDIAN OF THE GALAXY. HE'S NOT A RACCOON, THOUGH.

ROCKET RACCOON

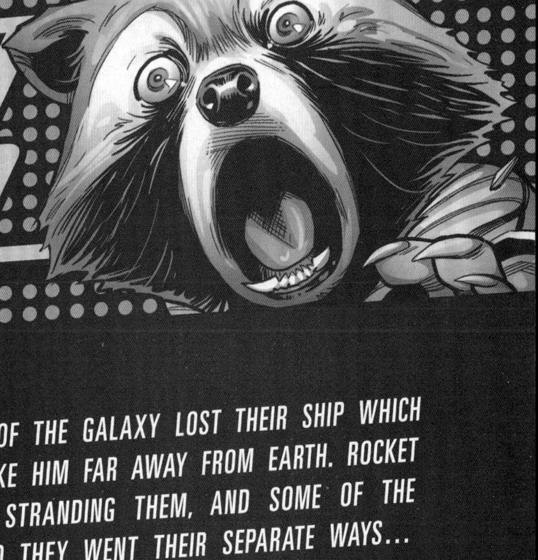

IN A CATACLYSMIC BATTLE ON EARTH, THE GUARDIANS OF THE GALAXY LOST THEIR SHIP WHICH ROCKET LOVED DEEPLY, IN PART FOR ITS ABILITY TO TAKE HIM FAR AWAY FROM EARTH. ROCKET BLAMED THE GUARDIANS' LEADER, PETER QUILL, FOR STRANDING THEM, AND SOME OF THE OTHERS WERE MAD ABOUT LESS IMPORTANT THINGS. SO THEY WENT THEIR SEPARATE WAYS...

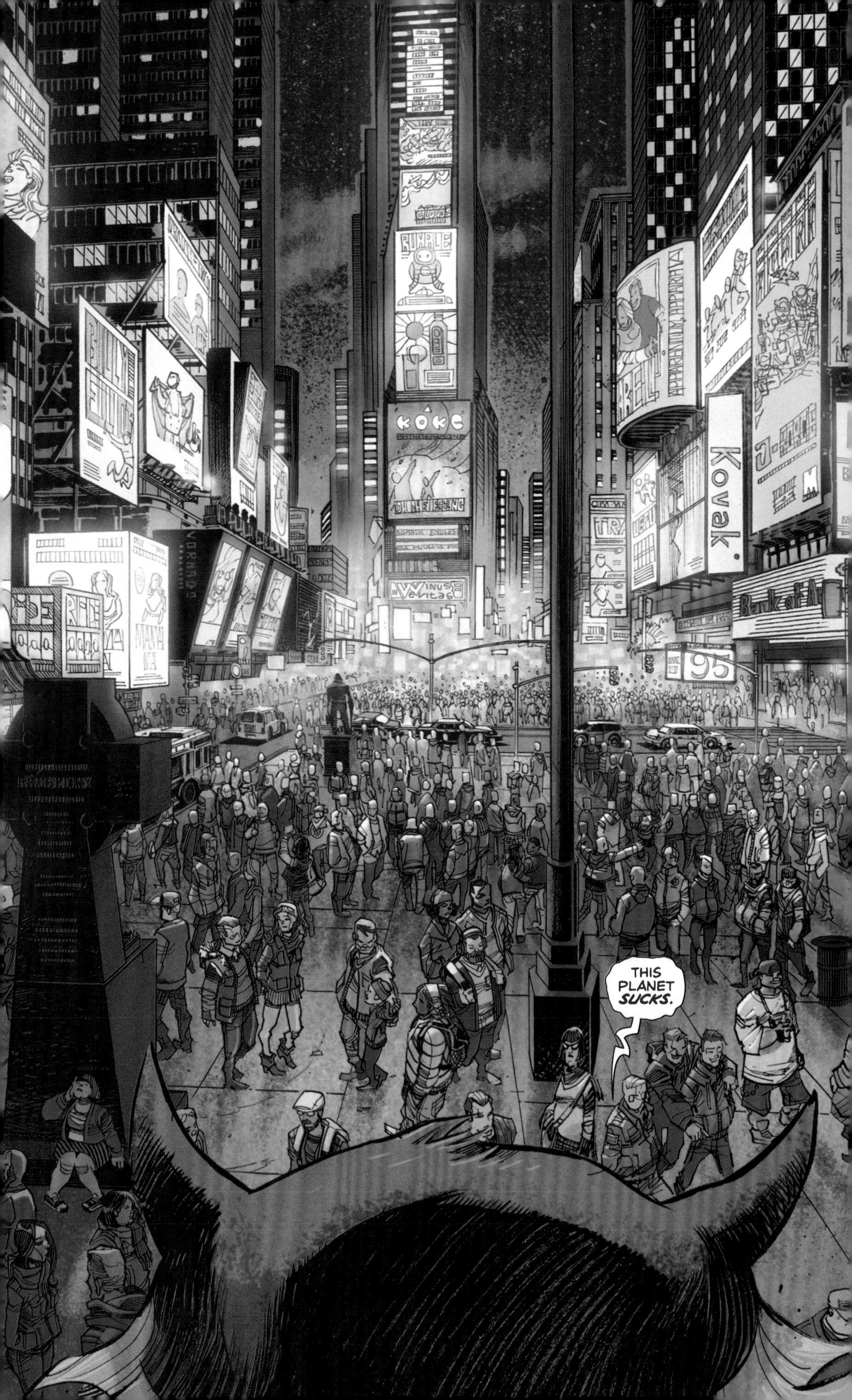
THIS PLANET *SUCKS.*
Kovak
95

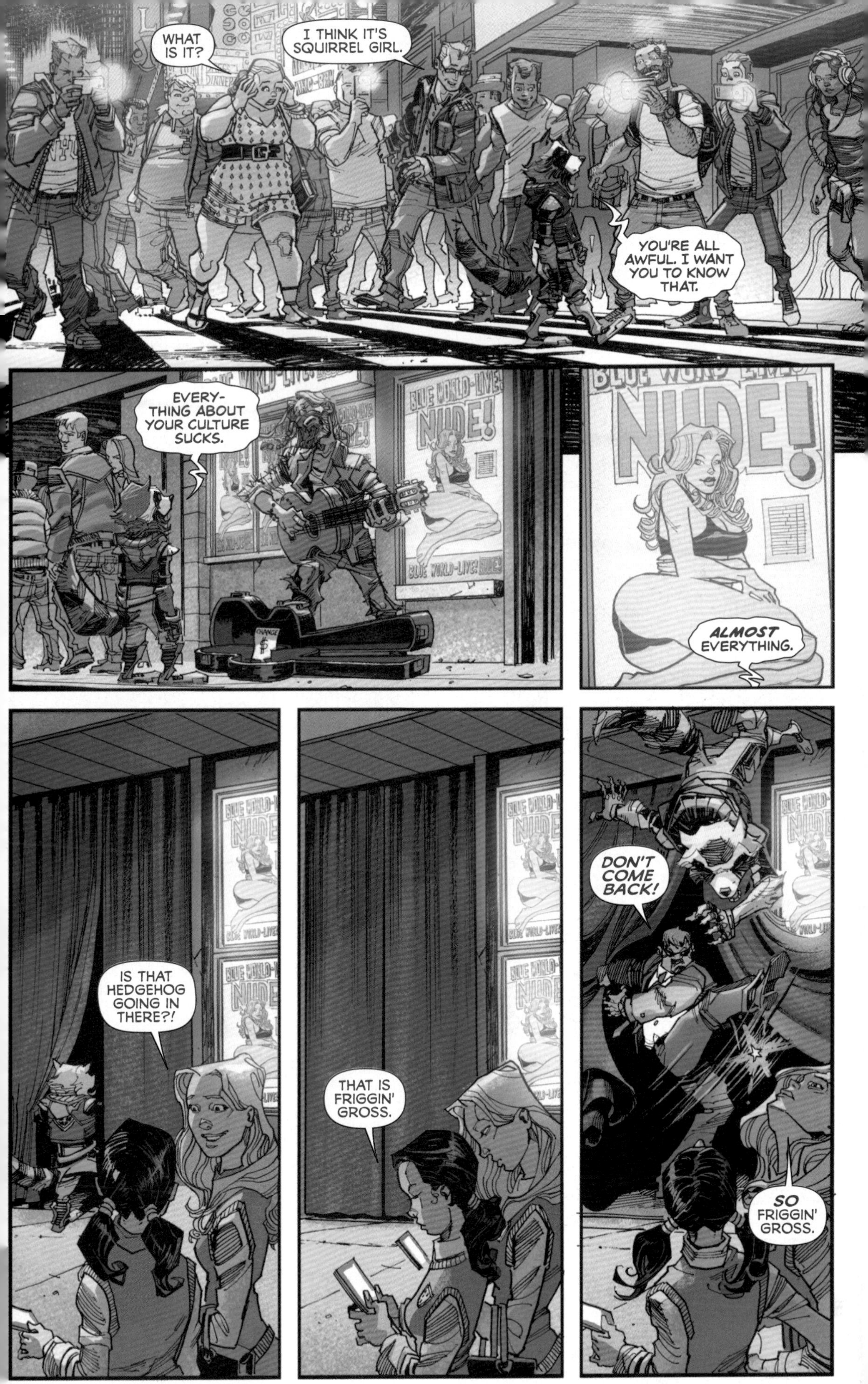
WHAT IS IT?
I THINK IT'S SQUIRREL GIRL.
YOU'RE ALL AWFUL. I WANT YOU TO KNOW THAT.
EVERY-THING ABOUT YOUR CULTURE SUCKS.
BLUE WORLD-LIVE! NUDE!
ALMOST EVERYTHING.
IS THAT HEDGEHOG GOING IN THERE?!
THAT IS FRIGGIN' GROSS.
DON'T COME BACK!
SO FRIGGIN' GROSS.

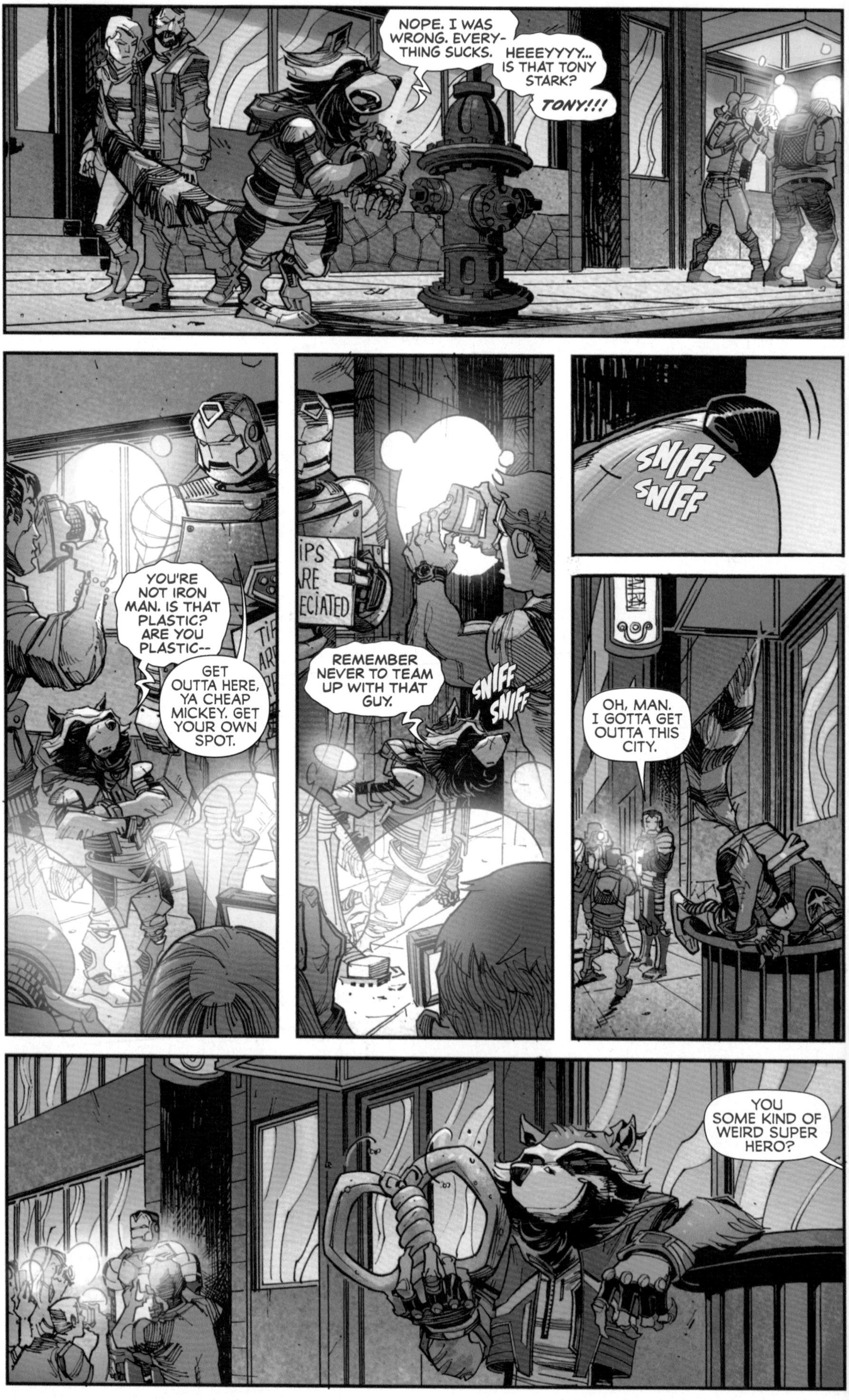
NOPE. I WAS WRONG. EVERYTHING SUCKS.
HEEEYYYY... IS THAT TONY STARK?
TONY!!!
YOU'RE NOT IRON MAN. IS THAT PLASTIC? ARE YOU PLASTIC--
GET OUTTA HERE, YA CHEAP MICKEY. GET YOUR OWN SPOT.
REMEMBER NEVER TO TEAM UP WITH THAT GUY.
SNIFF SNIFF
SNIFF SNIFF
OH, MAN. I GOTTA GET OUTTA THIS CITY.
YOU SOME KIND OF WEIRD SUPER HERO?

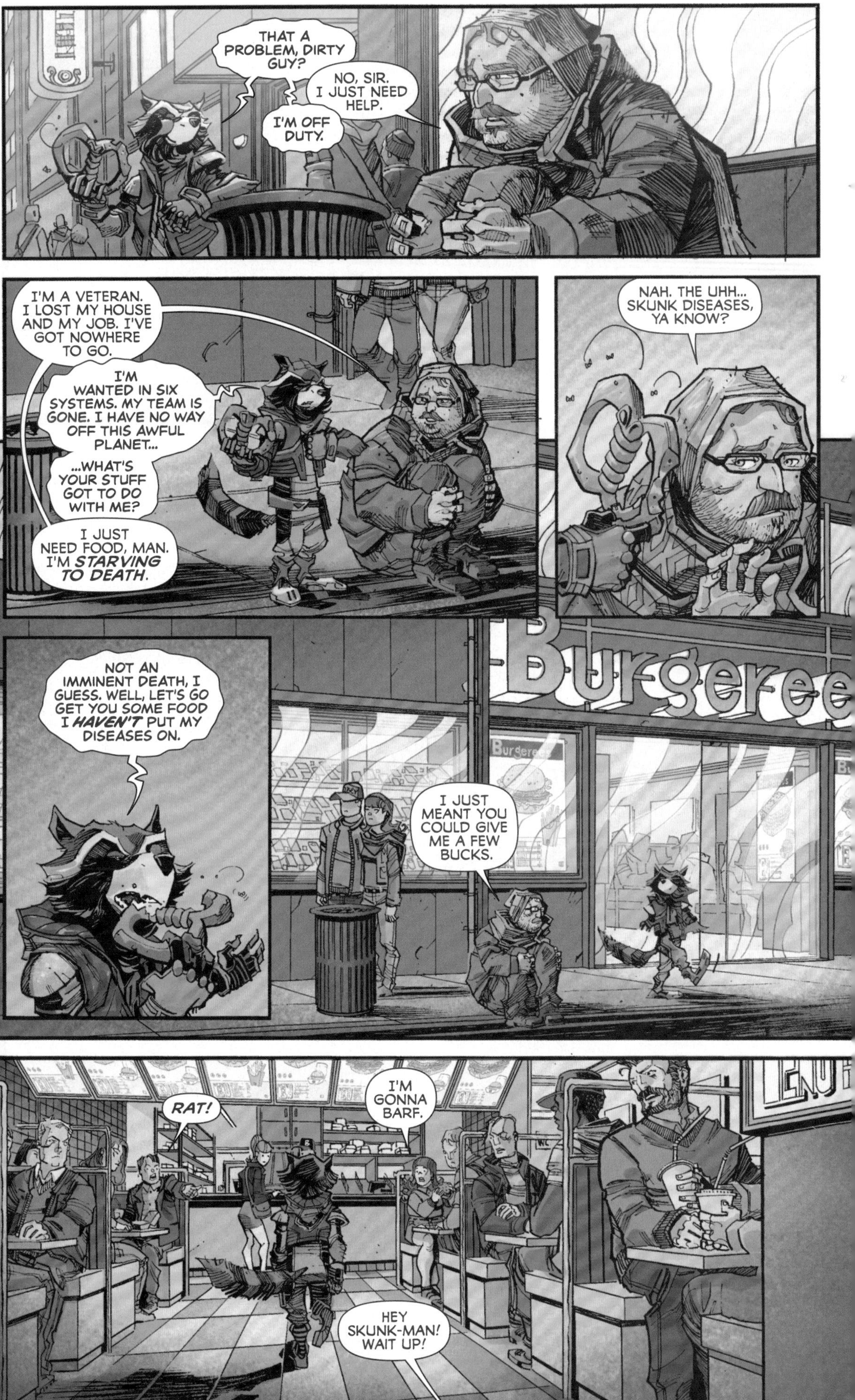
THAT A PROBLEM, DIRTY GUY?
NO, SIR. I JUST NEED HELP.
I'M OFF DUTY.
I'M A VETERAN. I LOST MY HOUSE AND MY JOB. I'VE GOT NOWHERE TO GO.
I'M WANTED IN SIX SYSTEMS. MY TEAM IS GONE. I HAVE NO WAY OFF THIS AWFUL PLANET...
...WHAT'S YOUR STUFF GOT TO DO WITH ME?
I JUST NEED FOOD, MAN. I'M STARVING TO DEATH.
NAH. THE UHH... SKUNK DISEASES, YA KNOW?
Burgeree
NOT AN IMMINENT DEATH, I GUESS. WELL, LET'S GO GET YOU SOME FOOD I HAVEN'T PUT MY DISEASES ON.
I JUST MEANT YOU COULD GIVE ME A FEW BUCKS.
RAT!
I'M GONNA BARF.
HEY SKUNK-MAN! WAIT UP!

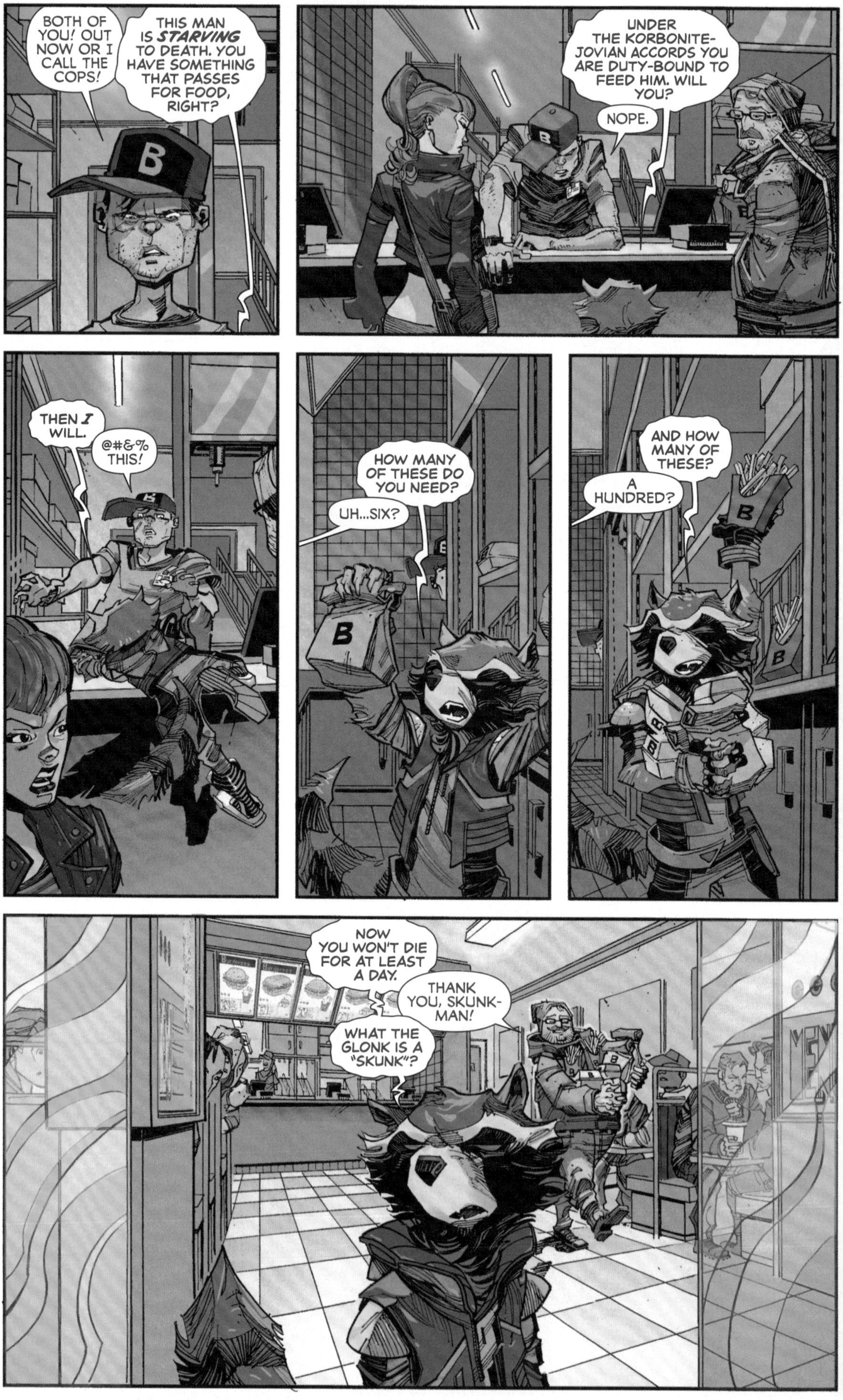
BOTH OF YOU! OUT NOW OR I CALL THE COPS!
THIS MAN IS STARVING TO DEATH. YOU HAVE SOMETHING THAT PASSES FOR FOOD, RIGHT?
UNDER THE KORBONITE-JOVIAN ACCORDS YOU ARE DUTY-BOUND TO FEED HIM. WILL YOU?
NOPE.
THEN I WILL.
@#&% THIS!
HOW MANY OF THESE DO YOU NEED?
UH...SIX?
AND HOW MANY OF THESE?
A HUNDRED?
NOW YOU WON'T DIE FOR AT LEAST A DAY.
THANK YOU, SKUNK-MAN!
WHAT THE GLONK IS A "SKUNK"?

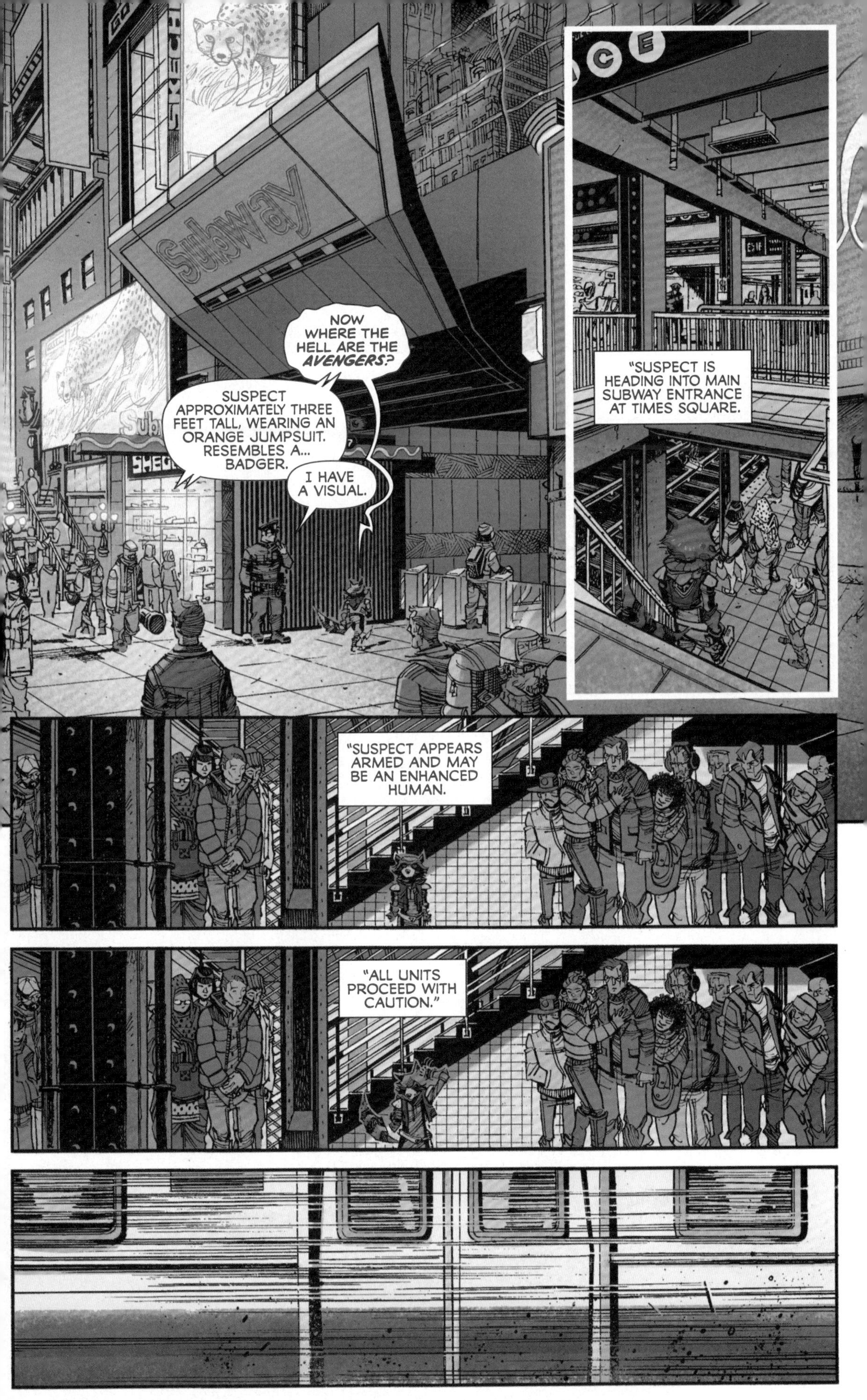
SUBWAY
NOW WHERE THE HELL ARE THE *AVENGERS?*
SUSPECT APPROXIMATELY THREE FEET TALL, WEARING AN ORANGE JUMPSUIT. RESEMBLES A... BADGER.
I HAVE A VISUAL.
"SUSPECT IS HEADING INTO MAIN SUBWAY ENTRANCE AT TIMES SQUARE.
"SUSPECT APPEARS ARMED AND MAY BE AN ENHANCED HUMAN.
"ALL UNITS PROCEED WITH CAUTION."

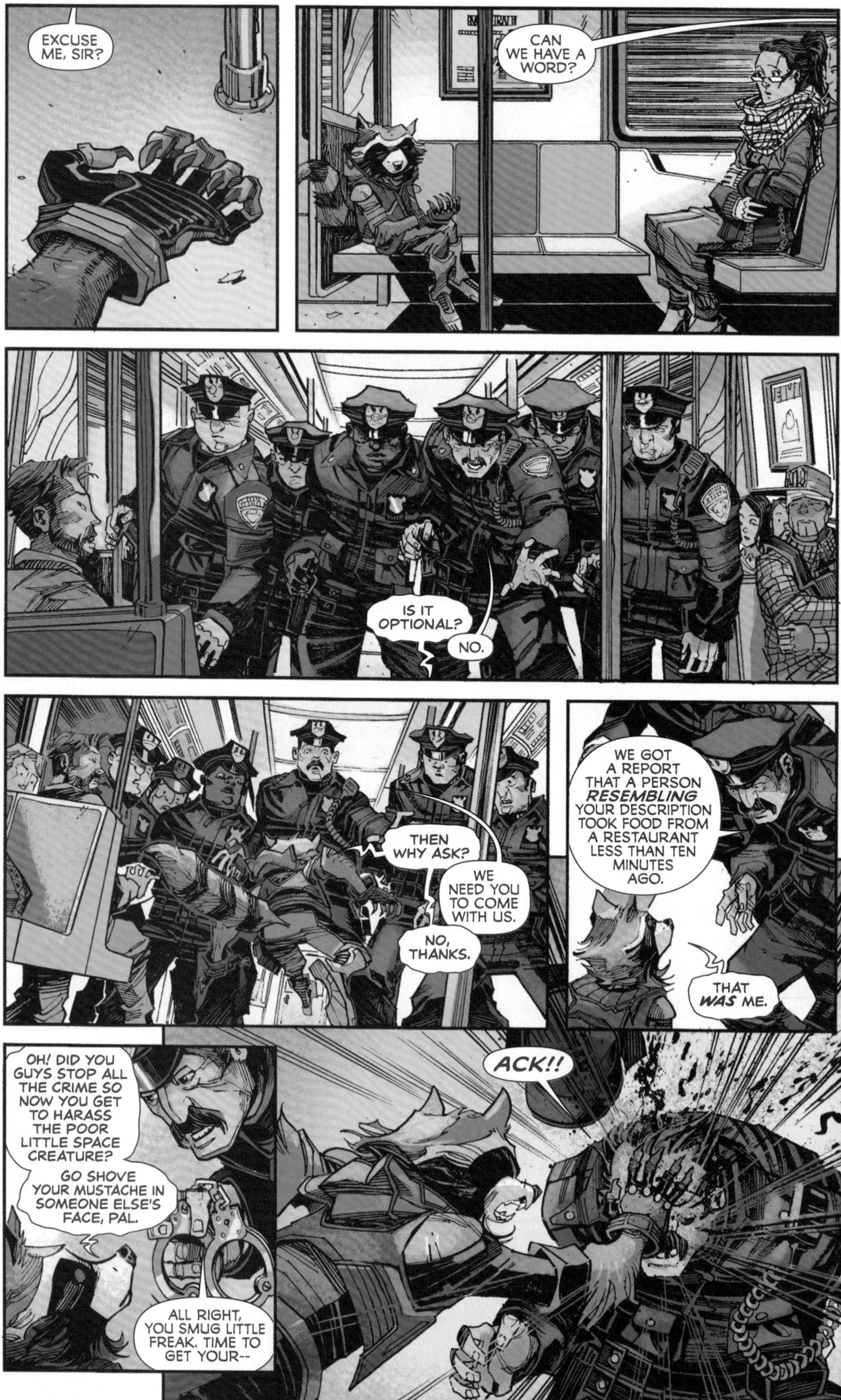
EXCUSE ME, SIR?
CAN WE HAVE A WORD?
IS IT OPTIONAL?
NO.
THEN WHY ASK?
WE NEED YOU TO COME WITH US.
NO, THANKS.
WE GOT A REPORT THAT A PERSON *RESEMBLING* YOUR DESCRIPTION TOOK FOOD FROM A RESTAURANT LESS THAN TEN MINUTES AGO.
THAT *WAS* ME.
OH! DID YOU GUYS STOP ALL THE CRIME SO NOW YOU GET TO HARASS THE POOR LITTLE SPACE CREATURE?
GO SHOVE YOUR MUSTACHE IN SOMEONE ELSE'S FACE, PAL.
ALL RIGHT, YOU SMUG LITTLE FREAK. TIME TO GET YOUR--
ACK!!

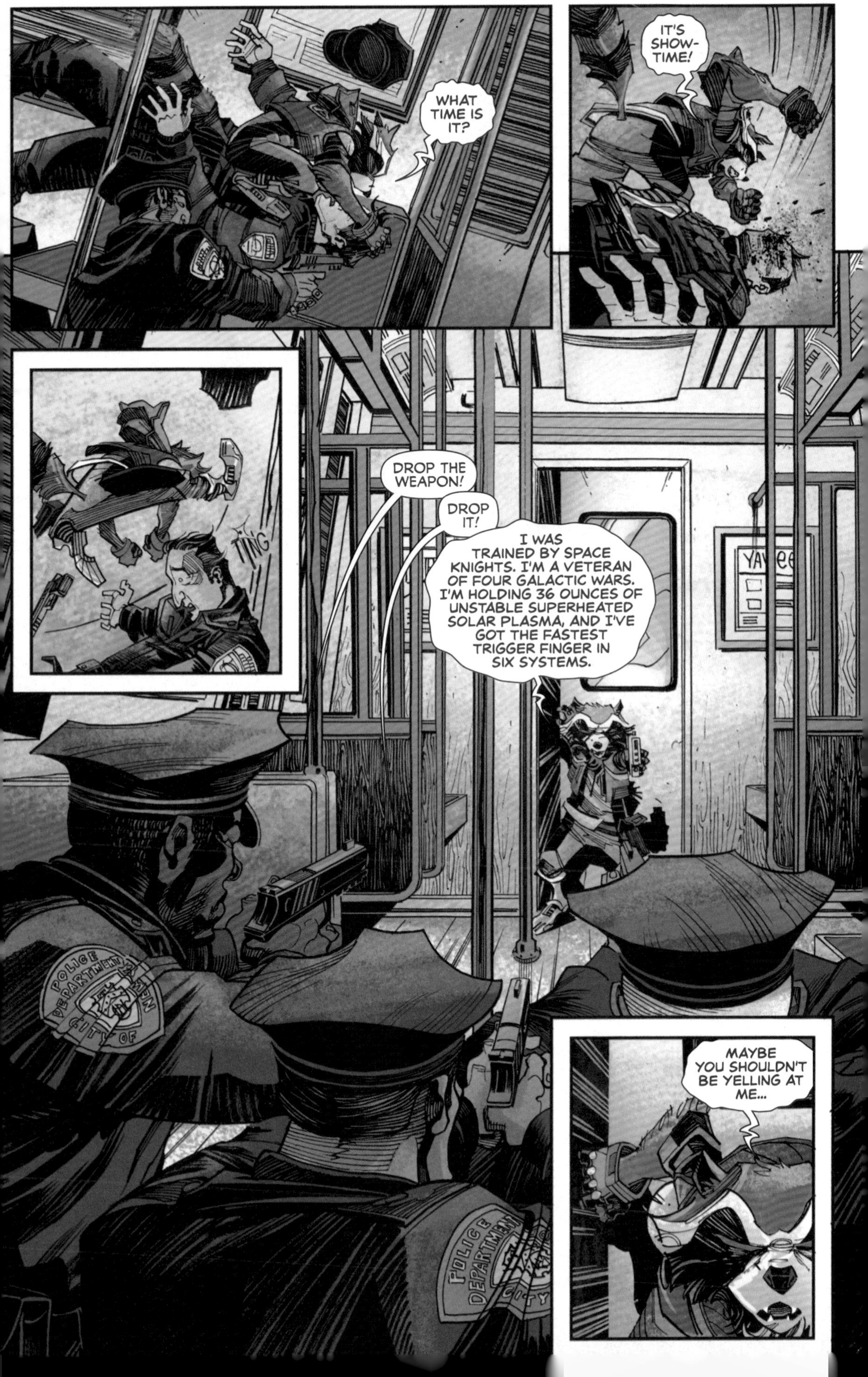
WHAT TIME IS IT?
IT'S SHOW-TIME!
FING
DROP THE WEAPON!
DROP IT!
I WAS TRAINED BY SPACE KNIGHTS. I'M A VETERAN OF FOUR GALACTIC WARS. I'M HOLDING 36 OUNCES OF UNSTABLE SUPERHEATED SOLAR PLASMA, AND I'VE GOT THE FASTEST TRIGGER FINGER IN SIX SYSTEMS.
MAYBE YOU SHOULDN'T BE YELLING AT ME...

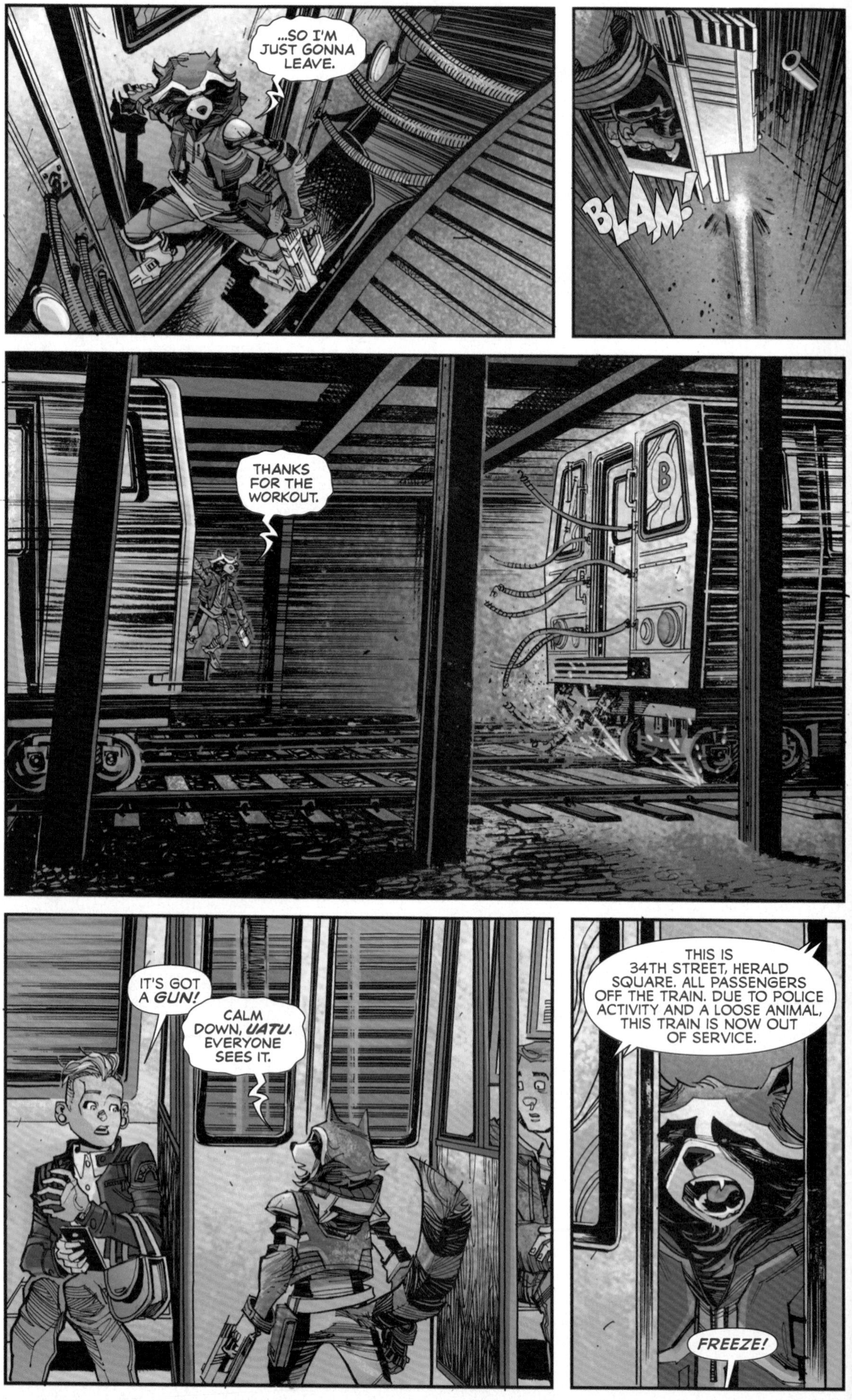
...SO I'M JUST GONNA LEAVE.
BLAM!
THANKS FOR THE WORKOUT.
B
IT'S GOT A *GUN!*
CALM DOWN, *UATU*. EVERYONE SEES IT.
THIS IS 34TH STREET, HERALD SQUARE. ALL PASSENGERS OFF THE TRAIN. DUE TO POLICE ACTIVITY AND A LOOSE ANIMAL, THIS TRAIN IS NOW OUT OF SERVICE.
FREEZE!

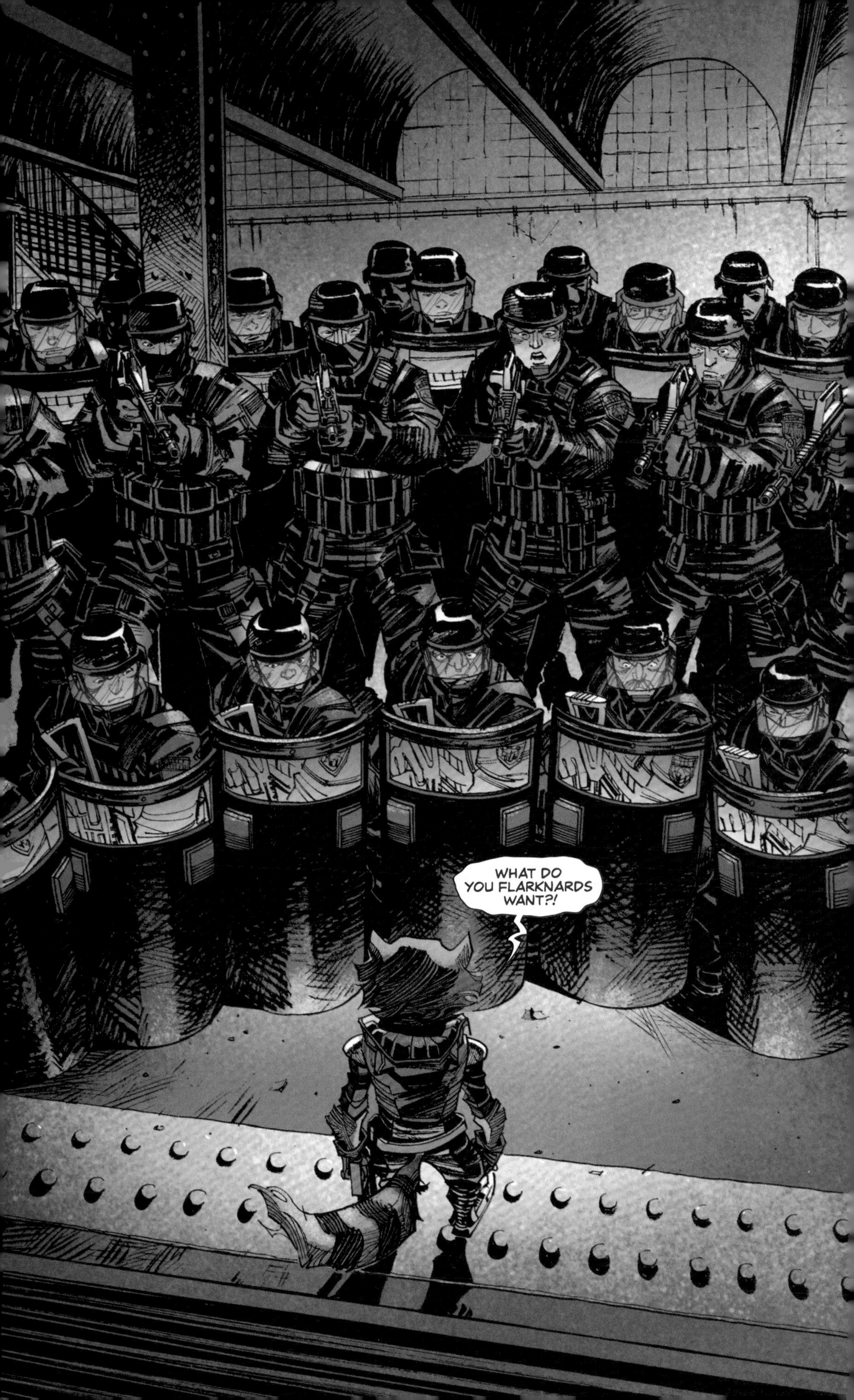
WHAT DO YOU FLARKNARDS WANT?!

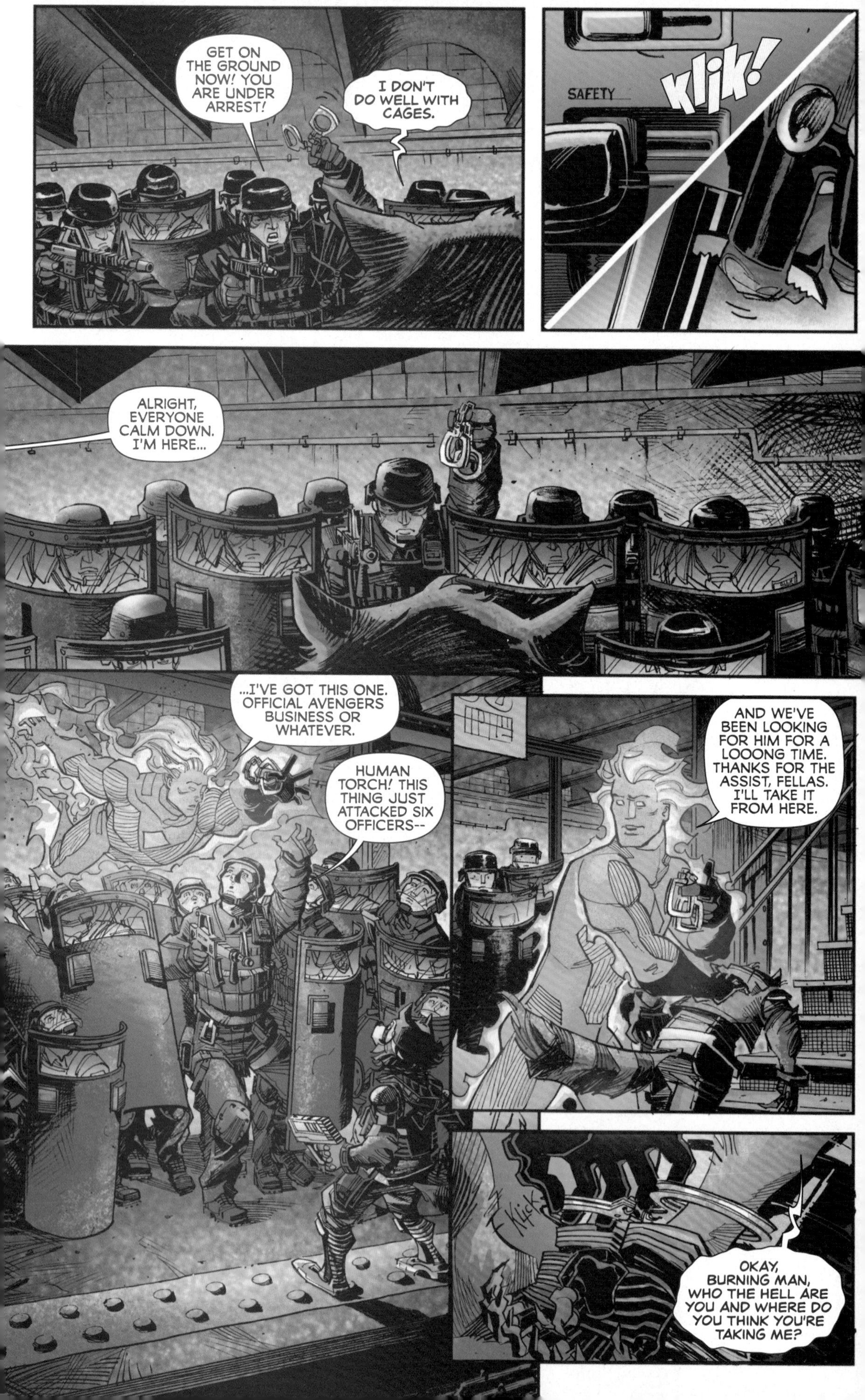
GET ON THE GROUND NOW! YOU ARE UNDER ARREST!
I DON'T DO WELL WITH CAGES.
SAFETY
KLIK!
ALRIGHT, EVERYONE CALM DOWN. I'M HERE...
...I'VE GOT THIS ONE. OFFICIAL AVENGERS BUSINESS OR WHATEVER.
HUMAN TORCH! THIS THING JUST ATTACKED SIX OFFICERS--
AND WE'VE BEEN LOOKING FOR HIM FOR A LOOONG TIME. THANKS FOR THE ASSIST, FELLAS. I'LL TAKE IT FROM HERE.
KLICK
OKAY, BURNING MAN, WHO THE HELL ARE YOU AND WHERE DO YOU THINK YOU'RE TAKING ME?

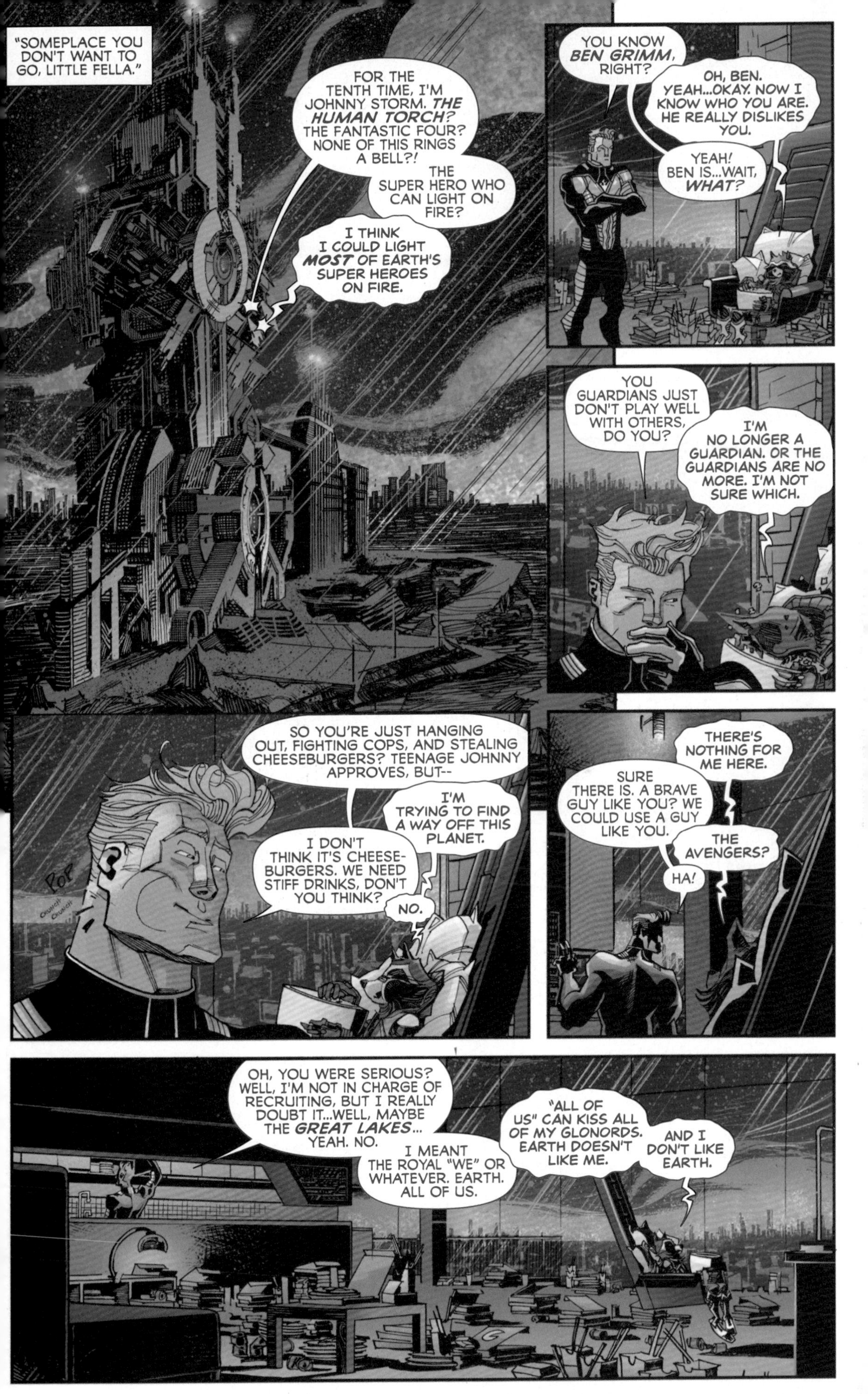
"SOMEPLACE YOU DON'T WANT TO GO, LITTLE FELLA."
FOR THE TENTH TIME, I'M JOHNNY STORM. THE HUMAN TORCH? THE FANTASTIC FOUR? NONE OF THIS RINGS A BELL?!
THE SUPER HERO WHO CAN LIGHT ON FIRE?
I THINK I COULD LIGHT MOST OF EARTH'S SUPER HEROES ON FIRE.
YOU KNOW BEN GRIMM, RIGHT?
OH, BEN. YEAH...OKAY. NOW I KNOW WHO YOU ARE. HE REALLY DISLIKES YOU.
YEAH! BEN IS...WAIT, WHAT?
YOU GUARDIANS JUST DON'T PLAY WELL WITH OTHERS, DO YOU?
I'M NO LONGER A GUARDIAN. OR THE GUARDIANS ARE NO MORE. I'M NOT SURE WHICH.
SO YOU'RE JUST HANGING OUT, FIGHTING COPS, AND STEALING CHEESEBURGERS? TEENAGE JOHNNY APPROVES, BUT--
I'M TRYING TO FIND A WAY OFF THIS PLANET.
I DON'T THINK IT'S CHEESE-BURGERS. WE NEED STIFF DRINKS, DON'T YOU THINK?
NO.
POP
CRUNCH CRUNCH
THERE'S NOTHING FOR ME HERE.
SURE THERE IS. A BRAVE GUY LIKE YOU? WE COULD USE A GUY LIKE YOU.
THE AVENGERS?
HA!
OH, YOU WERE SERIOUS? WELL, I'M NOT IN CHARGE OF RECRUITING, BUT I REALLY DOUBT IT...WELL, MAYBE THE GREAT LAKES... YEAH. NO.
I MEANT THE ROYAL "WE" OR WHATEVER. EARTH. ALL OF US.
"ALL OF US" CAN KISS ALL OF MY GLONORDS. EARTH DOESN'T LIKE ME.
AND I DON'T LIKE EARTH.

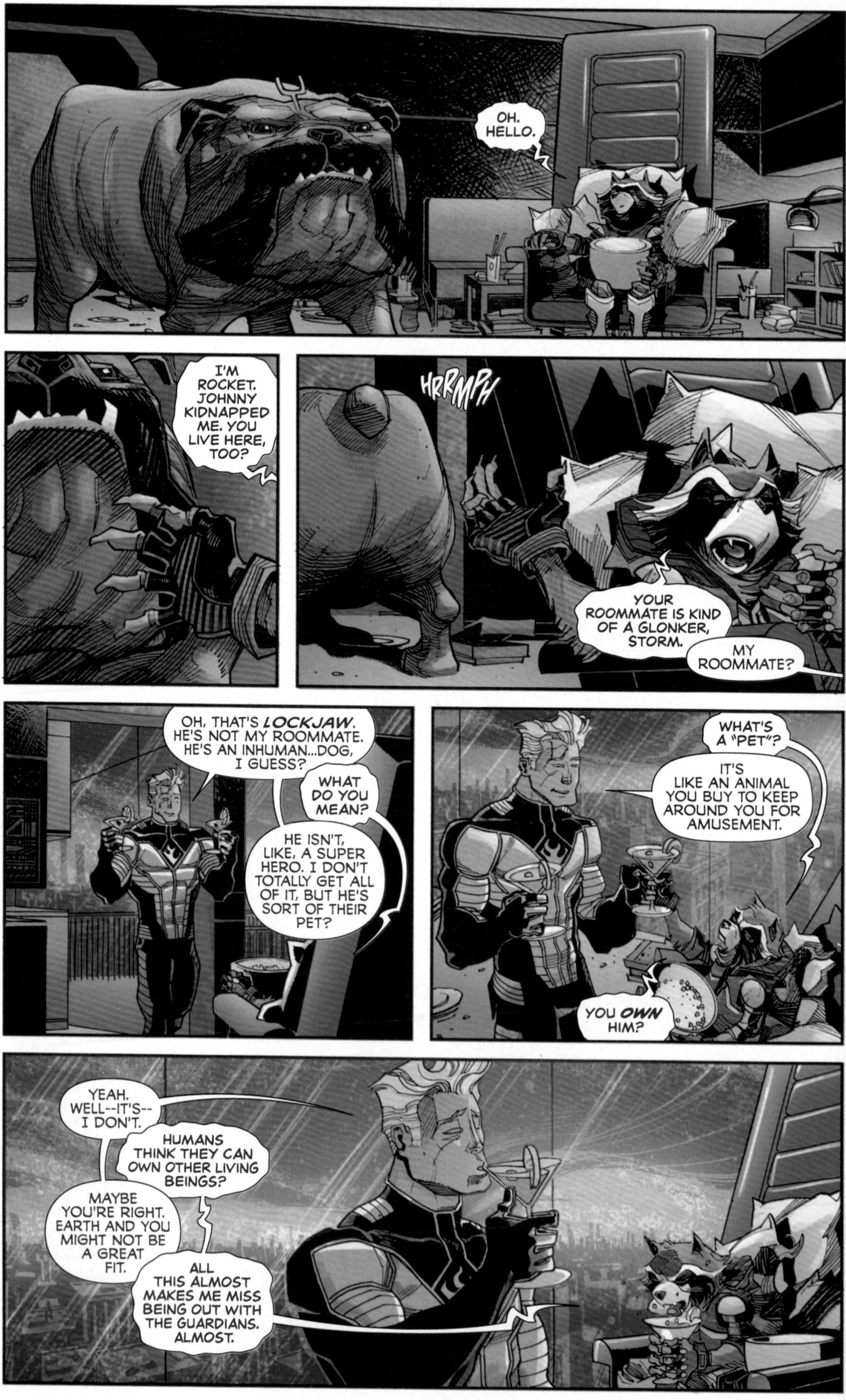
OH. HELLO.
I'M ROCKET. JOHNNY KIDNAPPED ME. YOU LIVE HERE, TOO?
HRRMPH
YOUR ROOMMATE IS KIND OF A GLONKER, STORM.
MY ROOMMATE?
OH, THAT'S LOCKJAW. HE'S NOT MY ROOMMATE. HE'S AN INHUMAN...DOG, I GUESS?
WHAT DO YOU MEAN?
HE ISN'T, LIKE, A SUPER HERO. I DON'T TOTALLY GET ALL OF IT, BUT HE'S SORT OF THEIR PET?
WHAT'S A "PET"?
IT'S LIKE AN ANIMAL YOU BUY TO KEEP AROUND YOU FOR AMUSEMENT.
YOU OWN HIM?
YEAH. WELL--IT'S-- I DON'T.
HUMANS THINK THEY CAN OWN OTHER LIVING BEINGS?
MAYBE YOU'RE RIGHT. EARTH AND YOU MIGHT NOT BE A GREAT FIT.
ALL THIS ALMOST MAKES ME MISS BEING OUT WITH THE GUARDIANS. ALMOST.

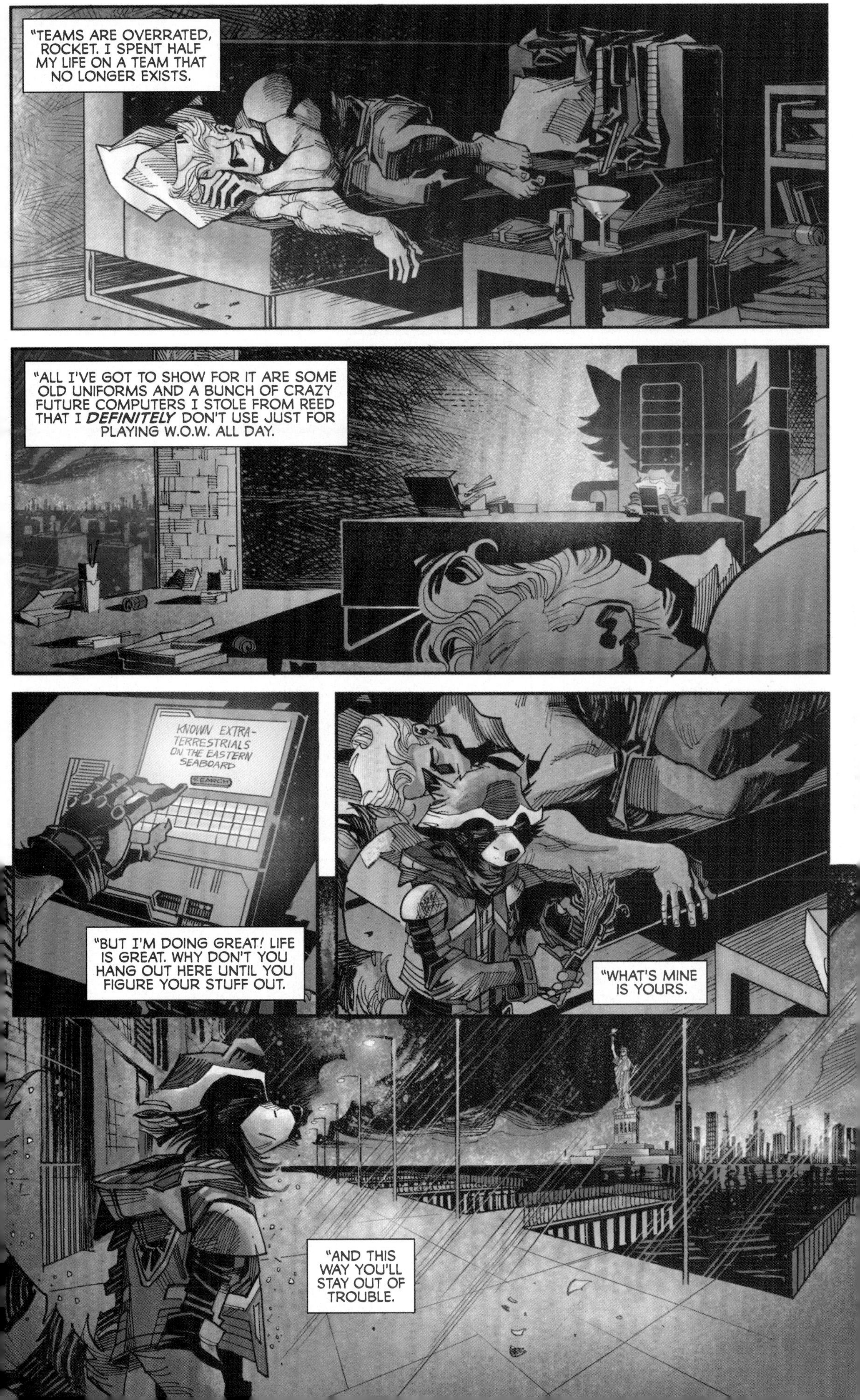
"TEAMS ARE OVERRATED, ROCKET. I SPENT HALF MY LIFE ON A TEAM THAT NO LONGER EXISTS.
"ALL I'VE GOT TO SHOW FOR IT ARE SOME OLD UNIFORMS AND A BUNCH OF CRAZY FUTURE COMPUTERS I STOLE FROM REED THAT I *DEFINITELY* DON'T USE JUST FOR PLAYING W.O.W. ALL DAY.
KNOWN EXTRA-TERRESTRIALS ON THE EASTERN SEABOARD
SEARCH
"BUT I'M DOING GREAT! LIFE IS GREAT. WHY DON'T YOU HANG OUT HERE UNTIL YOU FIGURE YOUR STUFF OUT.
"WHAT'S MINE IS YOURS.
"AND THIS WAY YOU'LL STAY OUT OF TROUBLE.

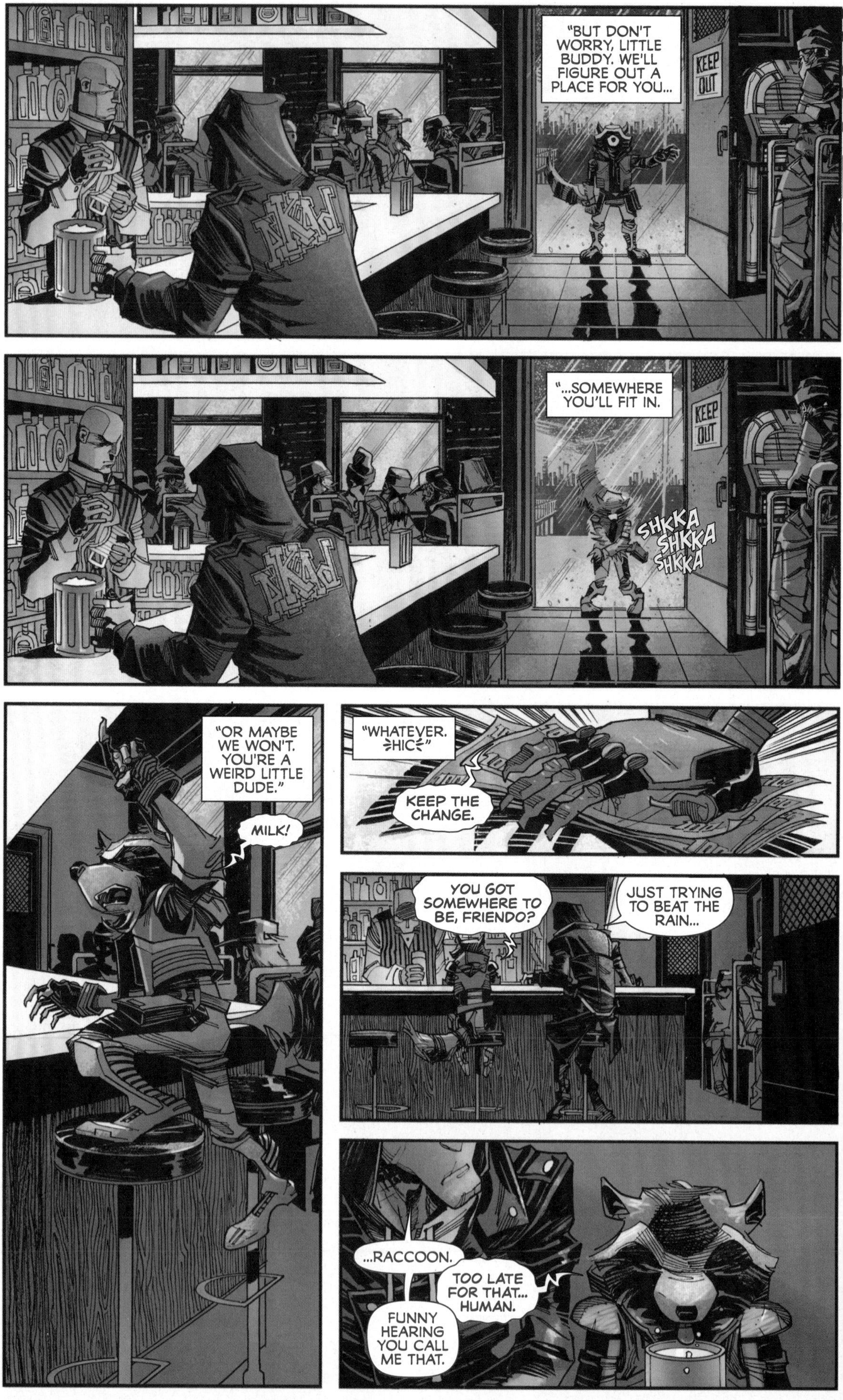
"BUT DON'T WORRY, LITTLE BUDDY. WE'LL FIGURE OUT A PLACE FOR YOU...
KEEP OUT
"...SOMEWHERE YOU'LL FIT IN.
KEEP OUT
SHKKA SHKKA SHKKA
"OR MAYBE WE WON'T. YOU'RE A WEIRD LITTLE DUDE."
MILK!
"WHATEVER. HIC"
KEEP THE CHANGE.
YOU GOT SOMEWHERE TO BE, FRIENDO?
JUST TRYING TO BEAT THE RAIN...
...RACCOON.
TOO LATE FOR THAT... HUMAN.
FUNNY HEARING YOU CALL ME THAT.

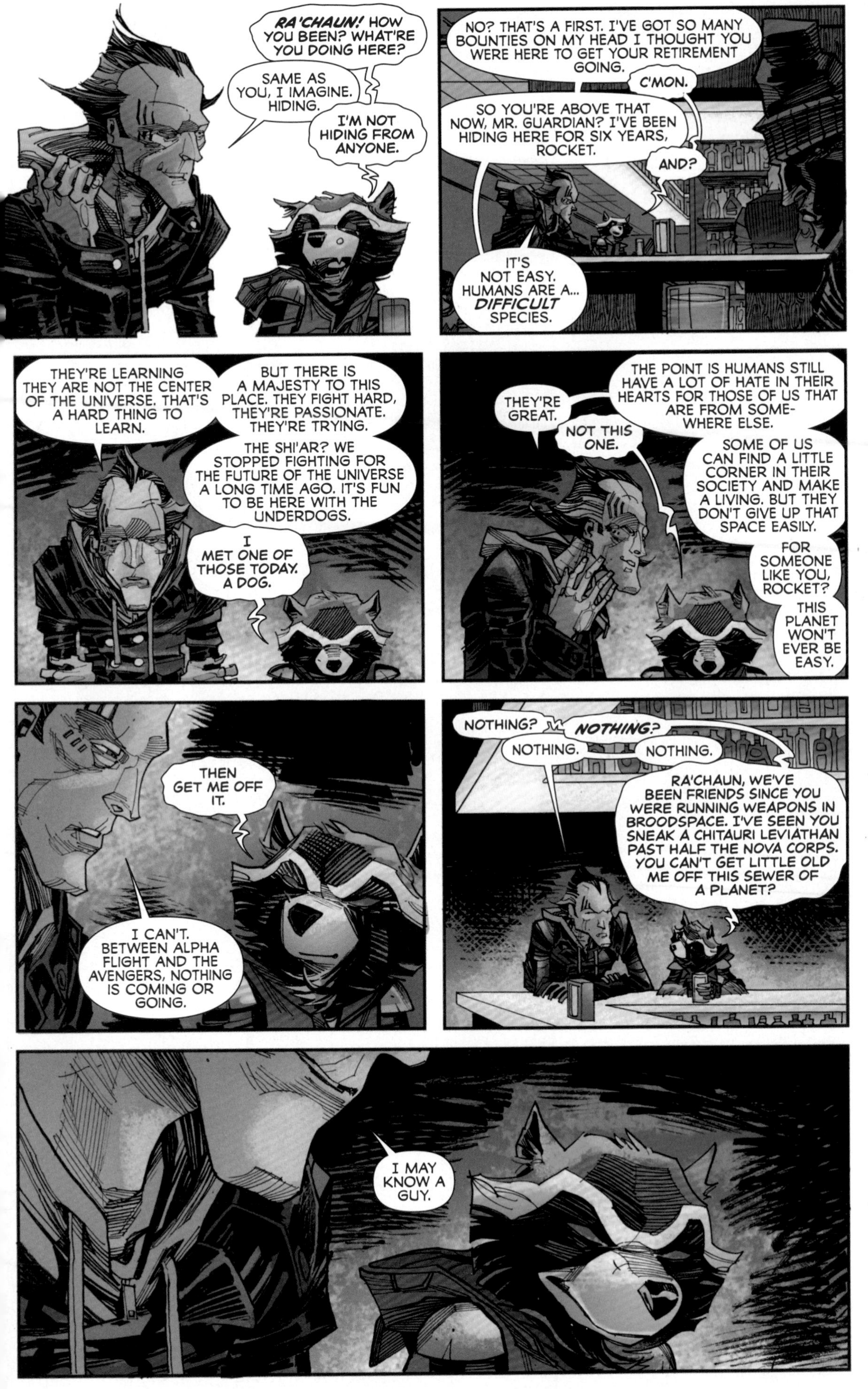
RA'CHAUN! HOW YOU BEEN? WHAT'RE YOU DOING HERE?
SAME AS YOU, I IMAGINE. HIDING.
I'M NOT HIDING FROM ANYONE.
NO? THAT'S A FIRST. I'VE GOT SO MANY BOUNTIES ON MY HEAD I THOUGHT YOU WERE HERE TO GET YOUR RETIREMENT GOING.
C'MON.
SO YOU'RE ABOVE THAT NOW, MR. GUARDIAN? I'VE BEEN HIDING HERE FOR SIX YEARS, ROCKET.
AND?
IT'S NOT EASY. HUMANS ARE A... DIFFICULT SPECIES.
THEY'RE LEARNING THEY ARE NOT THE CENTER OF THE UNIVERSE. THAT'S A HARD THING TO LEARN.
BUT THERE IS A MAJESTY TO THIS PLACE. THEY FIGHT HARD, THEY'RE PASSIONATE. THEY'RE TRYING.
THE SHI'AR? WE STOPPED FIGHTING FOR THE FUTURE OF THE UNIVERSE A LONG TIME AGO. IT'S FUN TO BE HERE WITH THE UNDERDOGS.
I MET ONE OF THOSE TODAY. A DOG.
THEY'RE GREAT.
THE POINT IS HUMANS STILL HAVE A LOT OF HATE IN THEIR HEARTS FOR THOSE OF US THAT ARE FROM SOME-WHERE ELSE.
NOT THIS ONE.
SOME OF US CAN FIND A LITTLE CORNER IN THEIR SOCIETY AND MAKE A LIVING. BUT THEY DON'T GIVE UP THAT SPACE EASILY.
FOR SOMEONE LIKE YOU, ROCKET?
THIS PLANET WON'T EVER BE EASY.
THEN GET ME OFF IT.
I CAN'T. BETWEEN ALPHA FLIGHT AND THE AVENGERS, NOTHING IS COMING OR GOING.
NOTHING?
NOTHING?
NOTHING.
NOTHING.
RA'CHAUN, WE'VE BEEN FRIENDS SINCE YOU WERE RUNNING WEAPONS IN BROODSPACE. I'VE SEEN YOU SNEAK A CHITAURI LEVIATHAN PAST HALF THE NOVA CORPS. YOU CAN'T GET LITTLE OLD ME OFF THIS SEWER OF A PLANET?
I MAY KNOW A GUY.

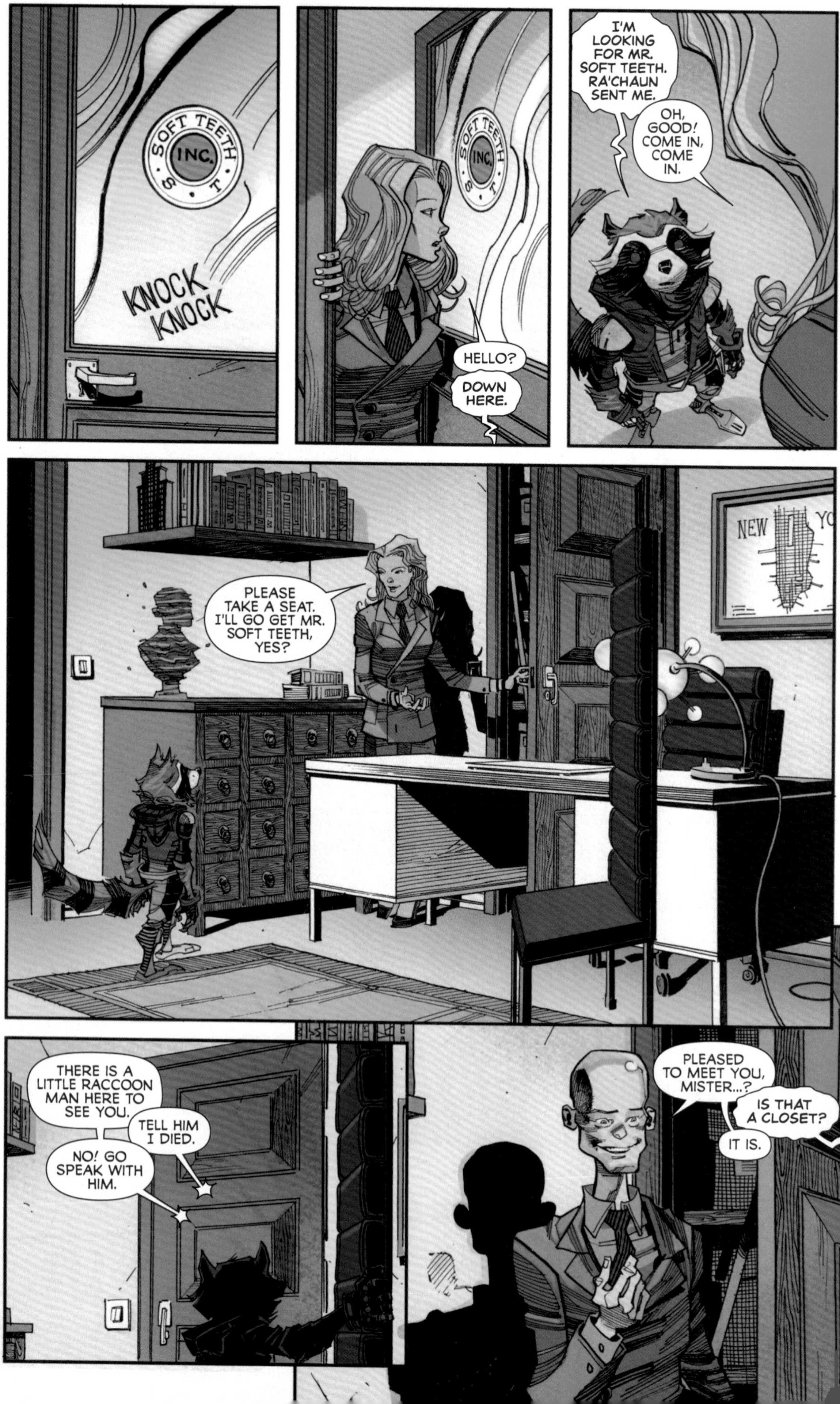

SOFT TEETH INC. S T
KNOCK KNOCK
SOFT TEETH INC. S T
HELLO?
DOWN HERE.
I'M LOOKING FOR MR. SOFT TEETH. RA'CHAUN SENT ME.
OH, GOOD! COME IN, COME IN.
NEW YO
PLEASE TAKE A SEAT. I'LL GO GET MR. SOFT TEETH, YES?
THERE IS A LITTLE RACCOON MAN HERE TO SEE YOU.
TELL HIM I DIED.
NO! GO SPEAK WITH HIM.
PLEASED TO MEET YOU, MISTER...?
IS THAT A CLOSET?
IT IS.

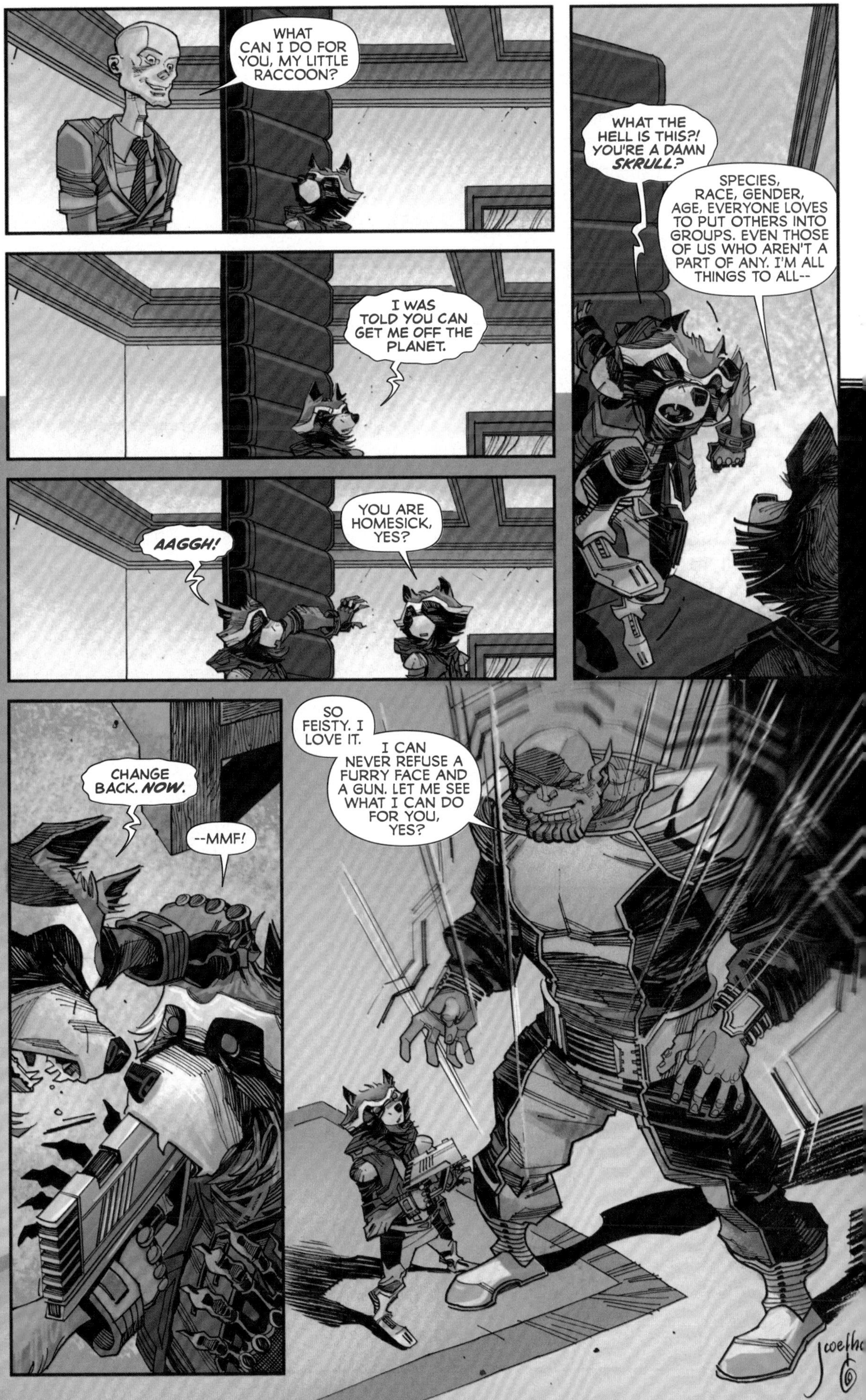
WHAT CAN I DO FOR YOU, MY LITTLE RACCOON?
I WAS TOLD YOU CAN GET ME OFF THE PLANET.
YOU ARE HOMESICK, YES?
AAGGH!
WHAT THE HELL IS THIS?! YOU'RE A DAMN SKRULL?
SPECIES, RACE, GENDER, AGE, EVERYONE LOVES TO PUT OTHERS INTO GROUPS. EVEN THOSE OF US WHO AREN'T A PART OF ANY. I'M ALL THINGS TO ALL--
CHANGE BACK. NOW.
--MMF!
SO FEISTY. I LOVE IT.
I CAN NEVER REFUSE A FURRY FACE AND A GUN. LET ME SEE WHAT I CAN DO FOR YOU, YES?

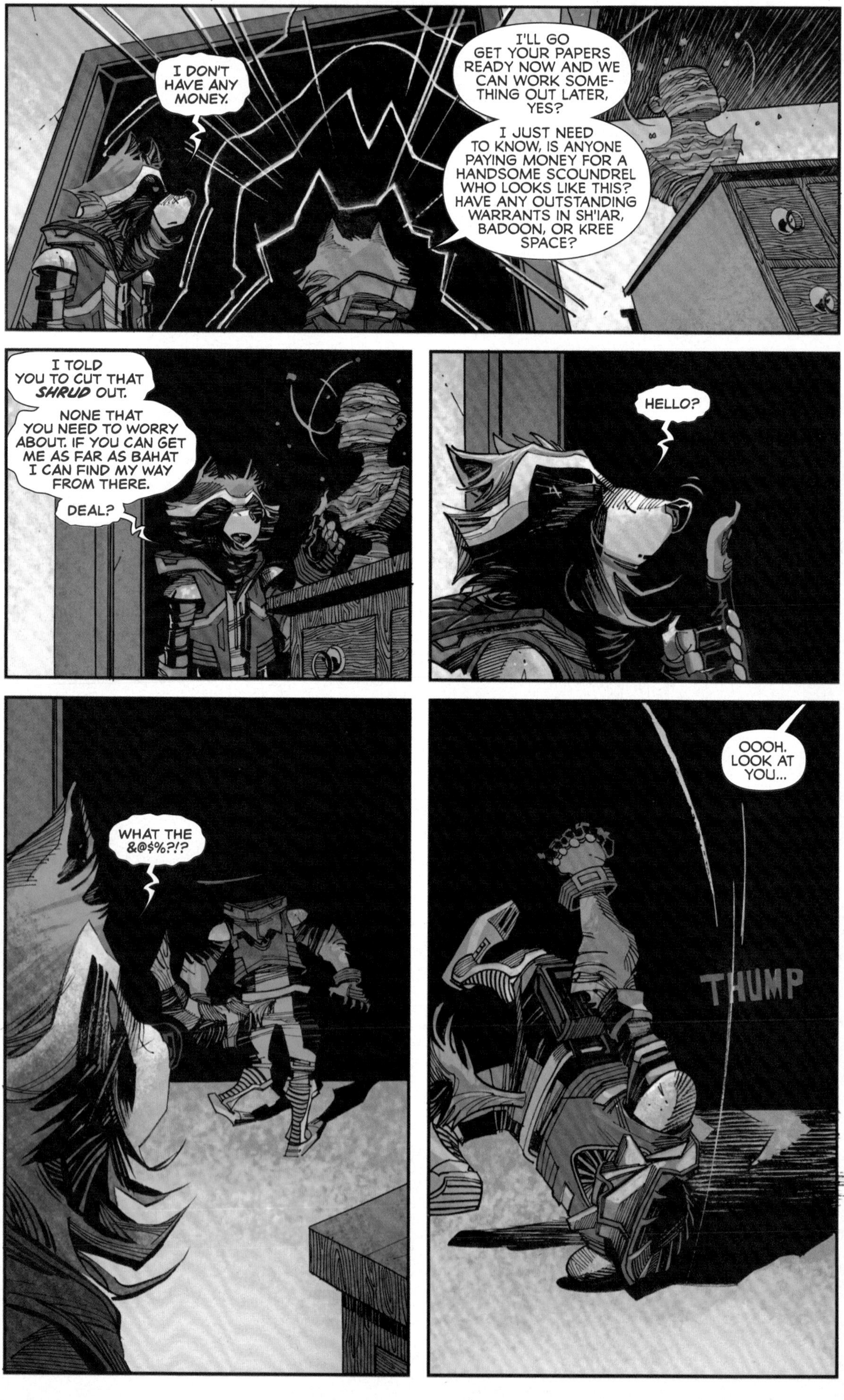
I DON'T HAVE ANY MONEY.
I'LL GO GET YOUR PAPERS READY NOW AND WE CAN WORK SOMETHING OUT LATER, YES?
I JUST NEED TO KNOW, IS ANYONE PAYING MONEY FOR A HANDSOME SCOUNDREL WHO LOOKS LIKE THIS? HAVE ANY OUTSTANDING WARRANTS IN SH'IAR, BADOON, OR KREE SPACE?
I TOLD YOU TO CUT THAT SHRUD OUT.
NONE THAT YOU NEED TO WORRY ABOUT. IF YOU CAN GET ME AS FAR AS BAHAT I CAN FIND MY WAY FROM THERE.
DEAL?
HELLO?
WHAT THE &@$%?!?
OOOH. LOOK AT YOU...
THUMP

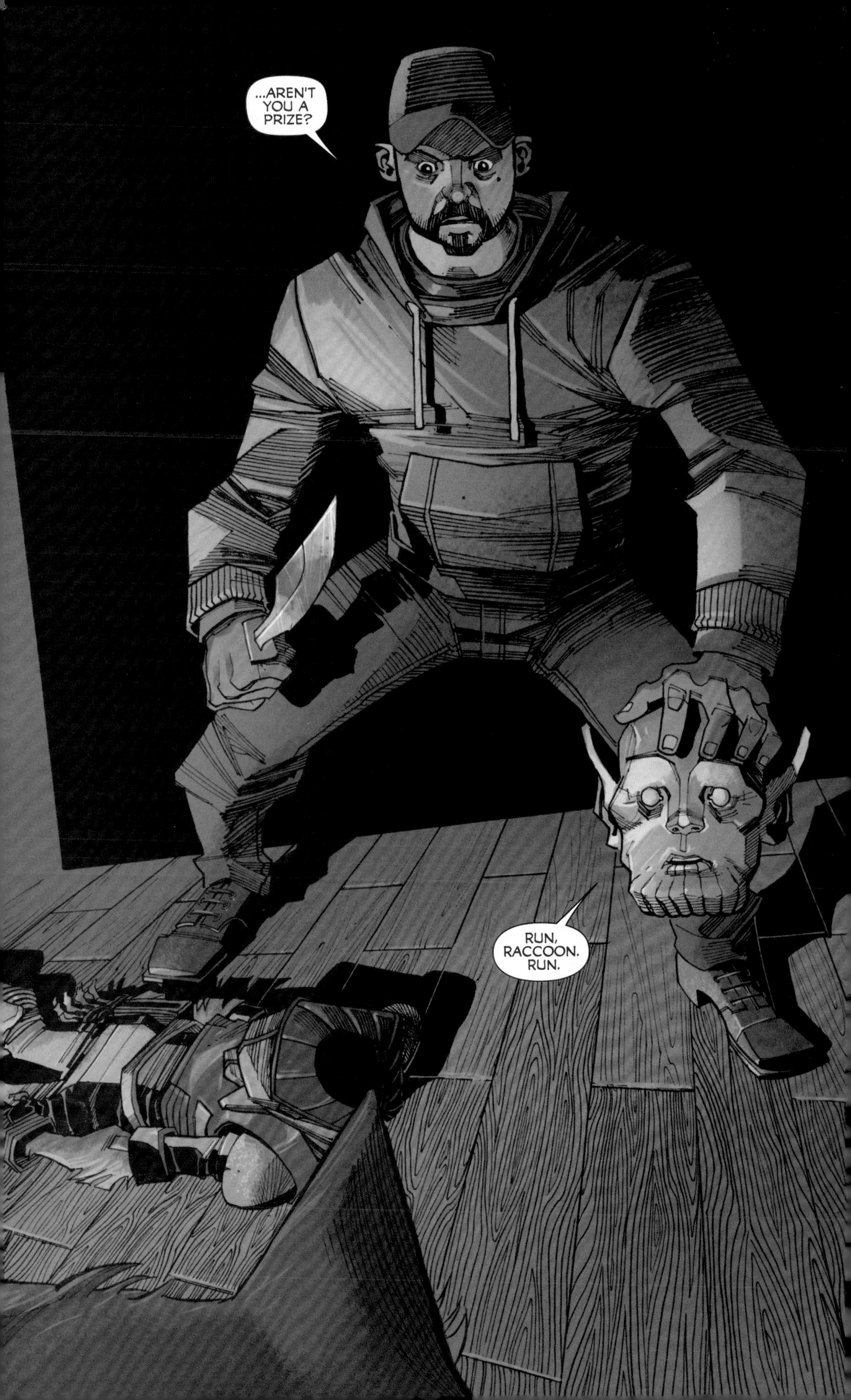
...AREN'T YOU A PRIZE?
RUN, RACCOON. RUN.

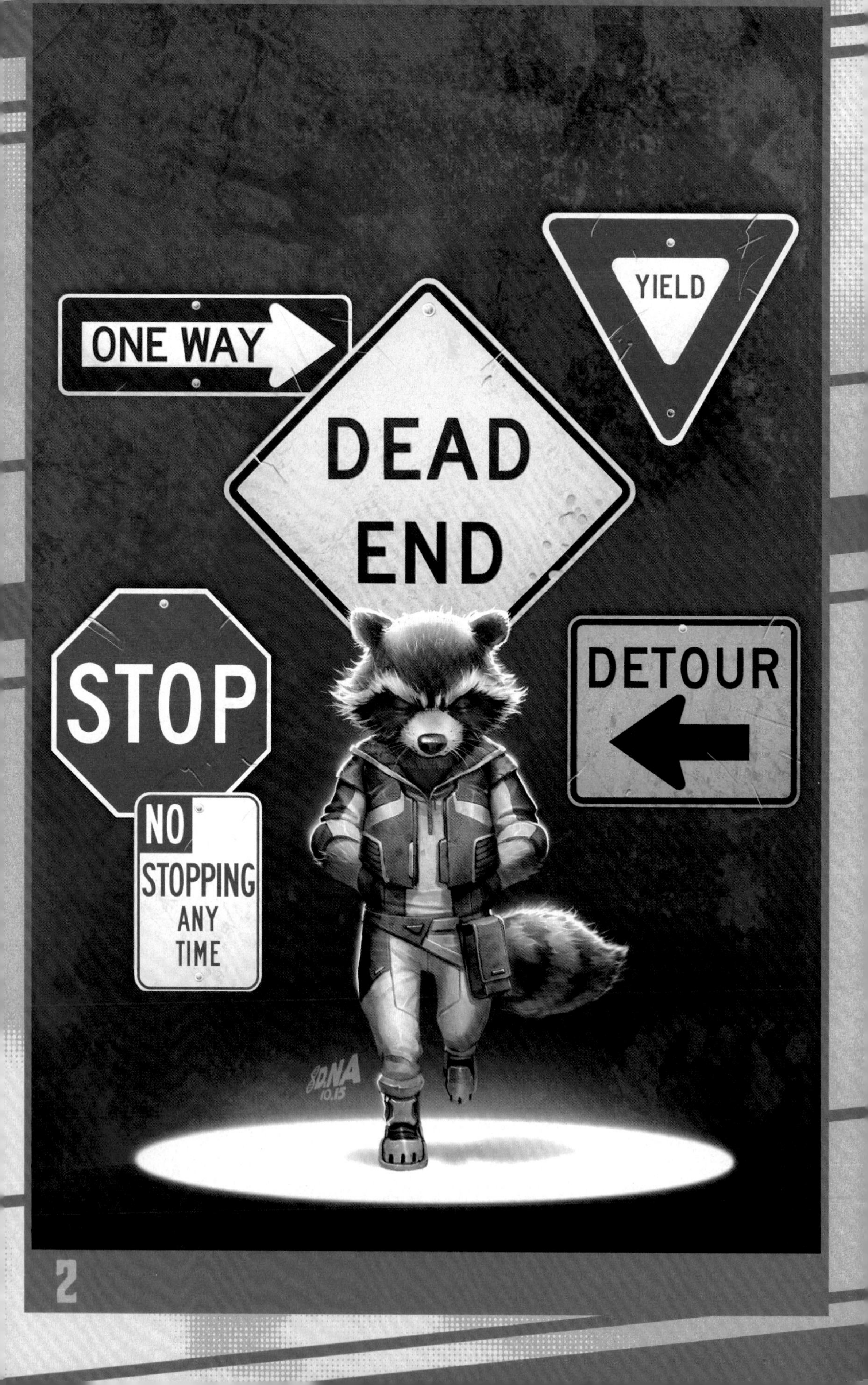
ONE WAY
DEAD END
YIELD
STOP
NO STOPPING ANY TIME
DETOUR

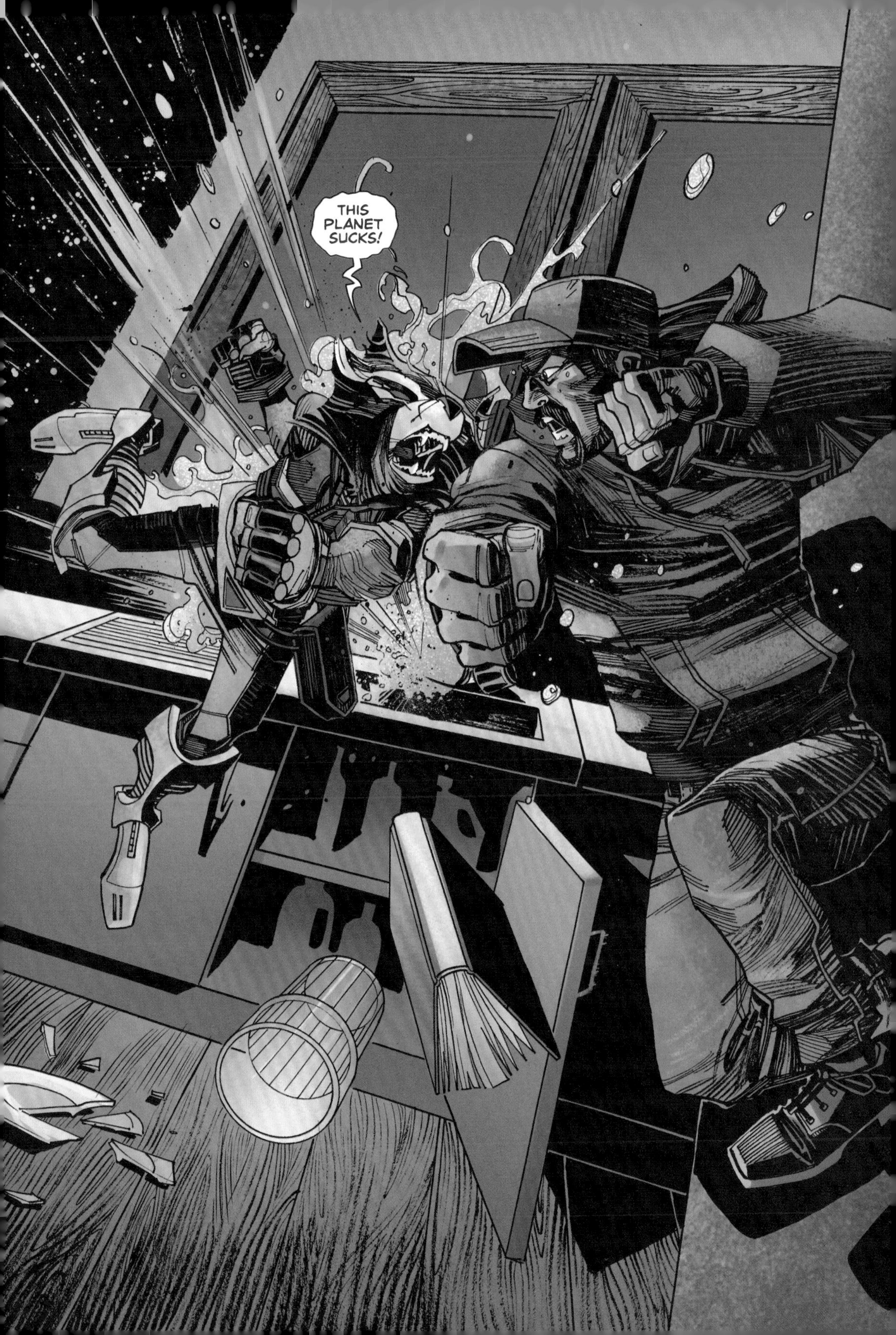
THIS PLANET SUCKS!

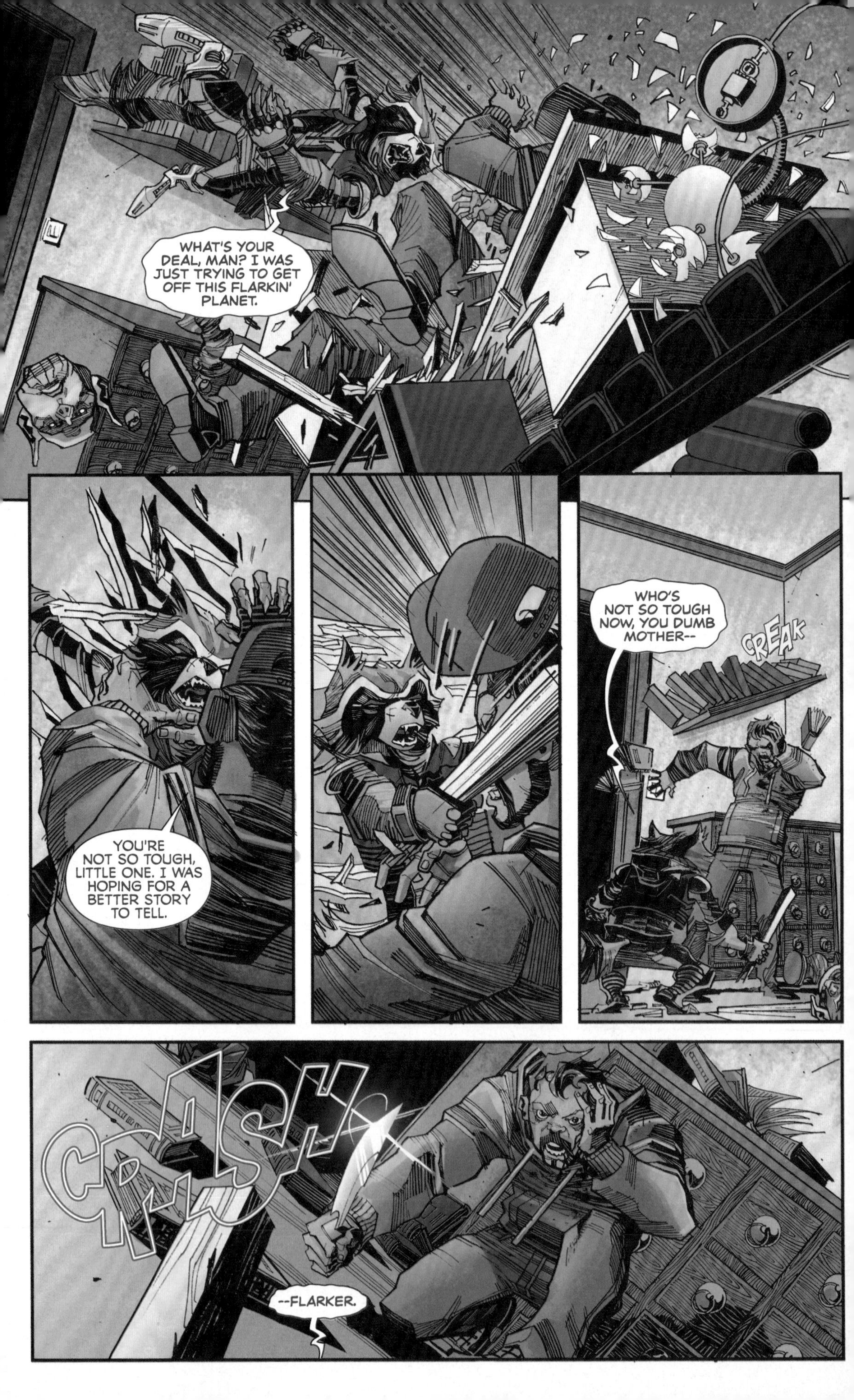
WHAT'S YOUR DEAL, MAN? I WAS JUST TRYING TO GET OFF THIS FLARKIN' PLANET.
YOU'RE NOT SO TOUGH, LITTLE ONE. I WAS HOPING FOR A BETTER STORY TO TELL.
WHO'S NOT SO TOUGH NOW, YOU DUMB MOTHER--
CREAK
CRASH
--FLARKER.

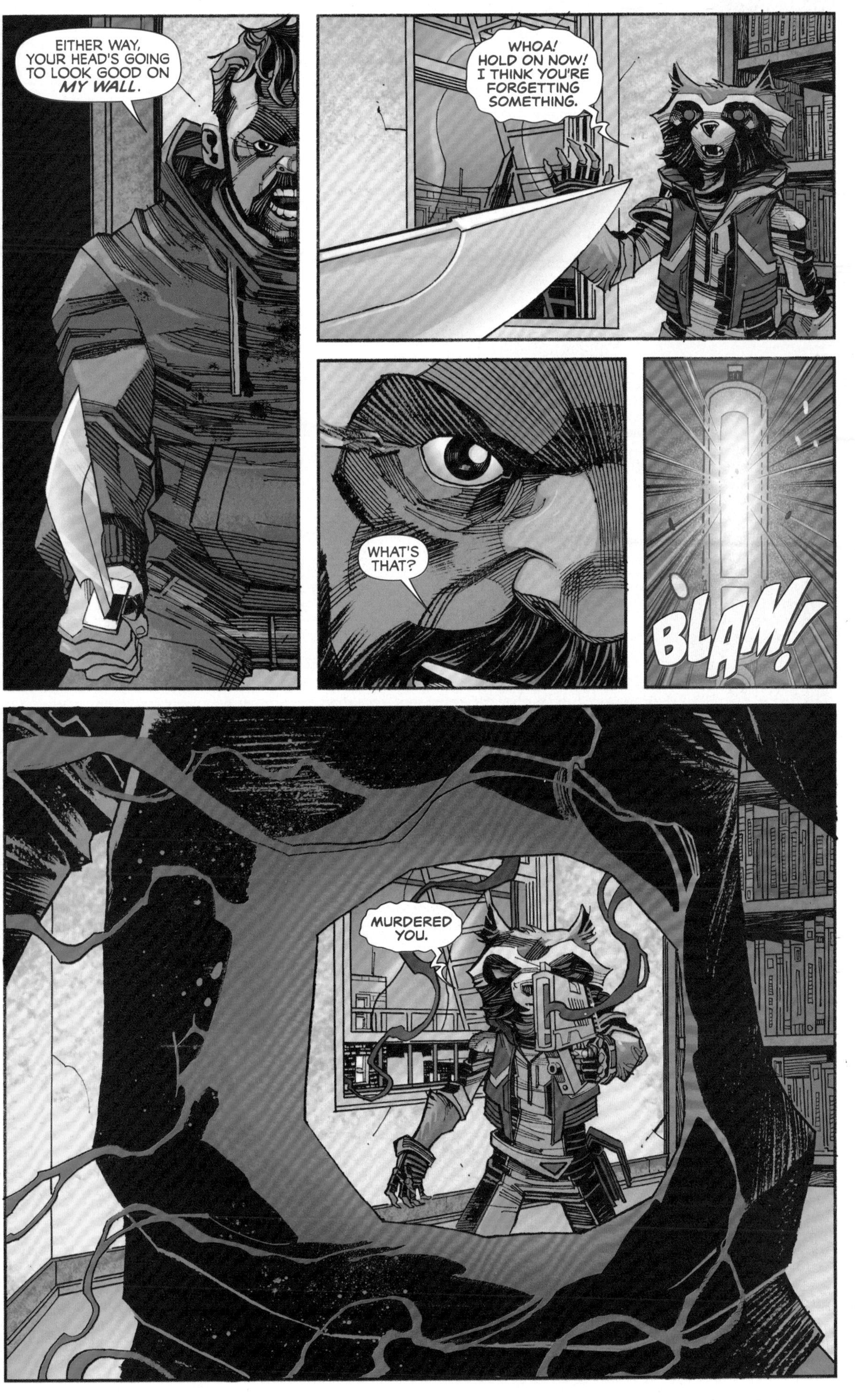
EITHER WAY, YOUR HEAD'S GOING TO LOOK GOOD ON MY WALL.
WHOA! HOLD ON NOW! I THINK YOU'RE FORGETTING SOMETHING.
WHAT'S THAT?
BLAM!
MURDERED YOU.

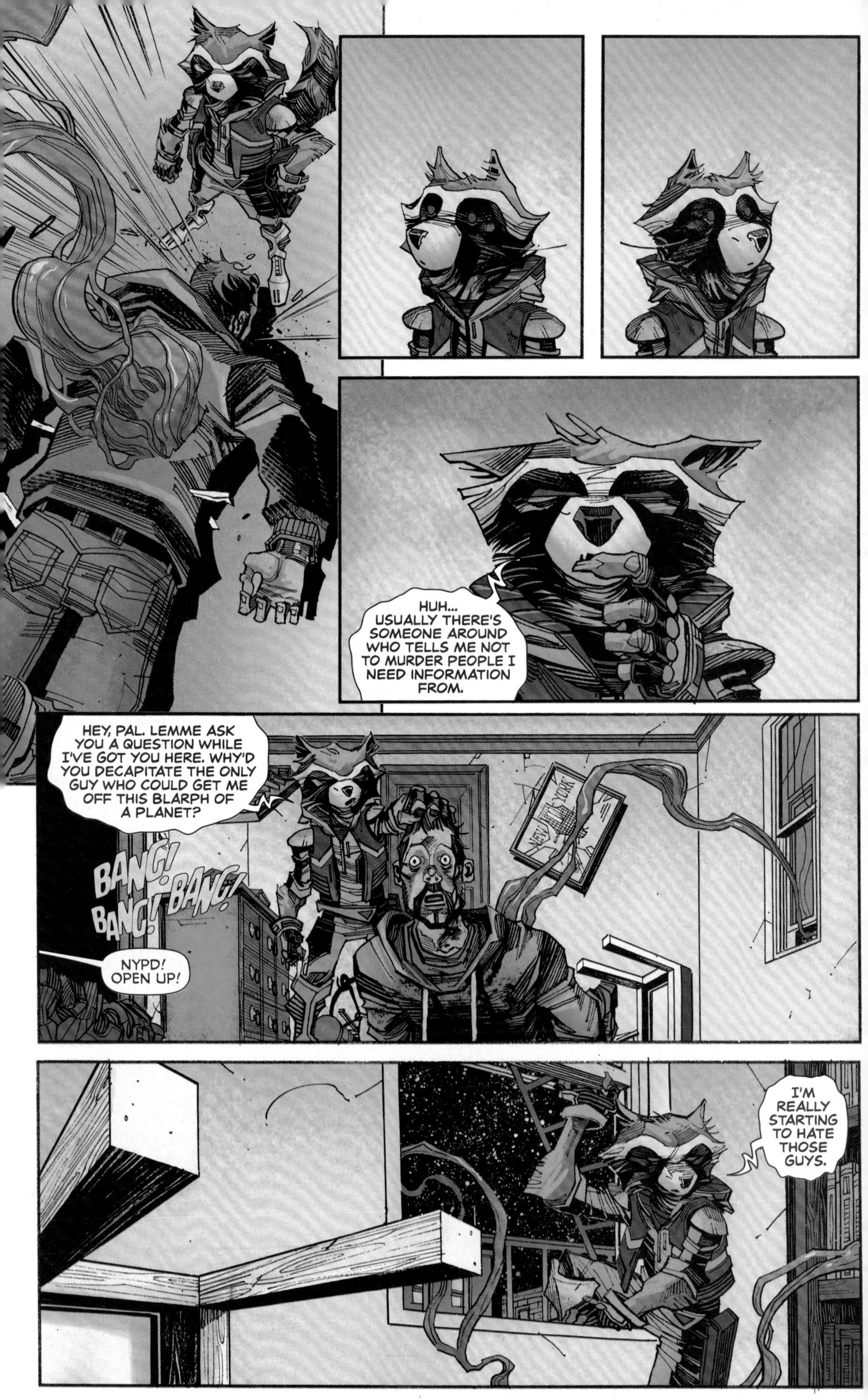
HUH... USUALLY THERE'S SOMEONE AROUND WHO TELLS ME NOT TO MURDER PEOPLE I NEED INFORMATION FROM.
HEY, PAL. LEMME ASK YOU A QUESTION WHILE I'VE GOT YOU HERE. WHY'D YOU DECAPITATE THE ONLY GUY WHO COULD GET ME OFF THIS BLARPH OF A PLANET?
NEW YORK
BANG! BANG! BANG!
NYPD! OPEN UP!
I'M REALLY STARTING TO HATE THOSE GUYS.

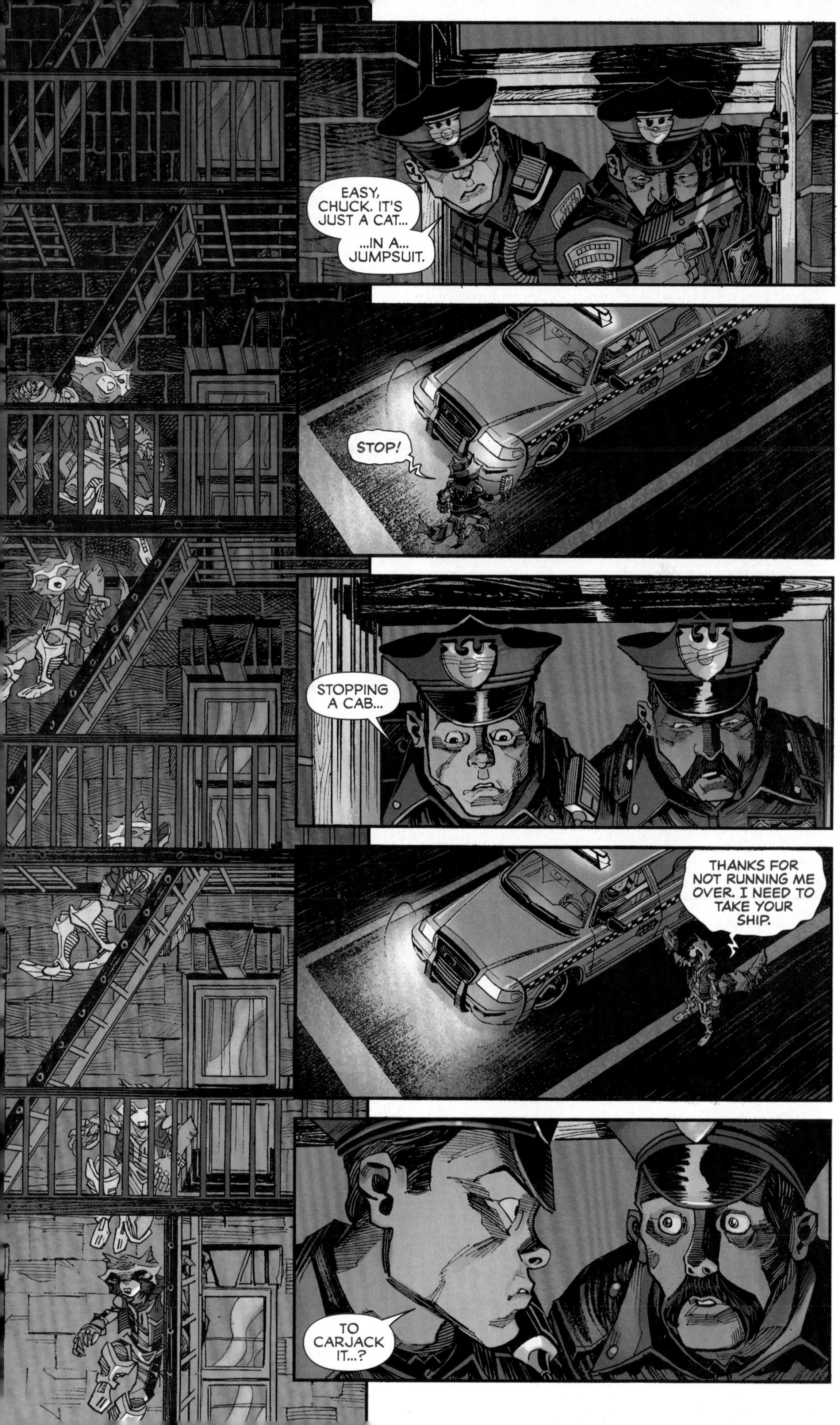
EASY, CHUCK. IT'S JUST A CAT...
...IN A... JUMPSUIT.
STOP!
STOPPING A CAB...
THANKS FOR NOT RUNNING ME OVER. I NEED TO TAKE YOUR SHIP.
TO CARJACK IT...?

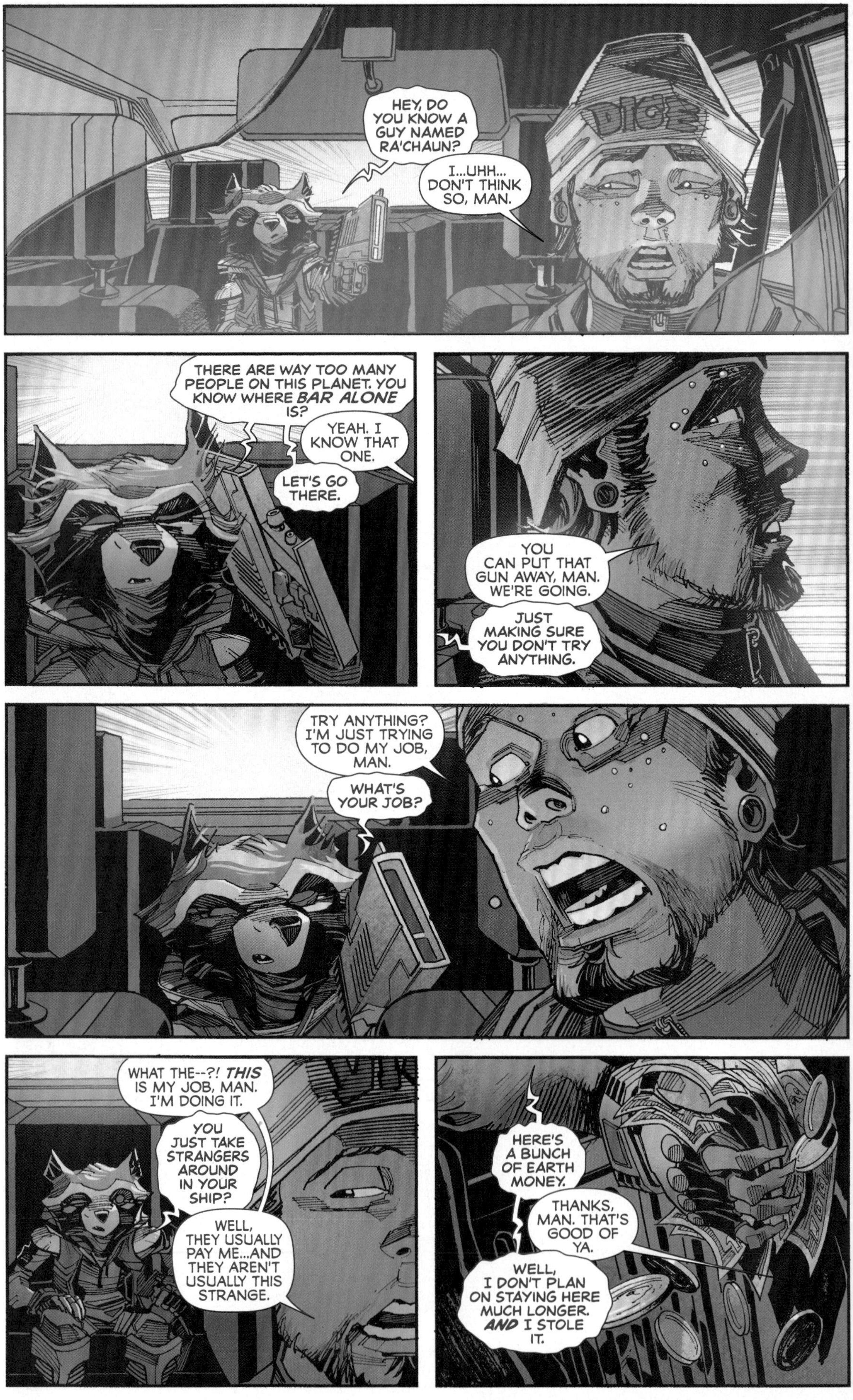
HEY, DO YOU KNOW A GUY NAMED RA'CHAUN?
I...UHH... DON'T THINK SO, MAN.
THERE ARE WAY TOO MANY PEOPLE ON THIS PLANET. YOU KNOW WHERE *BAR ALONE* IS?
YEAH. I KNOW THAT ONE.
LET'S GO THERE.
YOU CAN PUT THAT GUN AWAY, MAN. WE'RE GOING.
JUST MAKING SURE YOU DON'T TRY ANYTHING.
TRY ANYTHING? I'M JUST TRYING TO DO MY JOB, MAN.
WHAT'S YOUR JOB?
WHAT THE--?! *THIS* IS MY JOB, MAN. I'M DOING IT.
YOU JUST TAKE STRANGERS AROUND IN YOUR SHIP?
WELL, THEY USUALLY PAY ME...AND THEY AREN'T USUALLY THIS STRANGE.
HERE'S A BUNCH OF EARTH MONEY.
THANKS, MAN. THAT'S GOOD OF YA.
WELL, I DON'T PLAN ON STAYING HERE MUCH LONGER. ***AND*** I STOLE IT.

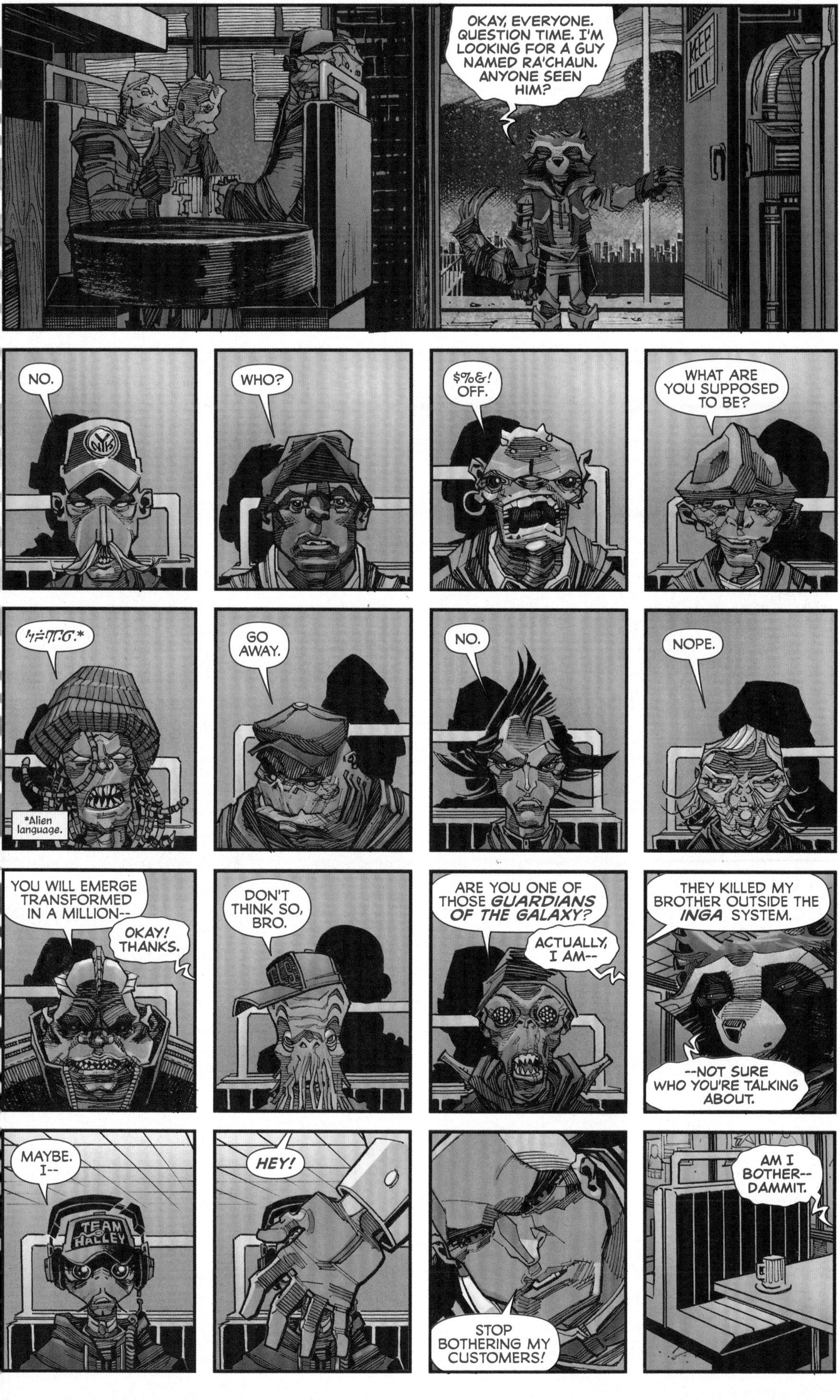
OKAY, EVERYONE. QUESTION TIME. I'M LOOKING FOR A GUY NAMED RA'CHAUN. ANYONE SEEN HIM?
KEEP OUT
NO.
WHO?
$%&! OFF.
WHAT ARE YOU SUPPOSED TO BE?
*Alien language.
GO AWAY.
NO.
NOPE.
YOU WILL EMERGE TRANSFORMED IN A MILLION--
OKAY! THANKS.
DON'T THINK SO, BRO.
ARE YOU ONE OF THOSE GUARDIANS OF THE GALAXY?
ACTUALLY, I AM--
THEY KILLED MY BROTHER OUTSIDE THE INGA SYSTEM.
--NOT SURE WHO YOU'RE TALKING ABOUT.
MAYBE. I--
TEAM HALLEY
HEY!
STOP BOTHERING MY CUSTOMERS!
AM I BOTHER--DAMMIT.

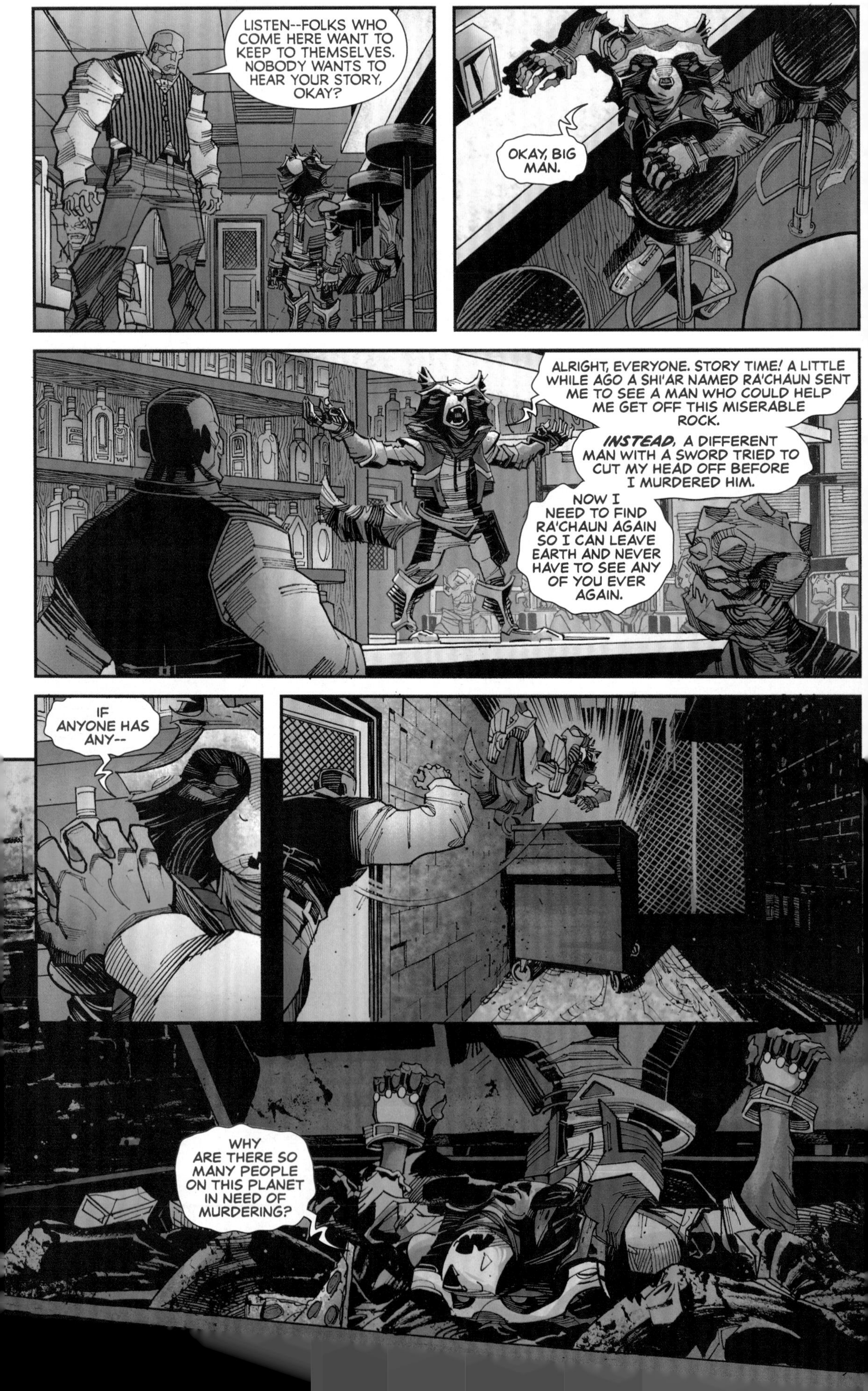
LISTEN--FOLKS WHO COME HERE WANT TO KEEP TO THEMSELVES. NOBODY WANTS TO HEAR YOUR STORY, OKAY?
OKAY, BIG MAN.
ALRIGHT, EVERYONE. STORY TIME! A LITTLE WHILE AGO A SHI'AR NAMED RA'CHAUN SENT ME TO SEE A MAN WHO COULD HELP ME GET OFF THIS MISERABLE ROCK.
INSTEAD, A DIFFERENT MAN WITH A SWORD TRIED TO CUT MY HEAD OFF BEFORE I MURDERED HIM.
NOW I NEED TO FIND RA'CHAUN AGAIN SO I CAN LEAVE EARTH AND NEVER HAVE TO SEE ANY OF YOU EVER AGAIN.
IF ANYONE HAS ANY--
WHY ARE THERE SO MANY PEOPLE ON THIS PLANET IN NEED OF MURDERING?

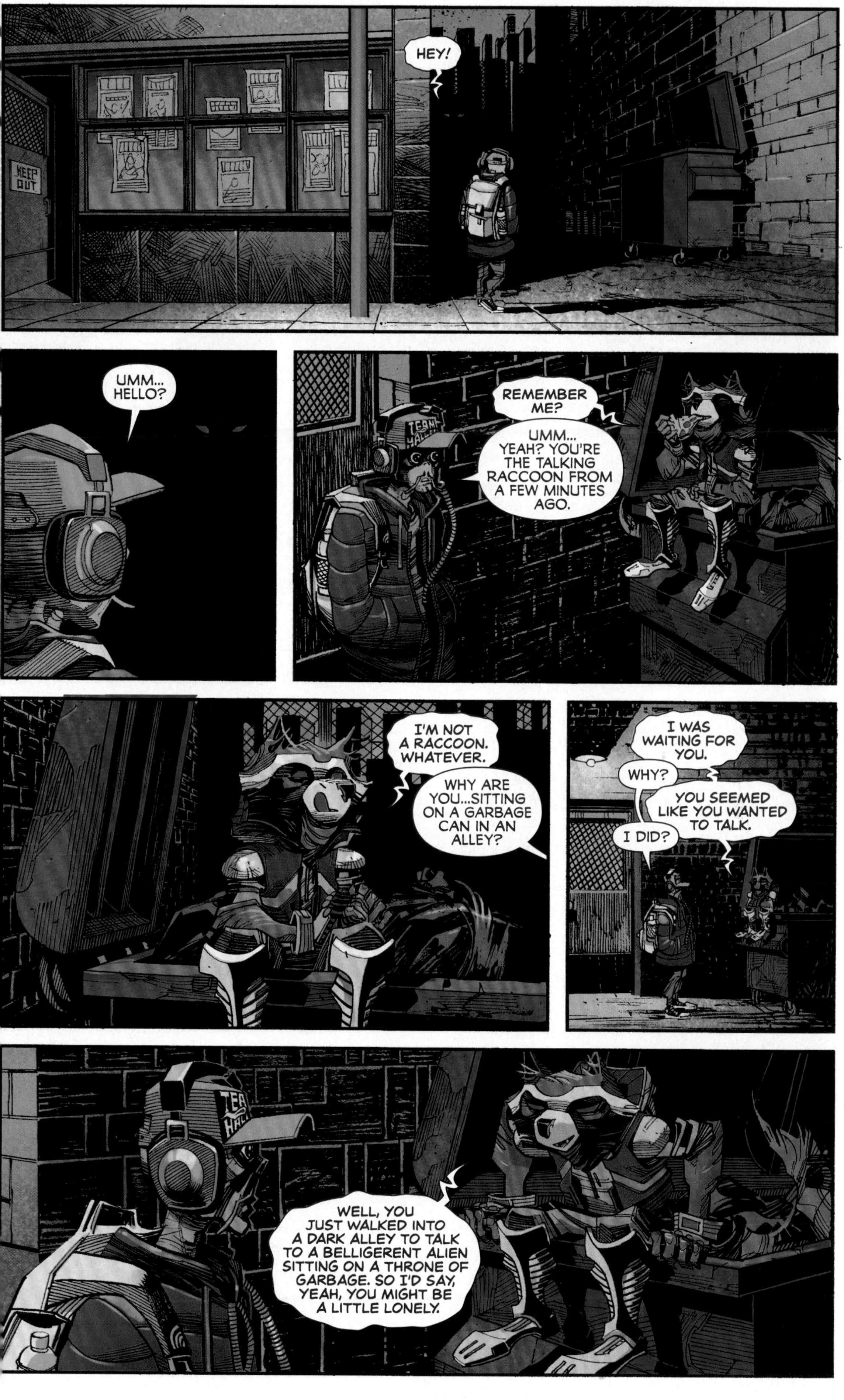
KEEP OUT
HEY!
UMM... HELLO?
REMEMBER ME?
UMM... YEAH? YOU'RE THE TALKING RACCOON FROM A FEW MINUTES AGO.
I'M NOT A RACCOON.
WHATEVER.
WHY ARE YOU...SITTING ON A GARBAGE CAN IN AN ALLEY?
I WAS WAITING FOR YOU.
WHY?
YOU SEEMED LIKE YOU WANTED TO TALK.
I DID?
WELL, YOU JUST WALKED INTO A DARK ALLEY TO TALK TO A BELLIGERENT ALIEN SITTING ON A THRONE OF GARBAGE. SO I'D SAY, YEAH, YOU MIGHT BE A LITTLE LONELY.

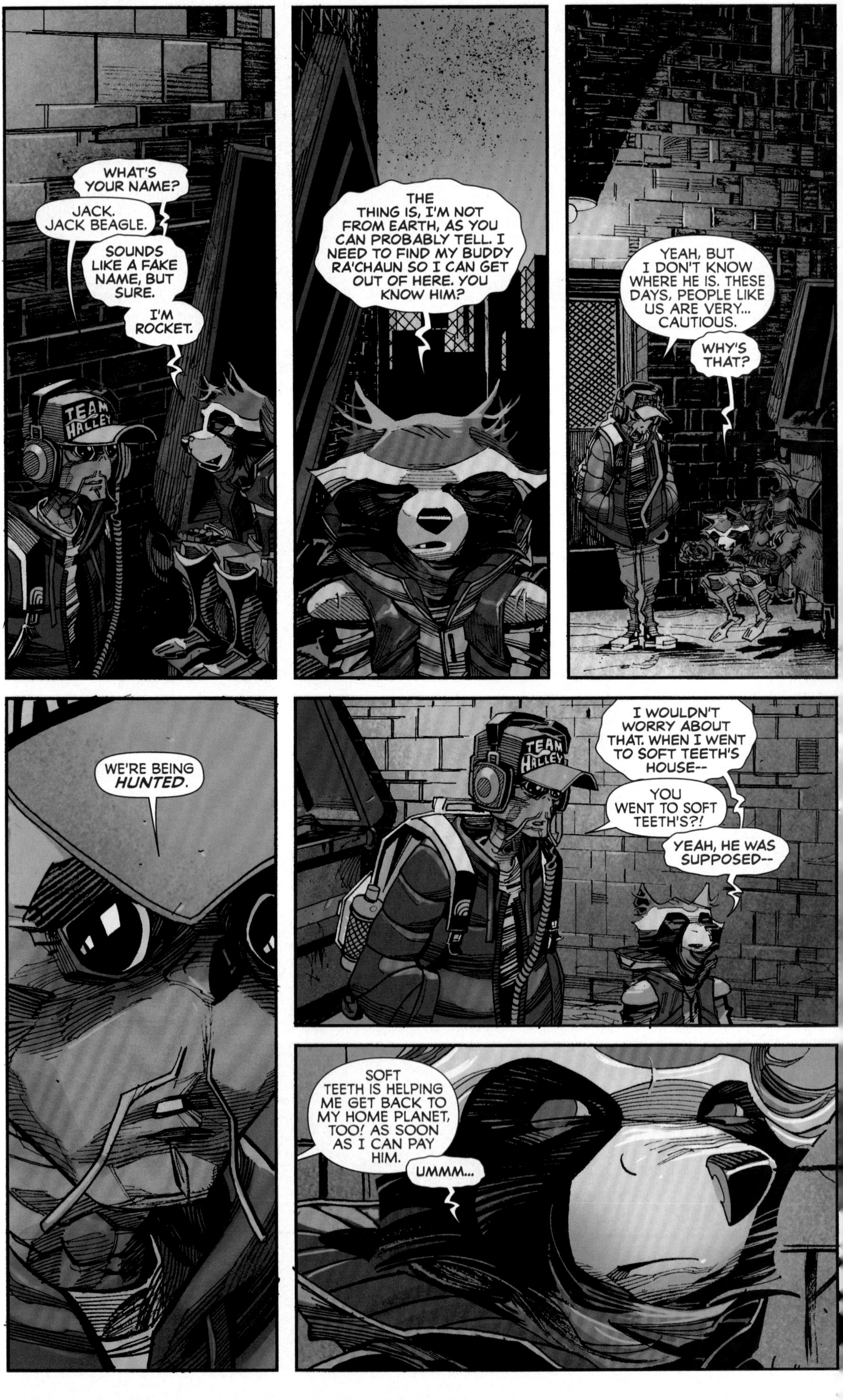
WHAT'S YOUR NAME?
JACK. JACK BEAGLE.
SOUNDS LIKE A FAKE NAME, BUT SURE.
I'M ROCKET.
TEAM HALLEY
THE THING IS, I'M NOT FROM EARTH, AS YOU CAN PROBABLY TELL. I NEED TO FIND MY BUDDY RA'CHAUN SO I CAN GET OUT OF HERE. YOU KNOW HIM?
YEAH, BUT I DON'T KNOW WHERE HE IS. THESE DAYS, PEOPLE LIKE US ARE VERY... CAUTIOUS.
WHY'S THAT?
WE'RE BEING *HUNTED*.
TEAM HALLEY
I WOULDN'T WORRY ABOUT THAT. WHEN I WENT TO SOFT TEETH'S HOUSE--
YOU WENT TO SOFT TEETH'S?!
YEAH, HE WAS SUPPOSED--
SOFT TEETH IS HELPING ME GET BACK TO MY HOME PLANET, TOO! AS SOON AS I CAN PAY HIM.
UMMM...

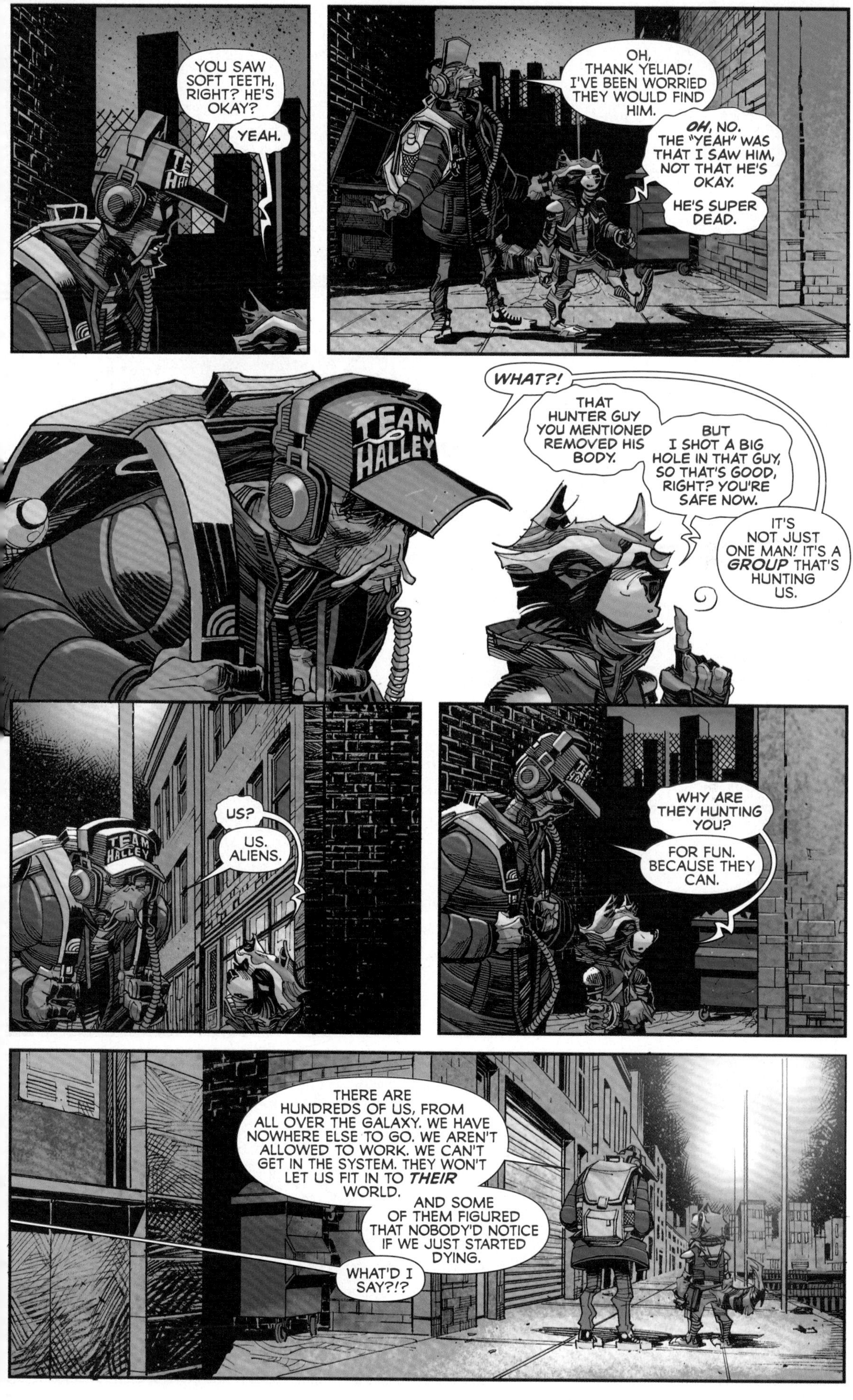
YOU SAW SOFT TEETH, RIGHT? HE'S OKAY?
YEAH.
OH, THANK YELIAD! I'VE BEEN WORRIED THEY WOULD FIND HIM.
OH, NO. THE "YEAH" WAS THAT I SAW HIM, NOT THAT HE'S OKAY.
HE'S SUPER DEAD.
WHAT?!
THAT HUNTER GUY YOU MENTIONED REMOVED HIS BODY.
BUT I SHOT A BIG HOLE IN THAT GUY, SO THAT'S GOOD, RIGHT? YOU'RE SAFE NOW.
IT'S NOT JUST ONE MAN! IT'S A GROUP THAT'S HUNTING US.
US?
US. ALIENS.
WHY ARE THEY HUNTING YOU?
FOR FUN. BECAUSE THEY CAN.
THERE ARE HUNDREDS OF US, FROM ALL OVER THE GALAXY. WE HAVE NOWHERE ELSE TO GO. WE AREN'T ALLOWED TO WORK. WE CAN'T GET IN THE SYSTEM. THEY WON'T LET US FIT IN TO THEIR WORLD.
AND SOME OF THEM FIGURED THAT NOBODY'D NOTICE IF WE JUST STARTED DYING.
WHAT'D I SAY?!?

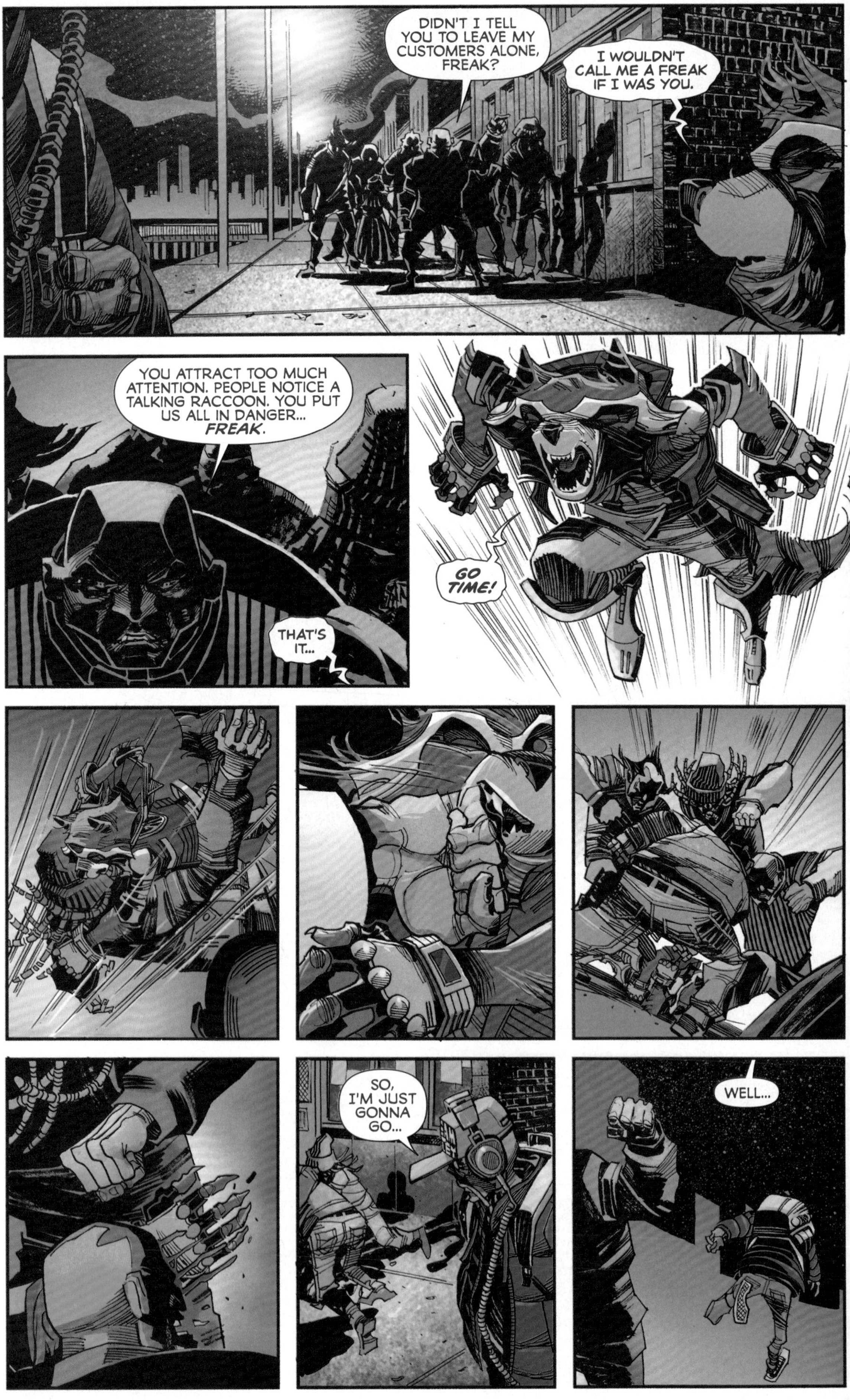
DIDN'T I TELL YOU TO LEAVE MY CUSTOMERS ALONE, FREAK?
I WOULDN'T CALL ME A FREAK IF I WAS YOU.
YOU ATTRACT TOO MUCH ATTENTION. PEOPLE NOTICE A TALKING RACCOON. YOU PUT US ALL IN DANGER... *FREAK*.
THAT'S IT...
GO TIME!
SO, I'M JUST GONNA GO...
WELL...

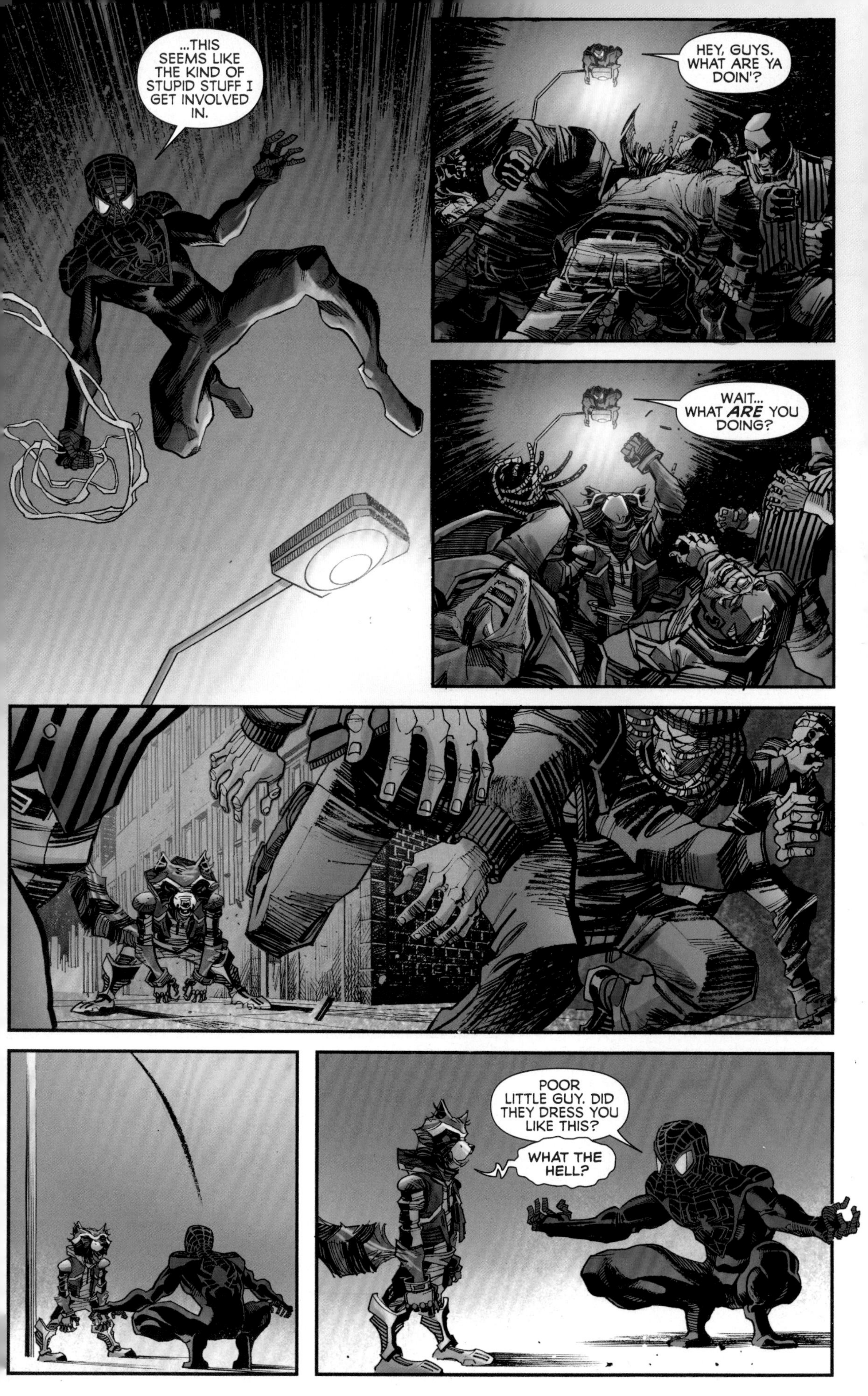
...THIS SEEMS LIKE THE KIND OF STUPID STUFF I GET INVOLVED IN.
HEY, GUYS. WHAT ARE YA DOIN'?
WAIT... WHAT *ARE* YOU DOING?
POOR LITTLE GUY. DID THEY DRESS YOU LIKE THIS?
WHAT THE HELL?

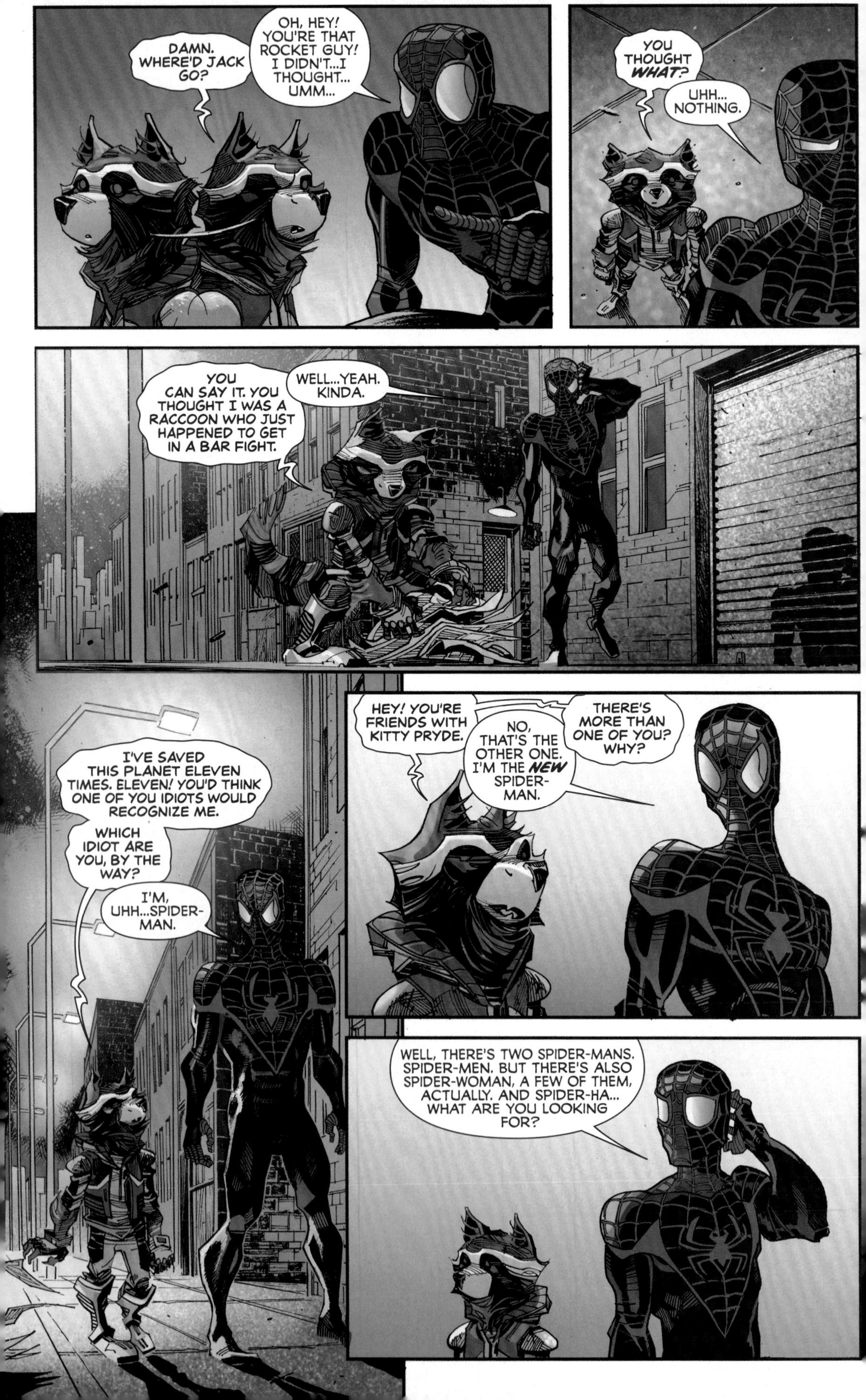
DAMN. WHERE'D JACK GO?
OH, HEY! YOU'RE THAT ROCKET GUY! I DIDN'T...I THOUGHT... UMM...
YOU THOUGHT *WHAT?*
UHH... NOTHING.
YOU CAN SAY IT. YOU THOUGHT I WAS A RACCOON WHO JUST HAPPENED TO GET IN A BAR FIGHT.
WELL...YEAH. KINDA.
I'VE SAVED THIS PLANET ELEVEN TIMES. ELEVEN! YOU'D THINK ONE OF YOU IDIOTS WOULD RECOGNIZE ME.
WHICH IDIOT ARE YOU, BY THE WAY?
I'M, UHH...SPIDER-MAN.
HEY! YOU'RE FRIENDS WITH KITTY PRYDE.
NO, THAT'S THE OTHER ONE. I'M THE *NEW* SPIDER-MAN.
THERE'S MORE THAN ONE OF YOU? WHY?
WELL, THERE'S TWO SPIDER-MANS. SPIDER-MEN. BUT THERE'S ALSO SPIDER-WOMAN, A FEW OF THEM, ACTUALLY. AND SPIDER-HA... WHAT ARE YOU LOOKING FOR?

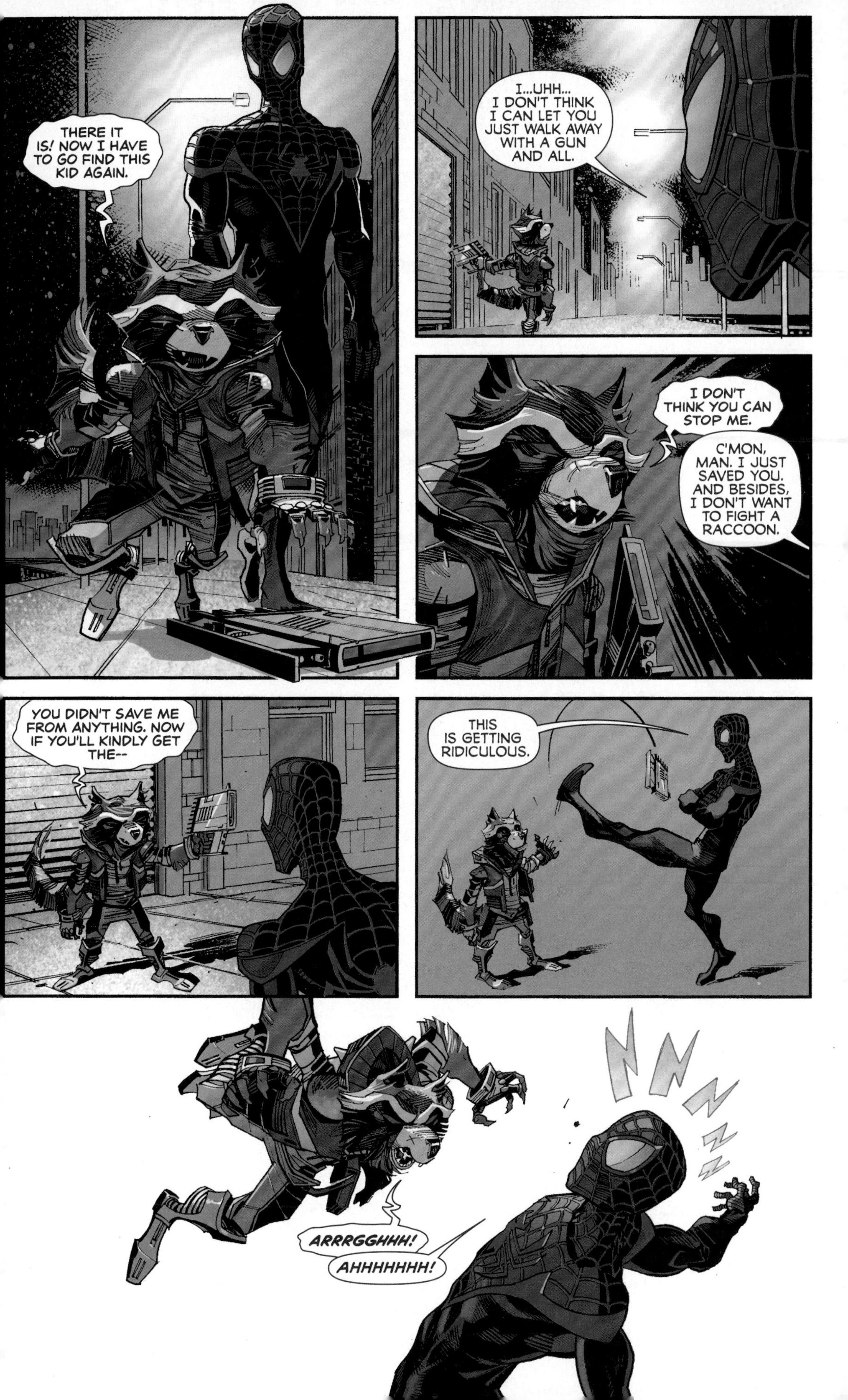
THERE IT IS! NOW I HAVE TO GO FIND THIS KID AGAIN.
I...UHH... I DON'T THINK I CAN LET YOU JUST WALK AWAY WITH A GUN AND ALL.
I DON'T THINK YOU CAN STOP ME.
C'MON, MAN. I JUST SAVED YOU. AND BESIDES, I DON'T WANT TO FIGHT A RACCOON.
YOU DIDN'T SAVE ME FROM ANYTHING. NOW IF YOU'LL KINDLY GET THE--
THIS IS GETTING RIDICULOUS.
NNNZZZ
ARRRGGHHH!
AHHHHHHH!

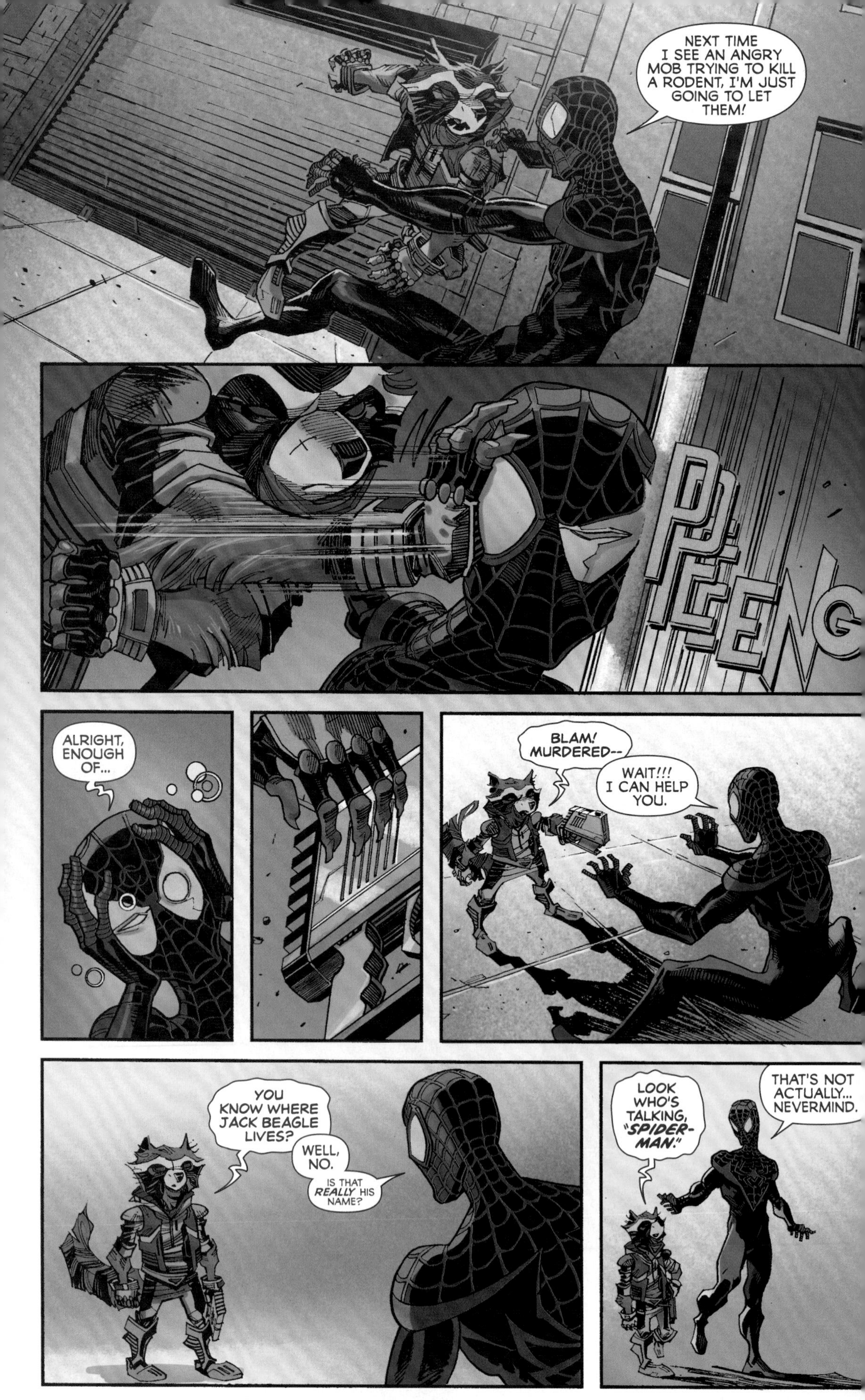
NEXT TIME I SEE AN ANGRY MOB TRYING TO KILL A RODENT, I'M JUST GOING TO LET THEM!
PEEENG
ALRIGHT, ENOUGH OF...
BLAM! MURDERED--
WAIT!!! I CAN HELP YOU.
YOU KNOW WHERE JACK BEAGLE LIVES?
WELL, NO.
IS THAT REALLY HIS NAME?
LOOK WHO'S TALKING, "SPIDER-MAN."
THAT'S NOT ACTUALLY... NEVERMIND.

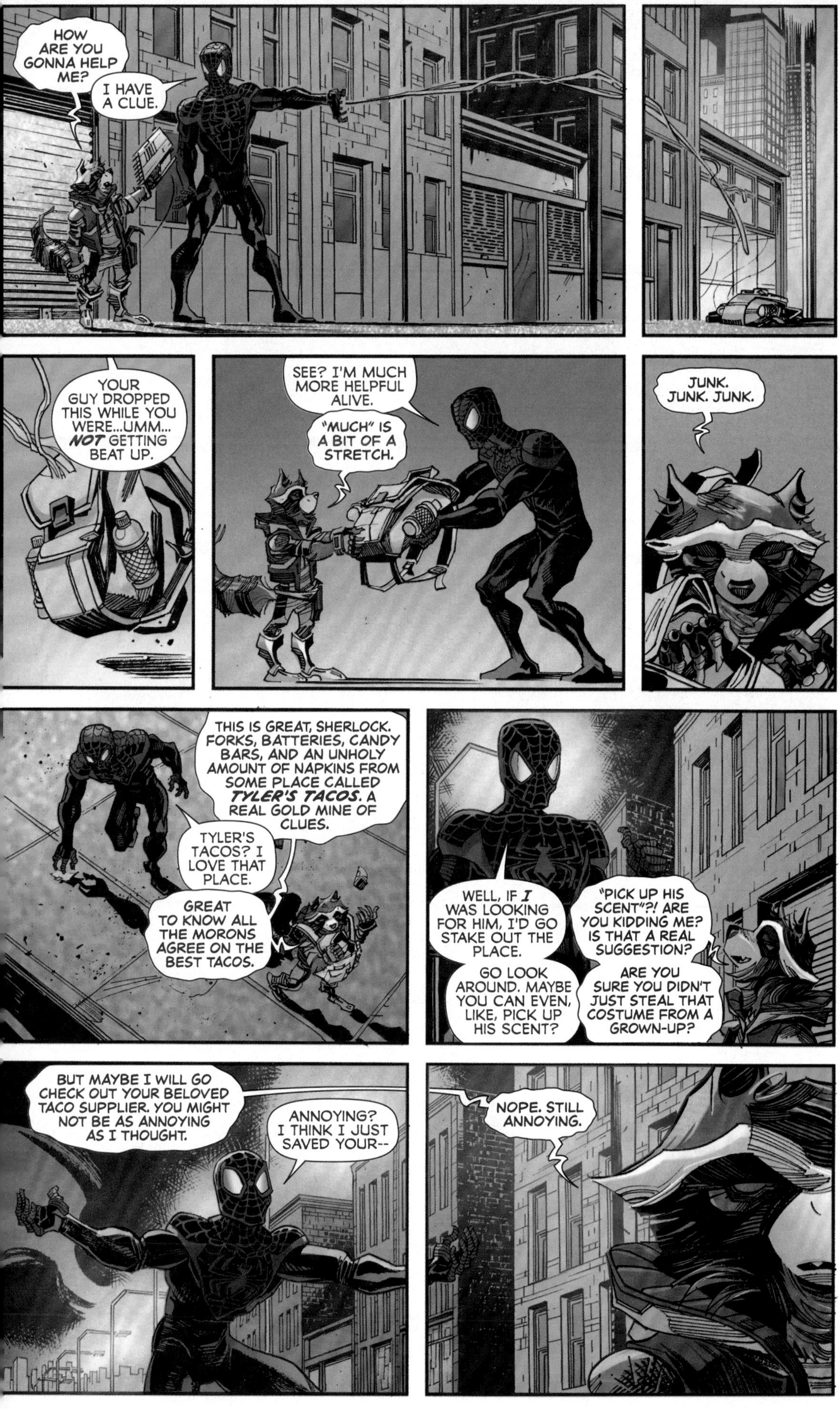
HOW ARE YOU GONNA HELP ME?
I HAVE A CLUE.
YOUR GUY DROPPED THIS WHILE YOU WERE...UMM... NOT GETTING BEAT UP.
SEE? I'M MUCH MORE HELPFUL ALIVE.
"MUCH" IS A BIT OF A STRETCH.
JUNK. JUNK. JUNK.
THIS IS GREAT, SHERLOCK. FORKS, BATTERIES, CANDY BARS, AND AN UNHOLY AMOUNT OF NAPKINS FROM SOME PLACE CALLED TYLER'S TACOS. A REAL GOLD MINE OF CLUES.
TYLER'S TACOS? I LOVE THAT PLACE.
GREAT TO KNOW ALL THE MORONS AGREE ON THE BEST TACOS.
WELL, IF I WAS LOOKING FOR HIM, I'D GO STAKE OUT THE PLACE.
GO LOOK AROUND. MAYBE YOU CAN EVEN, LIKE, PICK UP HIS SCENT?
"PICK UP HIS SCENT"?! ARE YOU KIDDING ME? IS THAT A REAL SUGGESTION?
ARE YOU SURE YOU DIDN'T JUST STEAL THAT COSTUME FROM A GROWN-UP?
BUT MAYBE I WILL GO CHECK OUT YOUR BELOVED TACO SUPPLIER. YOU MIGHT NOT BE AS ANNOYING AS I THOUGHT.
ANNOYING? I THINK I JUST SAVED YOUR--
NOPE. STILL ANNOYING.

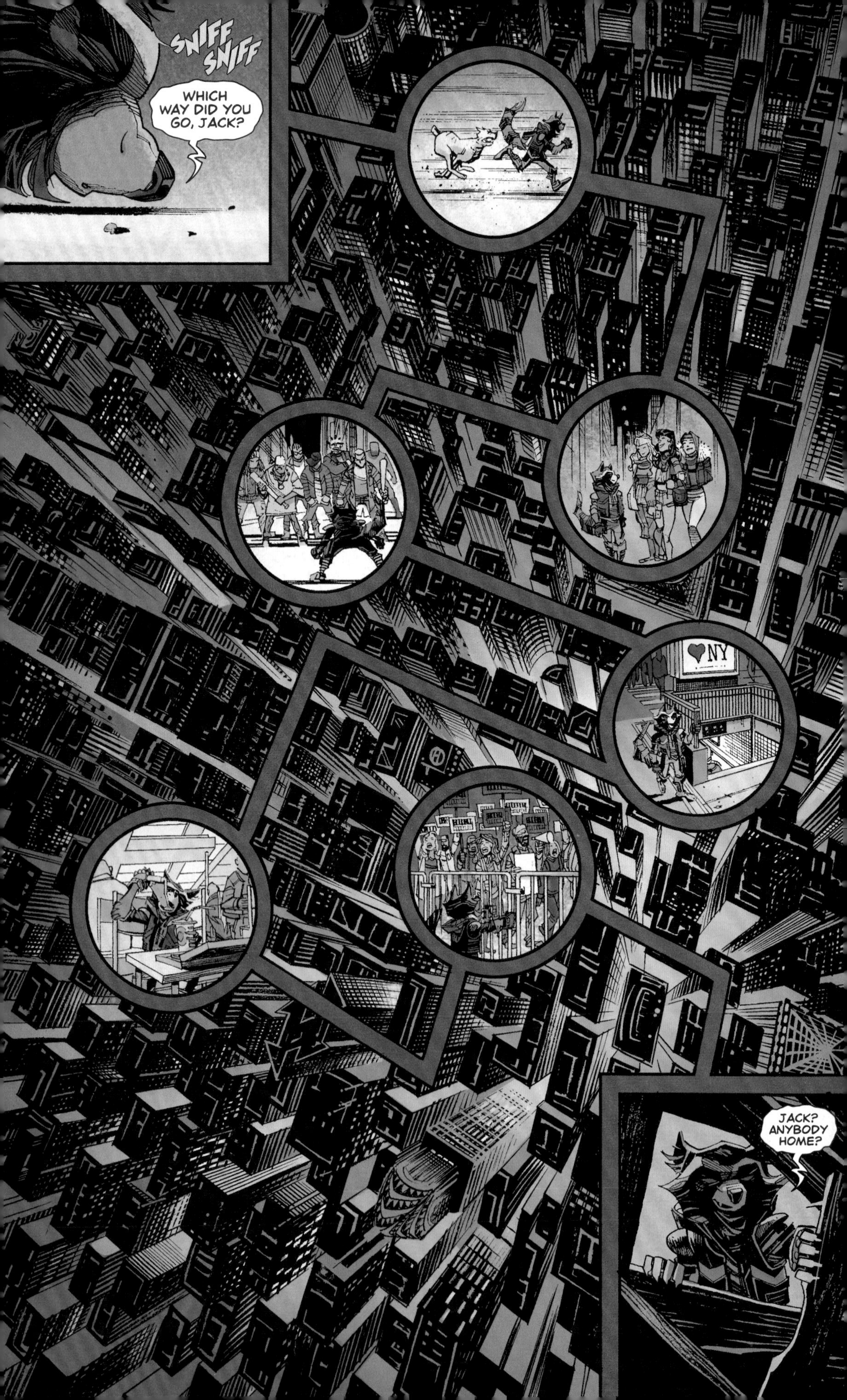
SNIFF SNIFF
WHICH WAY DID YOU GO, JACK?
NY
JACK? ANYBODY HOME?

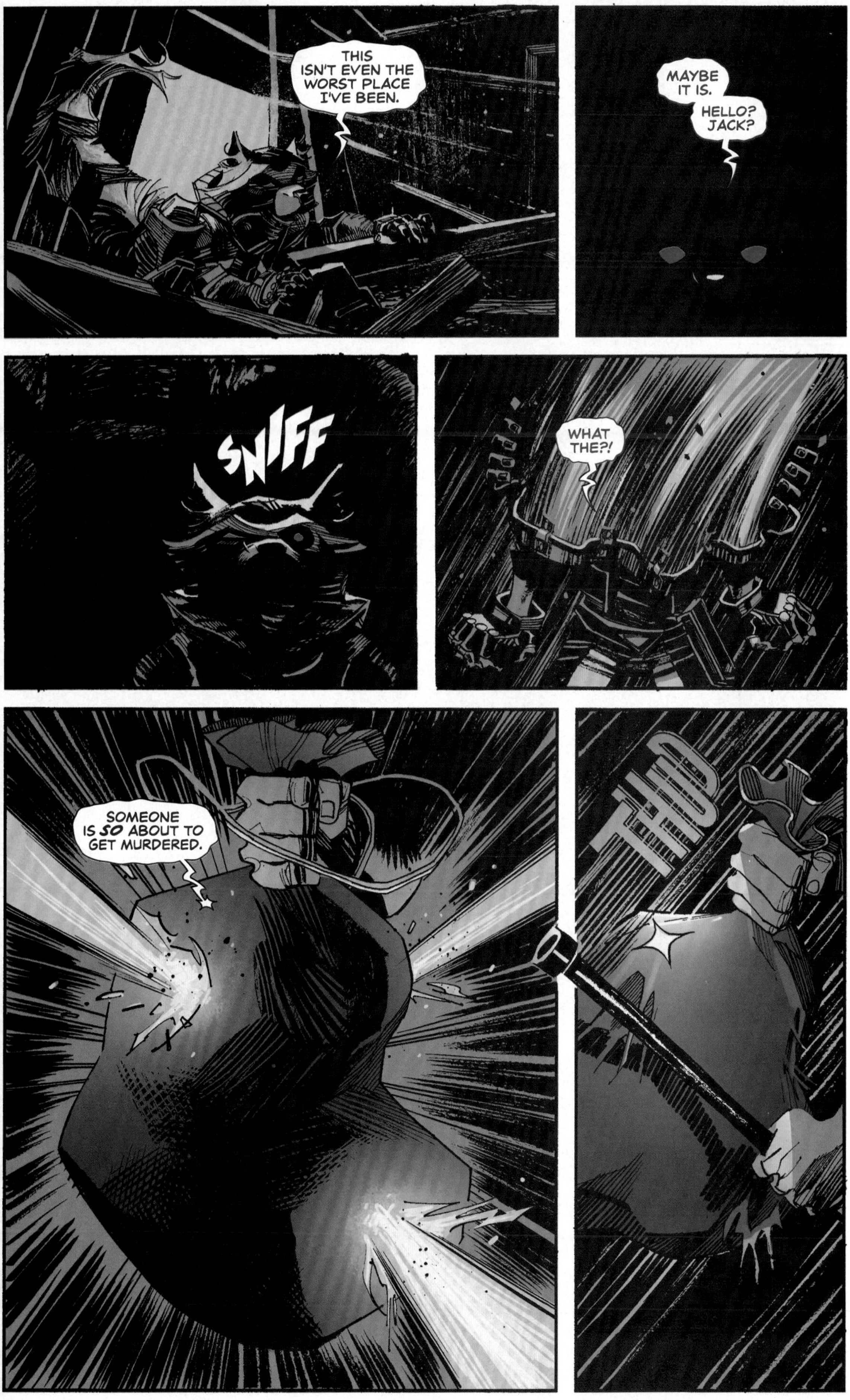
THIS ISN'T EVEN THE WORST PLACE I'VE BEEN.
MAYBE IT IS.
HELLO? JACK?
SNIFF
WHAT THE?!
SOMEONE IS SO ABOUT TO GET MURDERED.
THUD

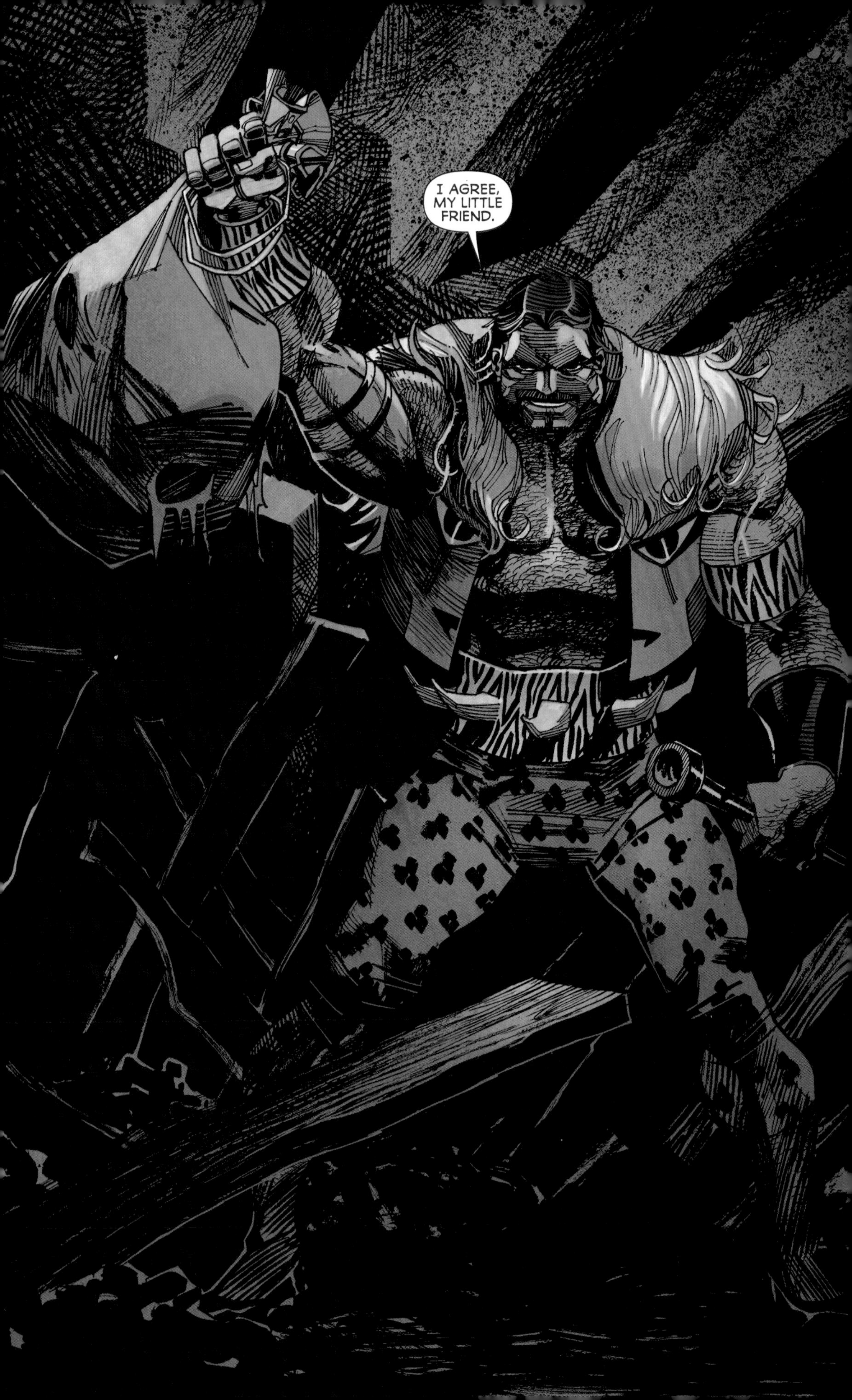
I AGREE, MY LITTLE FRIEND.

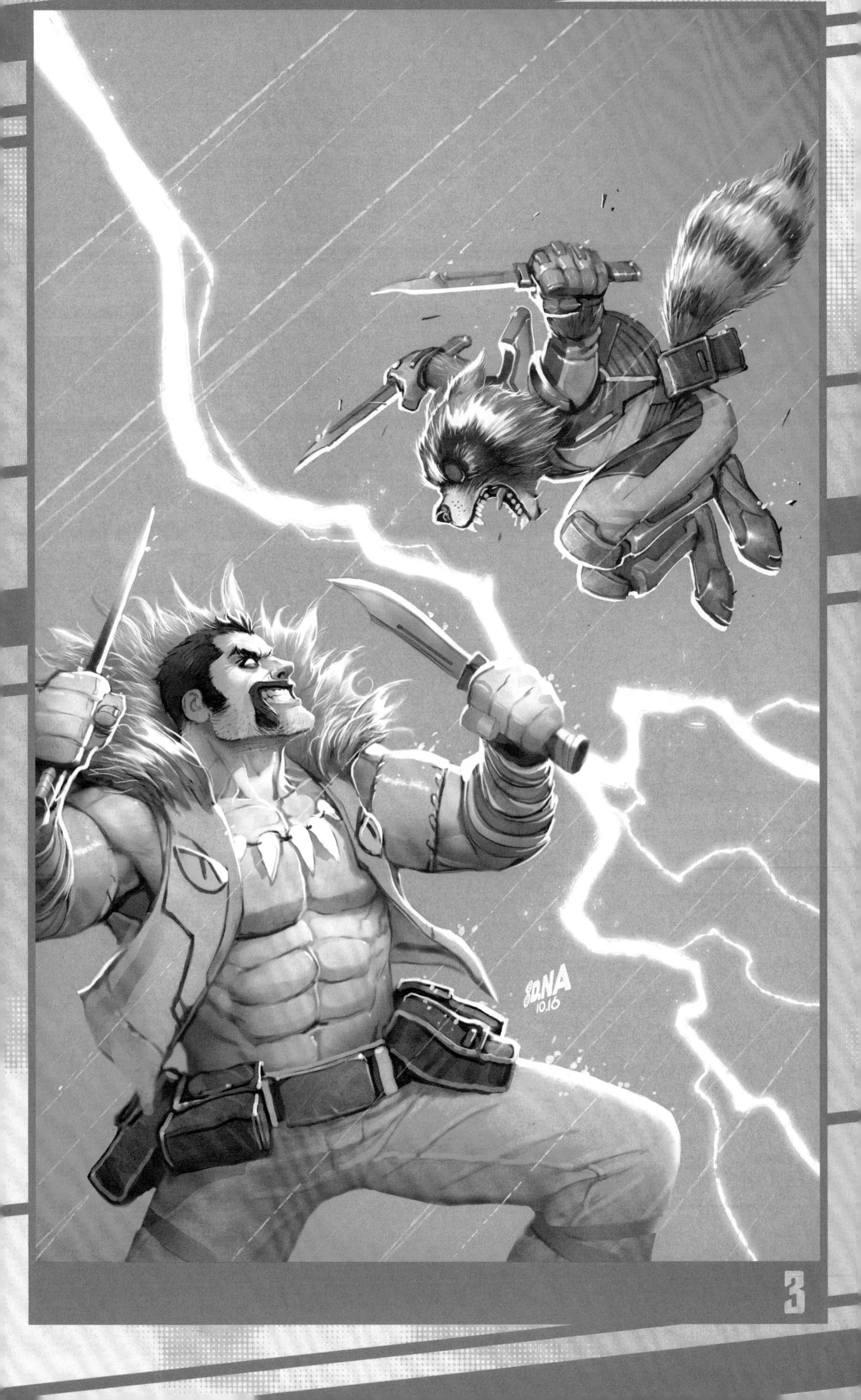
D.NA
10.16
3

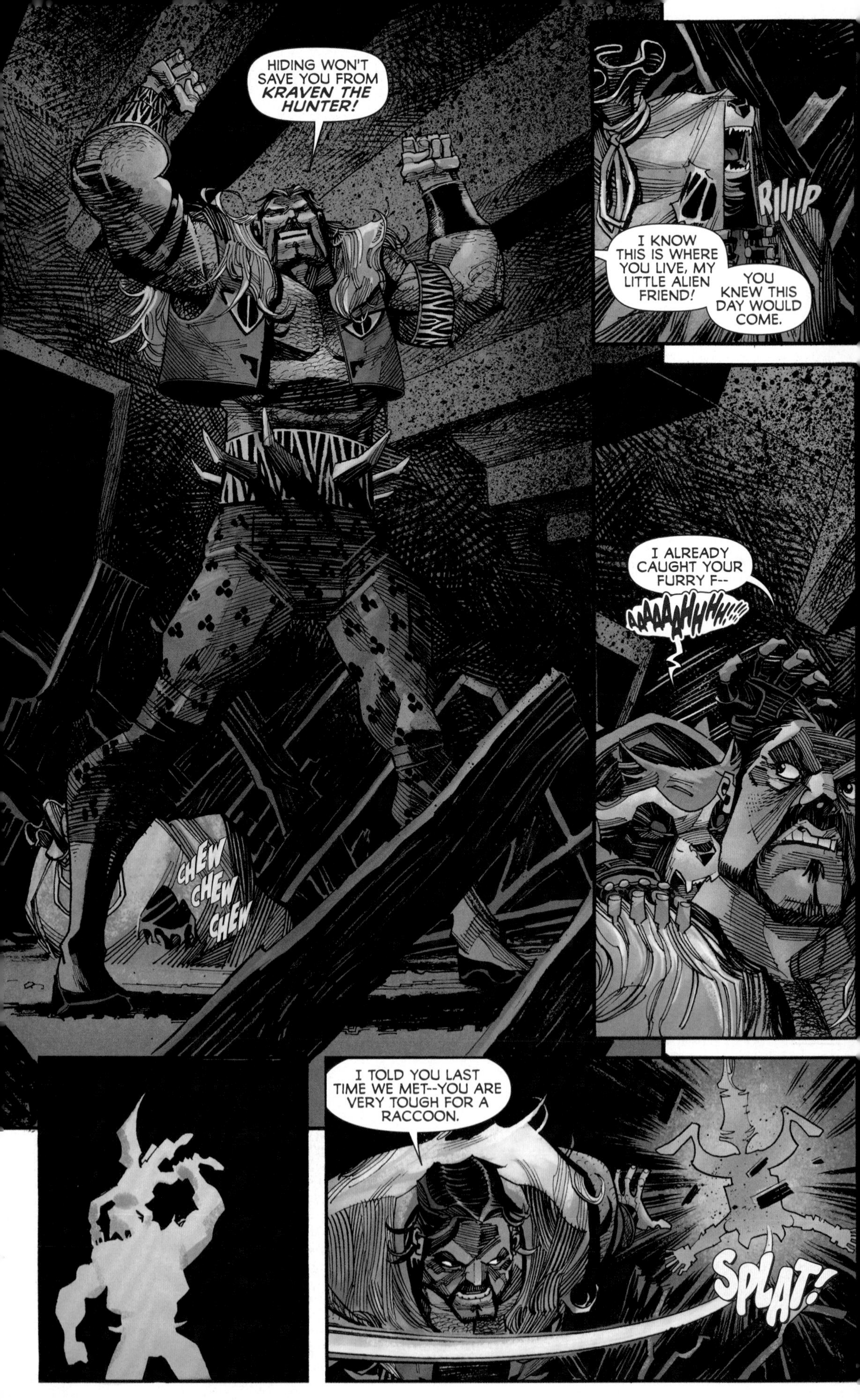
HIDING WON'T SAVE YOU FROM *KRAVEN THE HUNTER!*
CHEW CHEW CHEW
RIIIIP
I KNOW THIS IS WHERE YOU LIVE, MY LITTLE ALIEN FRIEND!
YOU KNEW THIS DAY WOULD COME.
I ALREADY CAUGHT YOUR FURRY F--
AAAAAAHHH!!!
I TOLD YOU LAST TIME WE MET--YOU ARE VERY TOUGH FOR A RACCOON.
SPLAT!

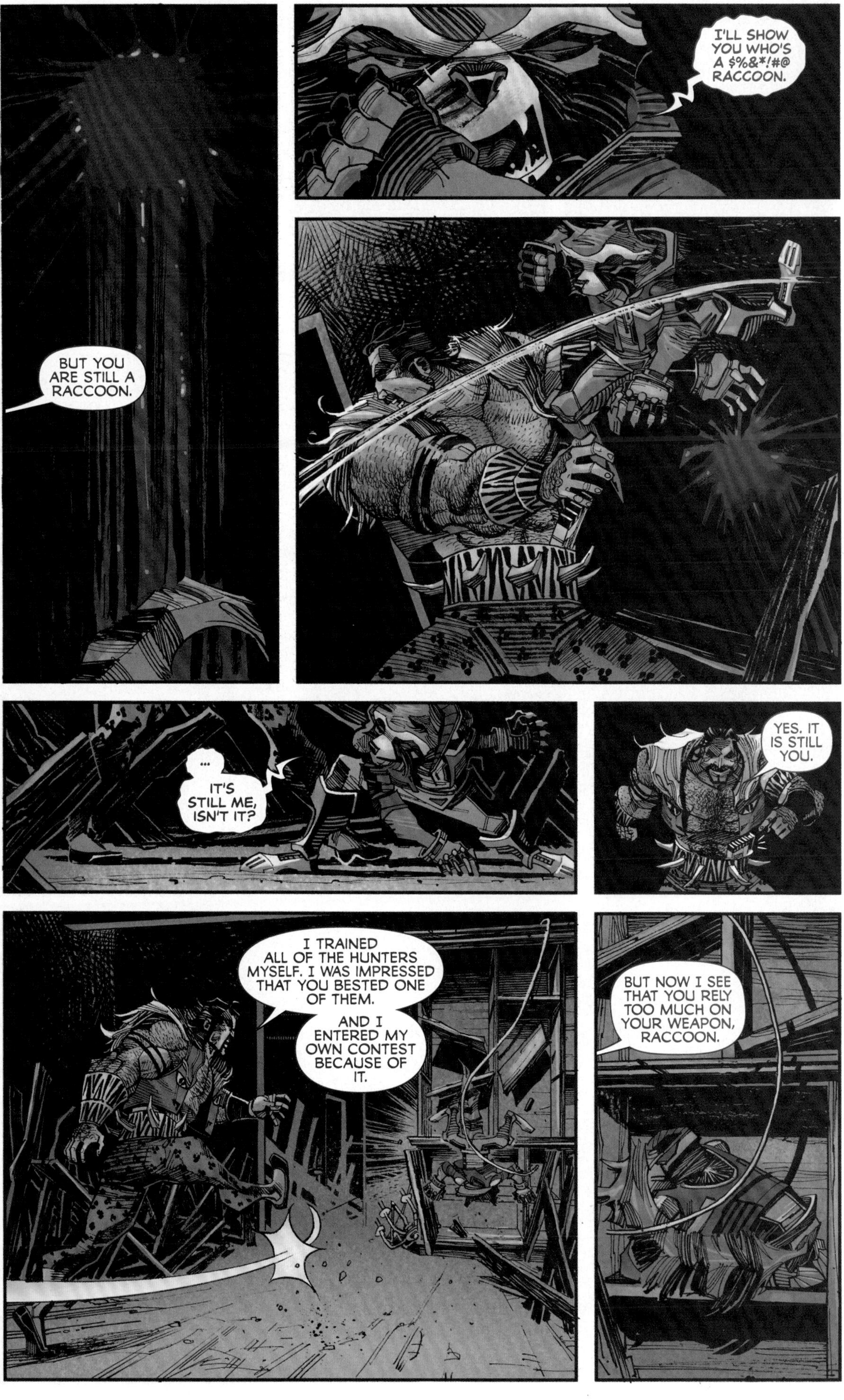
BUT YOU ARE STILL A RACCOON.
I'LL SHOW YOU WHO'S A $%&*!#@ RACCOON.
... IT'S STILL ME, ISN'T IT?
YES. IT IS STILL YOU.
I TRAINED ALL OF THE HUNTERS MYSELF. I WAS IMPRESSED THAT YOU BESTED ONE OF THEM.
AND I ENTERED MY OWN CONTEST BECAUSE OF IT.
BUT NOW I SEE THAT YOU RELY TOO MUCH ON YOUR WEAPON, RACCOON.

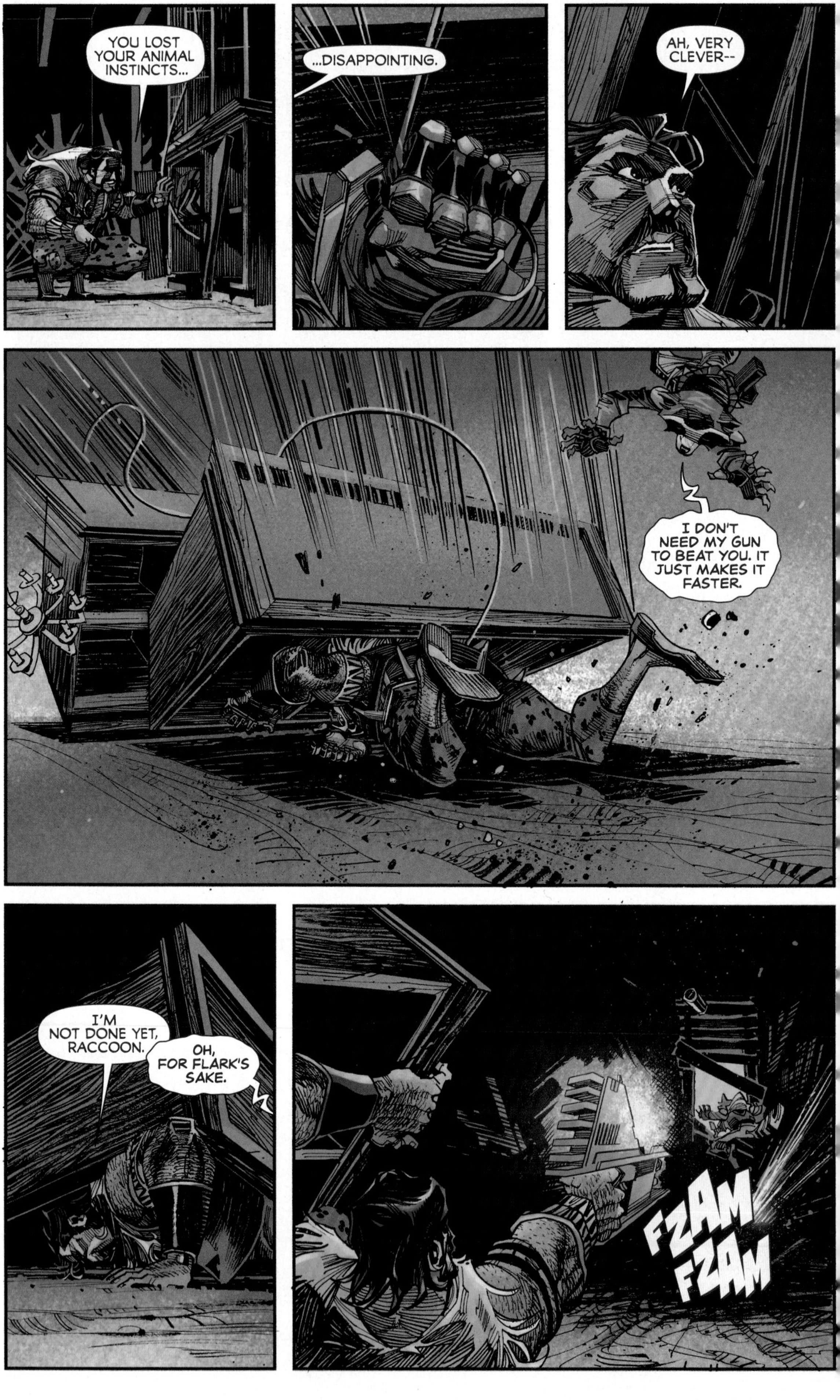
YOU LOST YOUR ANIMAL INSTINCTS...
...DISAPPOINTING.
AH, VERY CLEVER--
I DON'T NEED MY GUN TO BEAT YOU. IT JUST MAKES IT FASTER.
I'M NOT DONE YET, RACCOON.
OH, FOR FLARK'S SAKE.
FZAM
FZAM

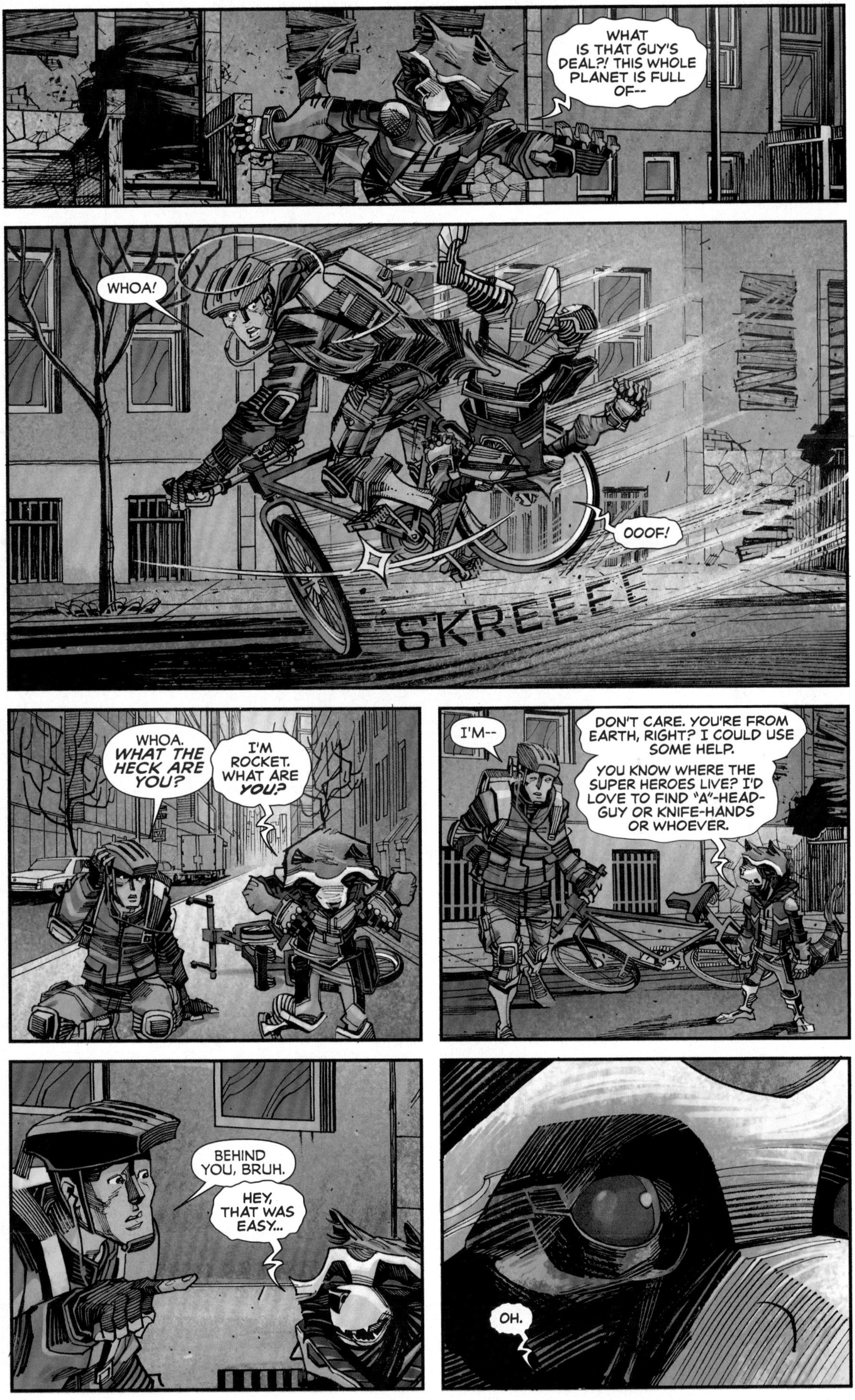
WHAT IS THAT GUY'S DEAL?! THIS WHOLE PLANET IS FULL OF--
WHOA!
OOOF!
SKREEEE
WHOA. WHAT THE HECK ARE YOU?
I'M ROCKET. WHAT ARE YOU?
I'M--
DON'T CARE. YOU'RE FROM EARTH, RIGHT? I COULD USE SOME HELP.
YOU KNOW WHERE THE SUPER HEROES LIVE? I'D LOVE TO FIND "A"-HEAD-GUY OR KNIFE-HANDS OR WHOEVER.
BEHIND YOU, BRUH.
HEY, THAT WAS EASY...
OH.

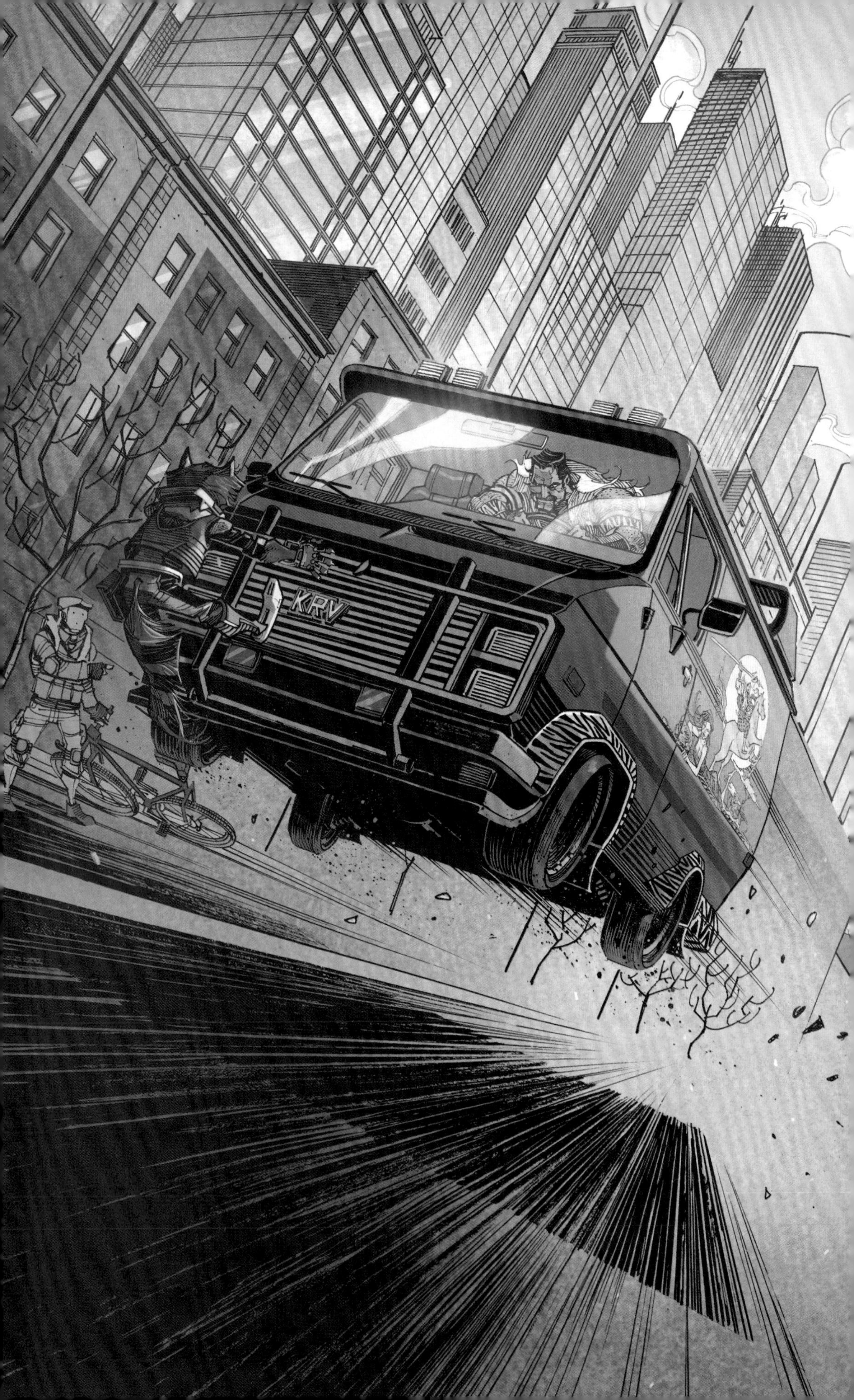
KRV

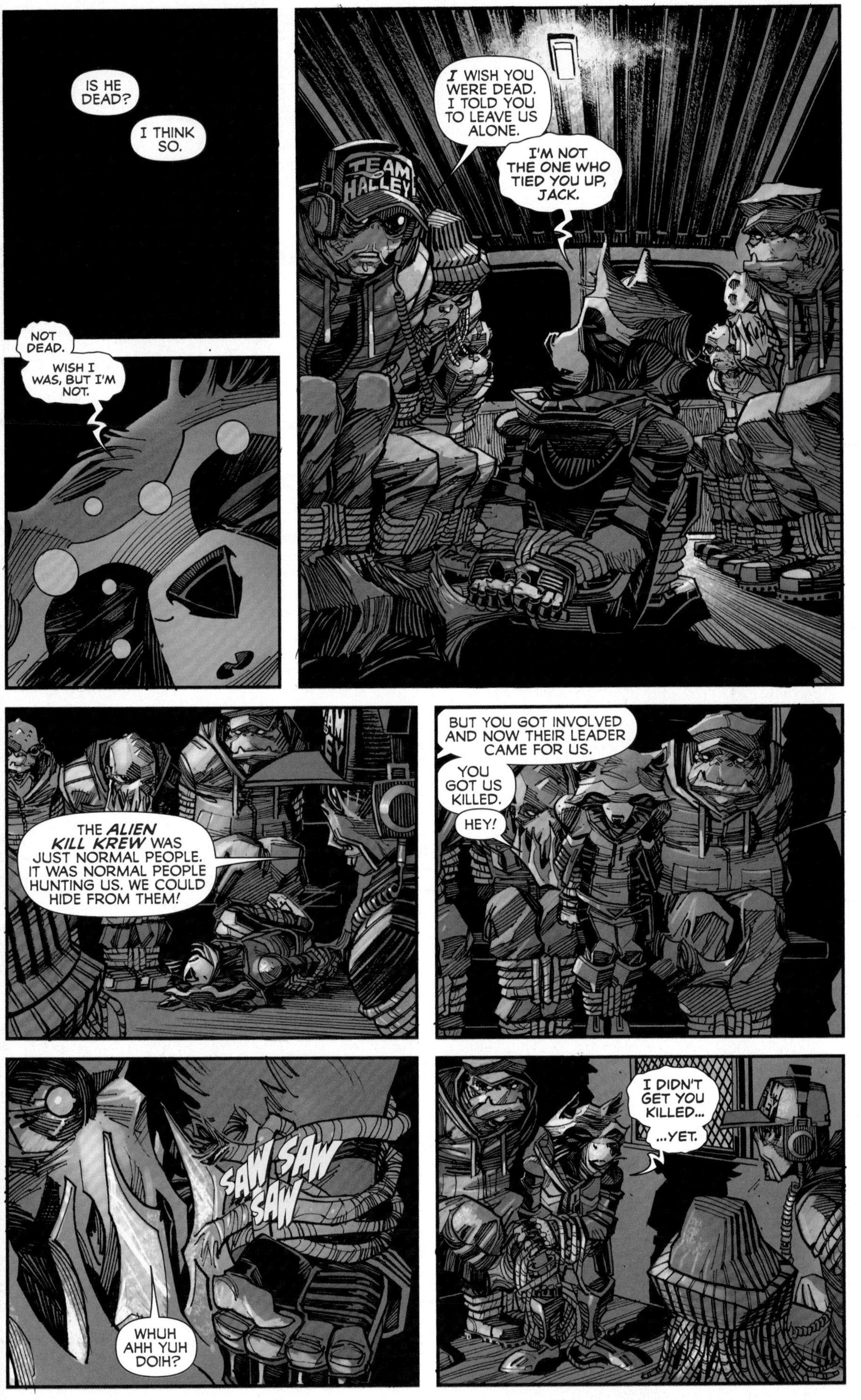
IS HE DEAD?
I THINK SO.
I WISH YOU WERE DEAD. I TOLD YOU TO LEAVE US ALONE.
I'M NOT THE ONE WHO TIED YOU UP, JACK.
TEAM HALLEY!
NOT DEAD.
WISH I WAS, BUT I'M NOT.
THE ALIEN KILL KREW WAS JUST NORMAL PEOPLE. IT WAS NORMAL PEOPLE HUNTING US. WE COULD HIDE FROM THEM!
BUT YOU GOT INVOLVED AND NOW THEIR LEADER CAME FOR US.
YOU GOT US KILLED.
HEY!
SAW SAW SAW
WHUH AHH YUH DOIH?
I DIDN'T GET YOU KILLED...
...YET.

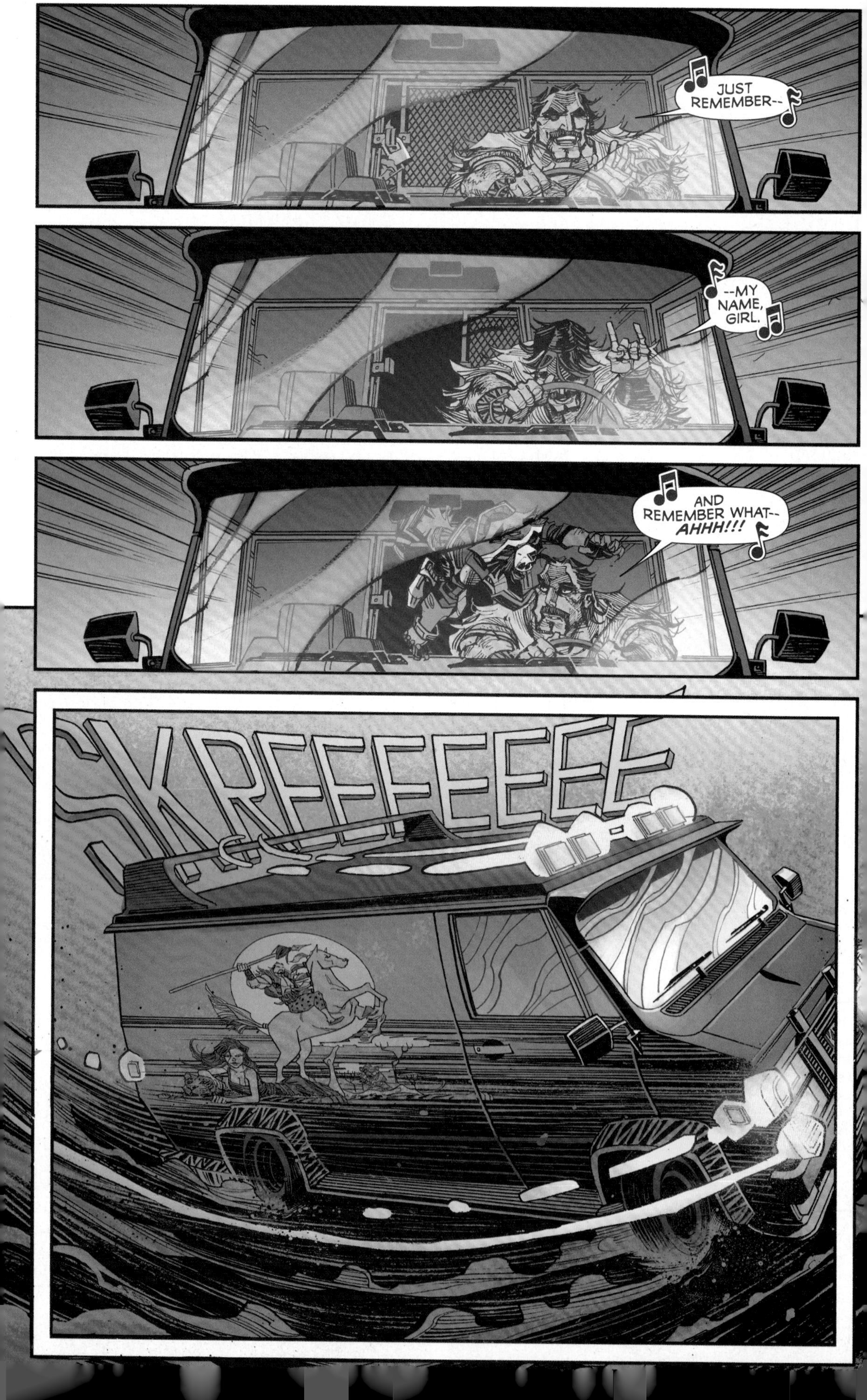
JUST REMEMBER--
--MY NAME, GIRL.
AND REMEMBER WHAT-- AHHH!!!
SKREEEEEEE

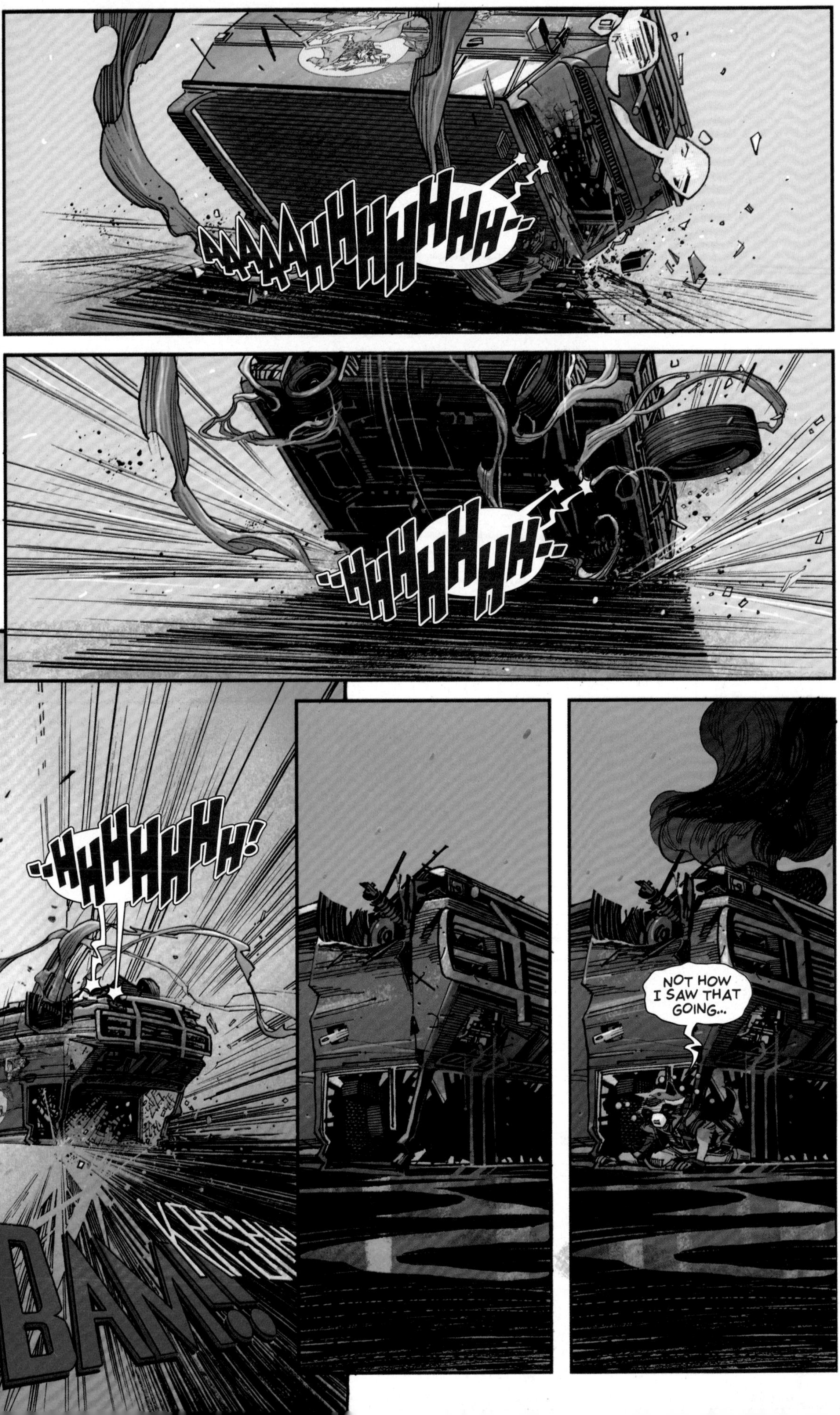
AAAAAHHHHHHH-
-HHHHHHHH-
-HHHHHHH!
BAM..
KRSHH
NOT HOW I SAW THAT GOING...

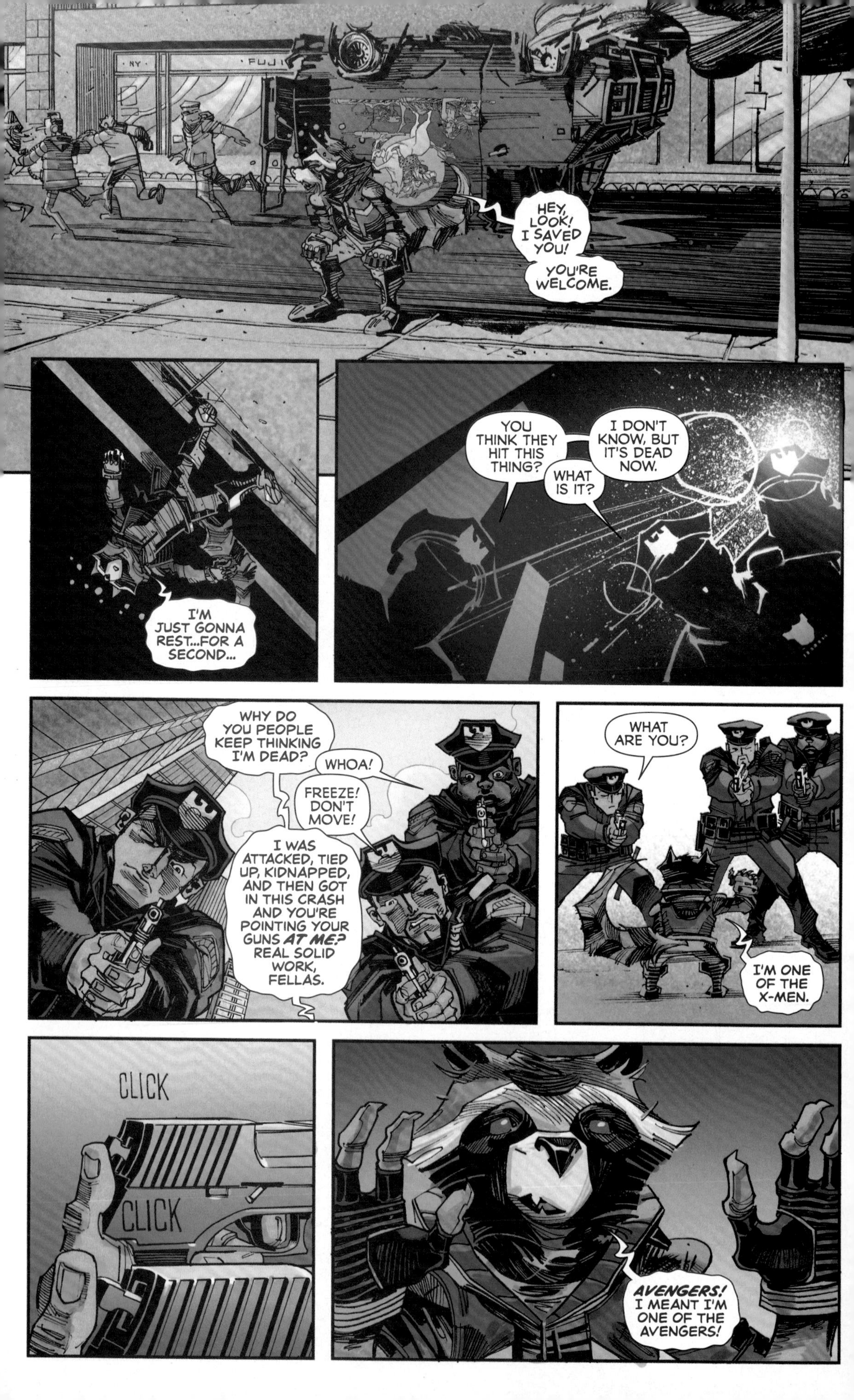
NY
FUJI
HEY, LOOK! I SAVED YOU!
YOU'RE WELCOME.
I'M JUST GONNA REST...FOR A SECOND...
YOU THINK THEY HIT THIS THING?
I DON'T KNOW, BUT IT'S DEAD NOW.
WHAT IS IT?
WHY DO YOU PEOPLE KEEP THINKING I'M DEAD?
WHOA!
FREEZE! DON'T MOVE!
I WAS ATTACKED, TIED UP, KIDNAPPED, AND THEN GOT IN THIS CRASH AND YOU'RE POINTING YOUR GUNS AT ME? REAL SOLID WORK, FELLAS.
WHAT ARE YOU?
I'M ONE OF THE X-MEN.
CLICK
CLICK
AVENGERS! I MEANT I'M ONE OF THE AVENGERS!

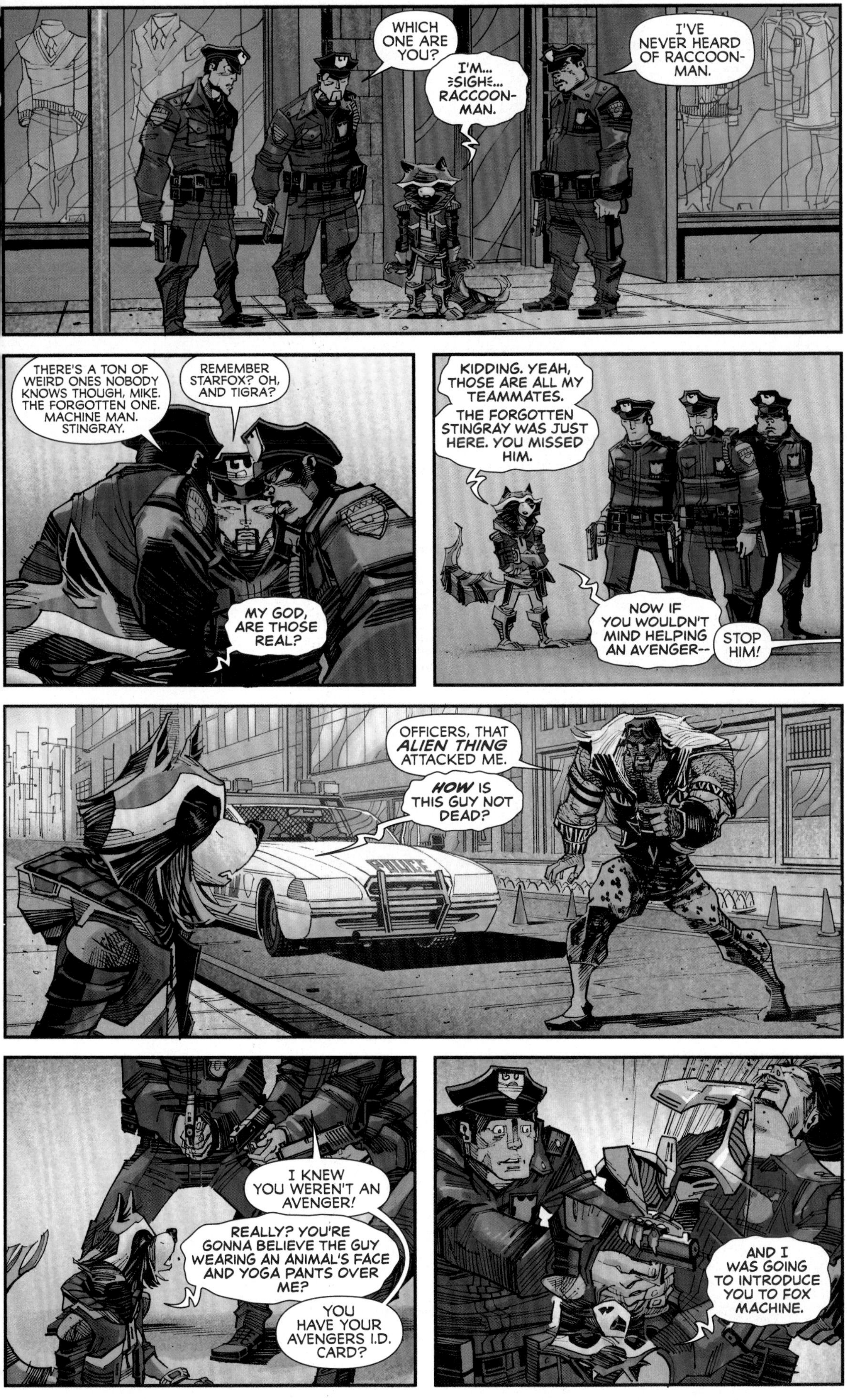
WHICH ONE ARE YOU?
I'M... SIGH... RACCOON-MAN.
I'VE NEVER HEARD OF RACCOON-MAN.
THERE'S A TON OF WEIRD ONES NOBODY KNOWS THOUGH, MIKE. THE FORGOTTEN ONE. MACHINE MAN. STINGRAY.
REMEMBER STARFOX? OH, AND TIGRA?
MY GOD, ARE THOSE REAL?
KIDDING. YEAH, THOSE ARE ALL MY TEAMMATES.
THE FORGOTTEN STINGRAY WAS JUST HERE. YOU MISSED HIM.
NOW IF YOU WOULDN'T MIND HELPING AN AVENGER--
STOP HIM!
OFFICERS, THAT *ALIEN THING* ATTACKED ME.
HOW IS THIS GUY NOT DEAD?
POLICE
I KNEW YOU WEREN'T AN AVENGER!
REALLY? YOU'RE GONNA BELIEVE THE GUY WEARING AN ANIMAL'S FACE AND YOGA PANTS OVER ME?
YOU HAVE YOUR AVENGERS I.D. CARD?
AND I WAS GOING TO INTRODUCE YOU TO FOX MACHINE.

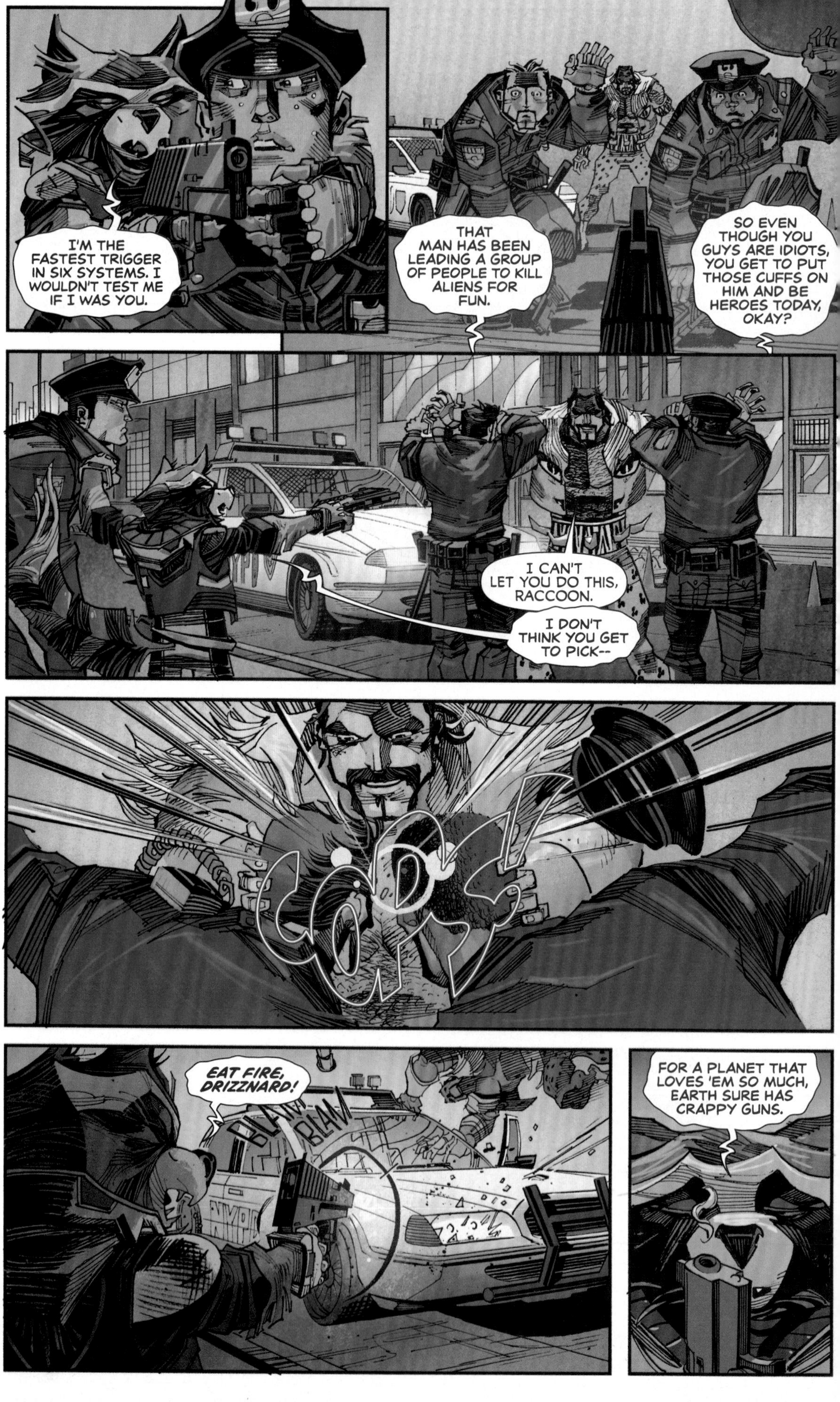
I'M THE FASTEST TRIGGER IN SIX SYSTEMS. I WOULDN'T TEST ME IF I WAS YOU.
THAT MAN HAS BEEN LEADING A GROUP OF PEOPLE TO KILL ALIENS FOR FUN.
SO EVEN THOUGH YOU GUYS ARE IDIOTS, YOU GET TO PUT THOSE CUFFS ON HIM AND BE HEROES TODAY, OKAY?
I CAN'T LET YOU DO THIS, RACCOON.
I DON'T THINK YOU GET TO PICK--
EAT FIRE, DRIZZNARD!
BLAM BLAM
FOR A PLANET THAT LOVES 'EM SO MUCH, EARTH SURE HAS CRAPPY GUNS.

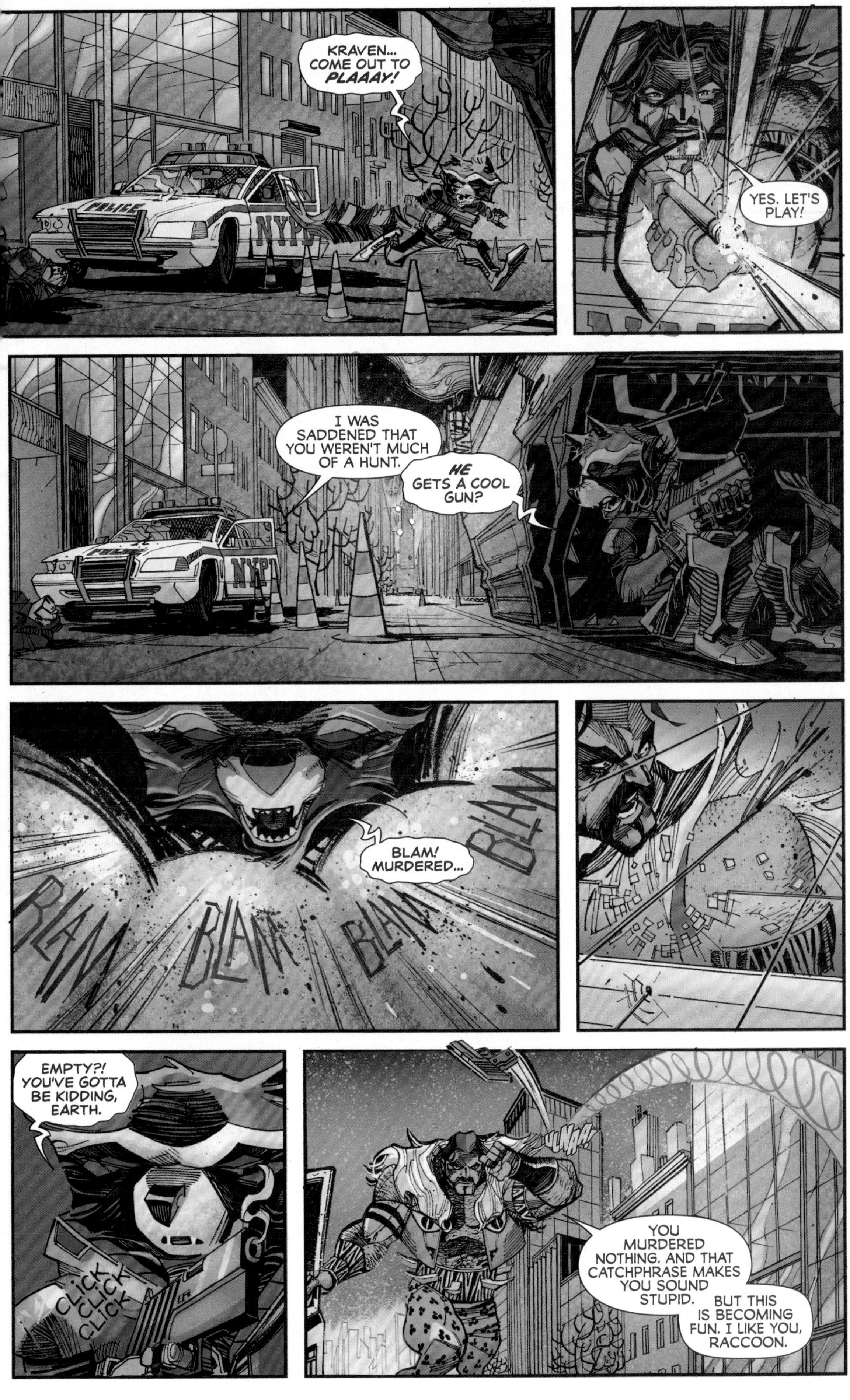
KRAVEN... COME OUT TO PLAAAY!
YES. LET'S PLAY!
I WAS SADDENED THAT YOU WEREN'T MUCH OF A HUNT.
HE GETS A COOL GUN?
BLAM! MURDERED...
BLAM BLAM BLAM BLAM
EMPTY?! YOU'VE GOTTA BE KIDDING, EARTH.
CLICK CLICK CLICK
ULNAA!
YOU MURDERED NOTHING. AND THAT CATCHPHRASE MAKES YOU SOUND STUPID.
BUT THIS IS BECOMING FUN. I LIKE YOU, RACCOON.

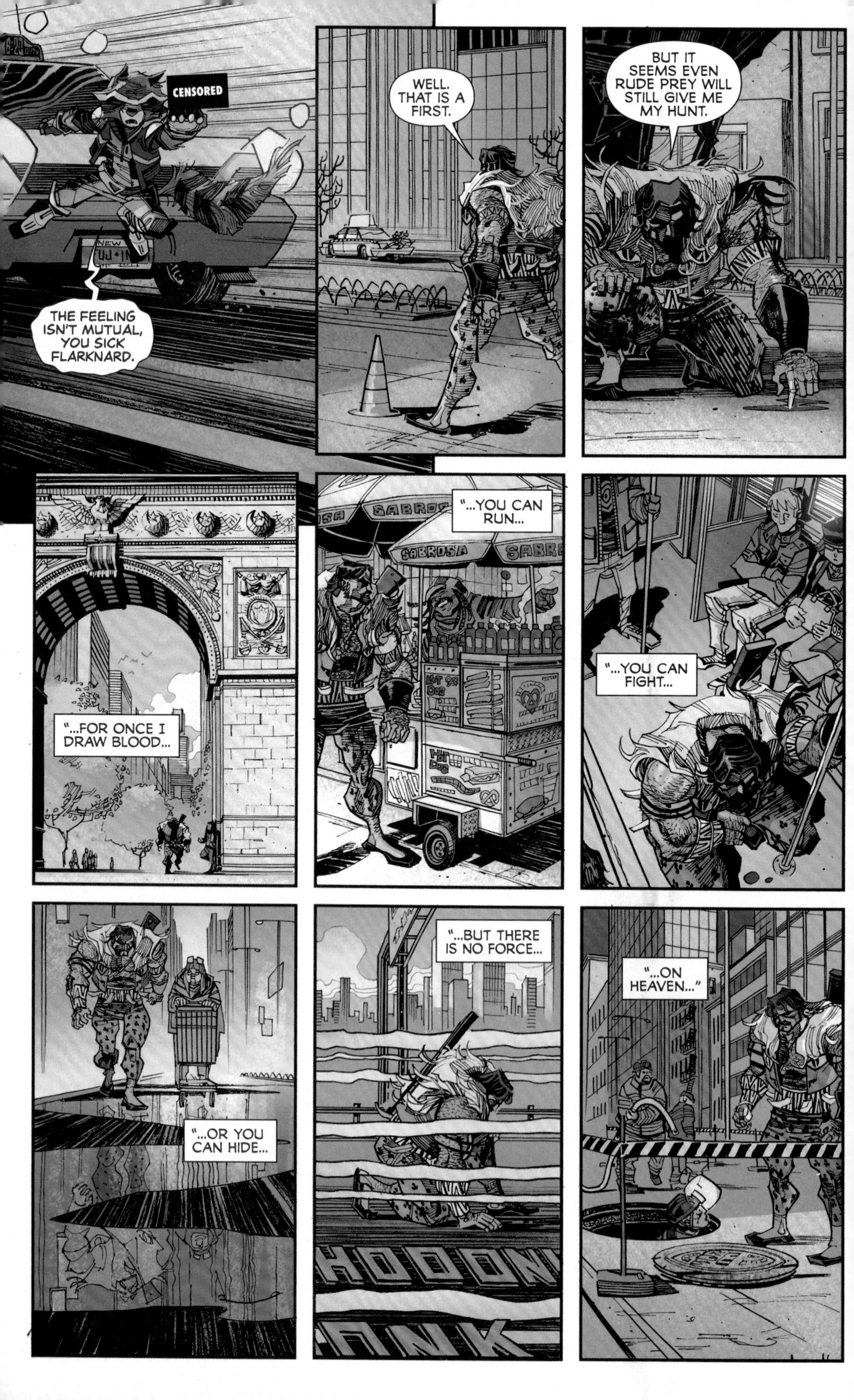
CENSORED
THE FEELING ISN'T MUTUAL, YOU SICK FLARKNARD.
WELL. THAT IS A FIRST.
BUT IT SEEMS EVEN RUDE PREY WILL STILL GIVE ME MY HUNT.
"...FOR ONCE I DRAW BLOOD...
SABROSA
"...YOU CAN RUN...
"...YOU CAN FIGHT...
"...OR YOU CAN HIDE...
"...BUT THERE IS NO FORCE...
HOOON
"...ON HEAVEN..."

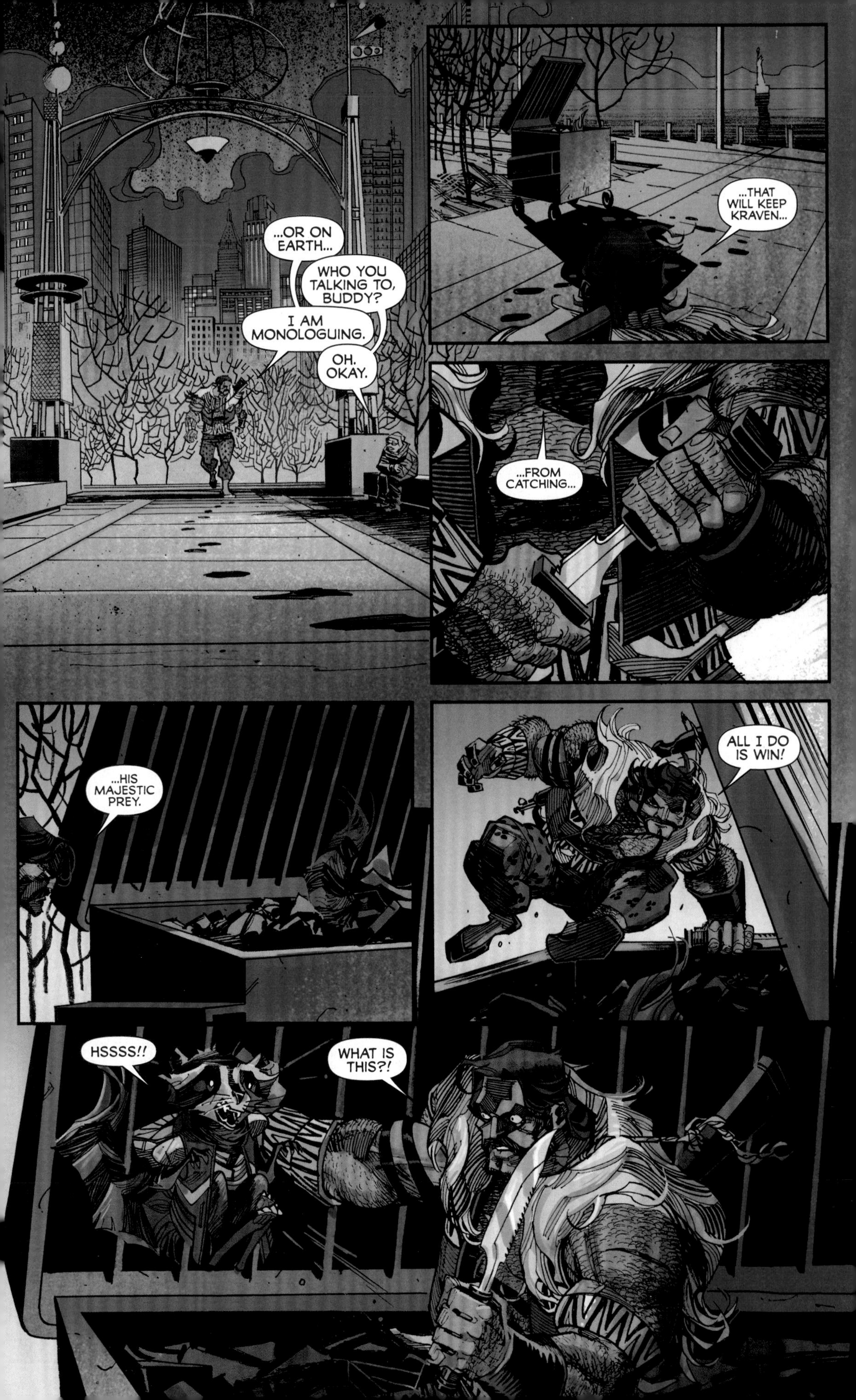
...OR ON EARTH...
WHO YOU TALKING TO, BUDDY?
I AM MONOLOGUING.
OH. OKAY.
...THAT WILL KEEP KRAVEN...
...FROM CATCHING...
...HIS MAJESTIC PREY.
ALL I DO IS WIN!
HSSSS!!
WHAT IS THIS?!

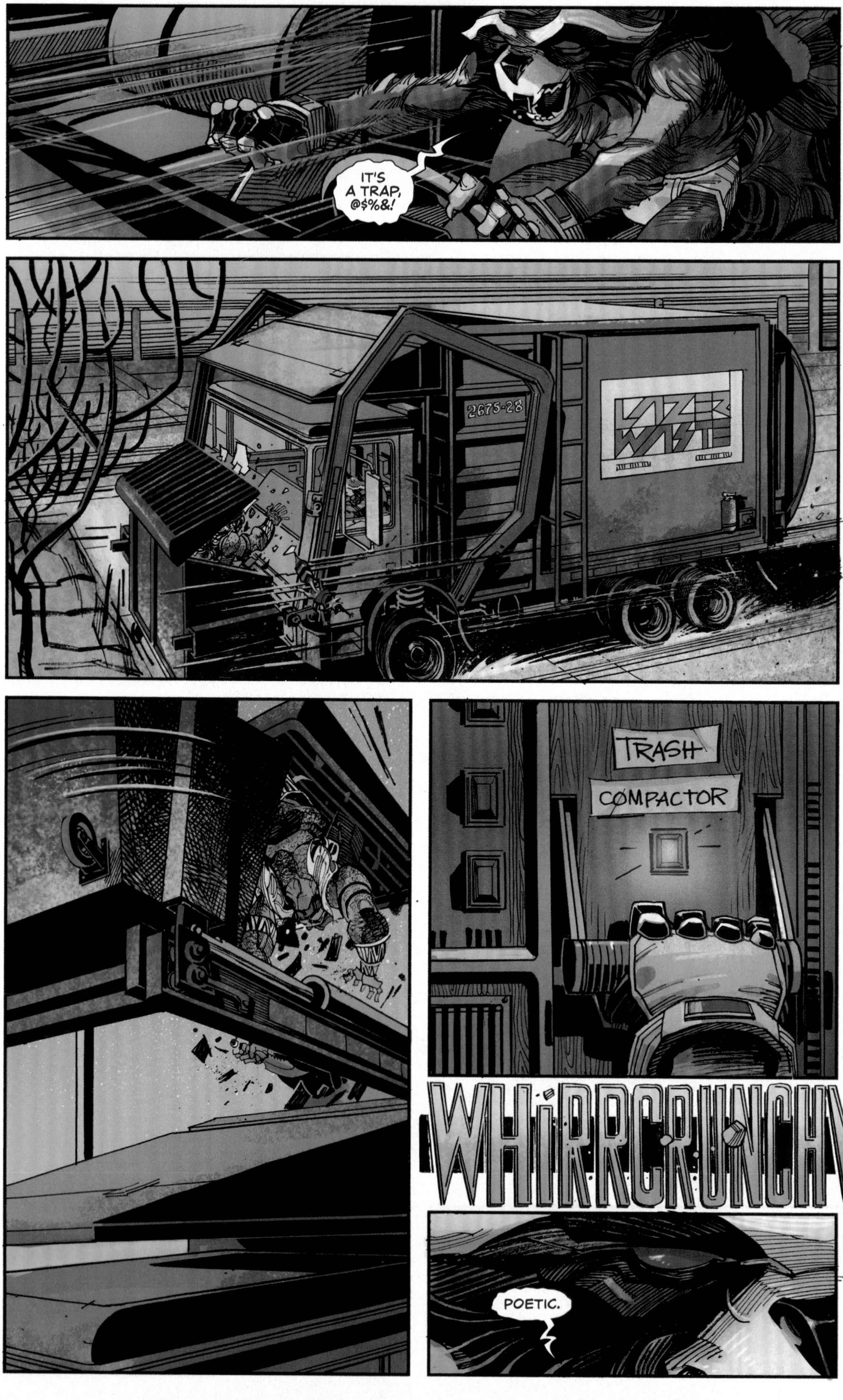
IT'S A TRAP, @$%&!
2675-28
TRASH
CØMPACTOR
WHIRRCRUNCH
POETIC.

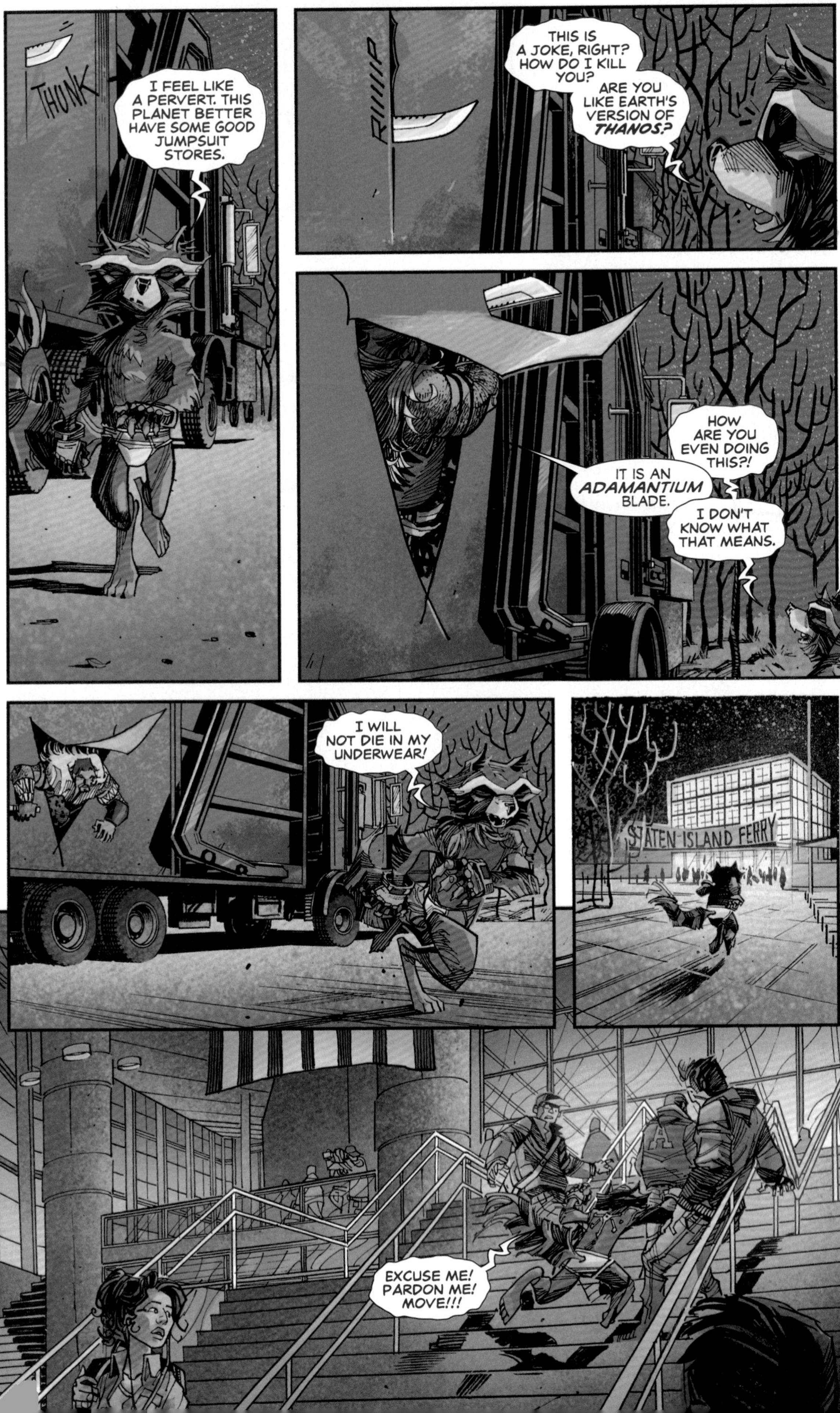
THUNK
I FEEL LIKE A PERVERT. THIS PLANET BETTER HAVE SOME GOOD JUMPSUIT STORES.
RIIIIP
THIS IS A JOKE, RIGHT? HOW DO I KILL YOU?
ARE YOU LIKE EARTH'S VERSION OF THANOS?
HOW ARE YOU EVEN DOING THIS?!
IT IS AN ADAMANTIUM BLADE.
I DON'T KNOW WHAT THAT MEANS.
I WILL NOT DIE IN MY UNDERWEAR!
STATEN ISLAND FERRY
EXCUSE ME! PARDON ME! MOVE!!!

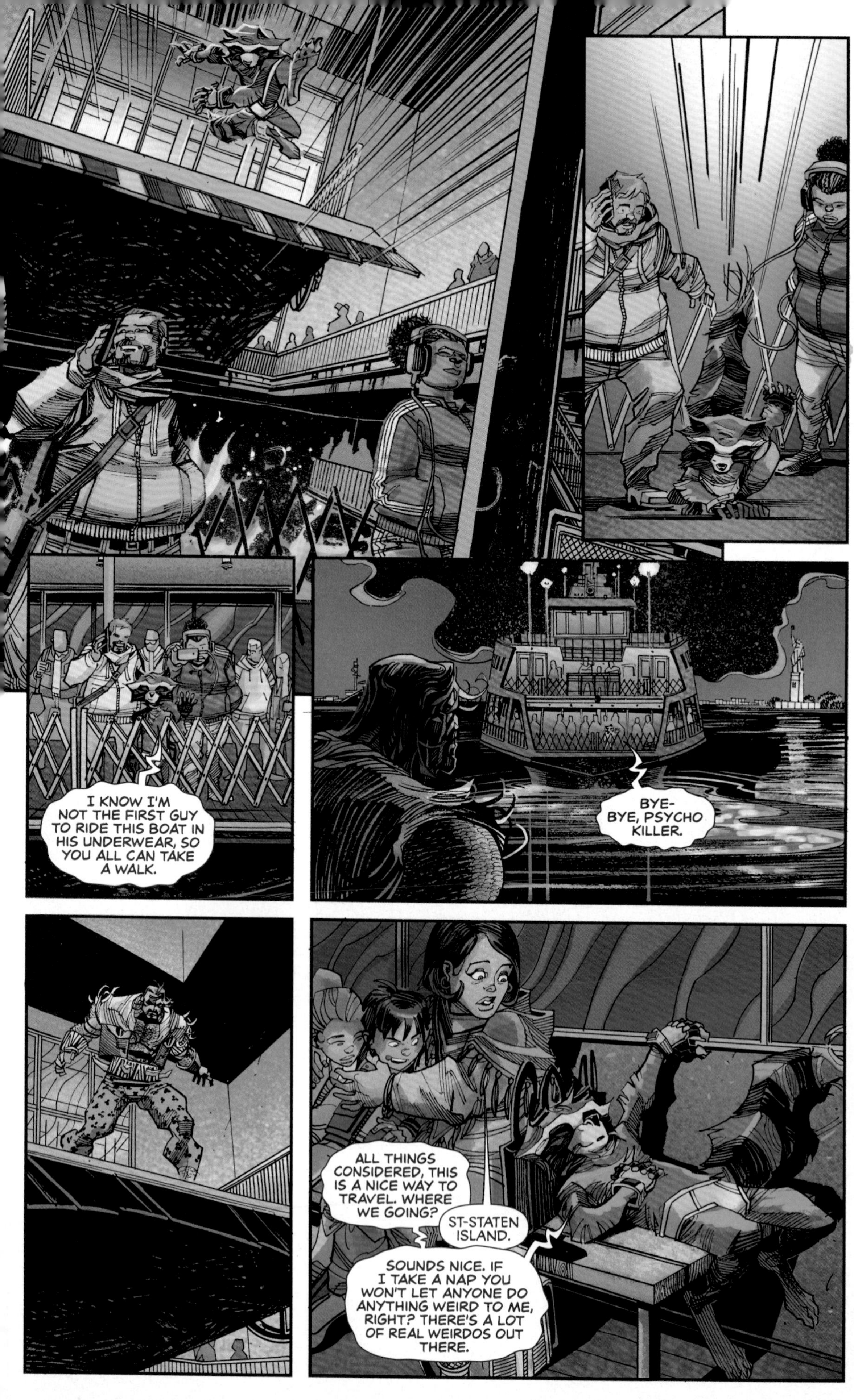
I KNOW I'M NOT THE FIRST GUY TO RIDE THIS BOAT IN HIS UNDERWEAR, SO YOU ALL CAN TAKE A WALK.
BYE-BYE, PSYCHO KILLER.
ALL THINGS CONSIDERED, THIS IS A NICE WAY TO TRAVEL. WHERE WE GOING?
ST-STATEN ISLAND.
SOUNDS NICE. IF I TAKE A NAP YOU WON'T LET ANYONE DO ANYTHING WEIRD TO ME, RIGHT? THERE'S A LOT OF REAL WEIRDOS OUT THERE.

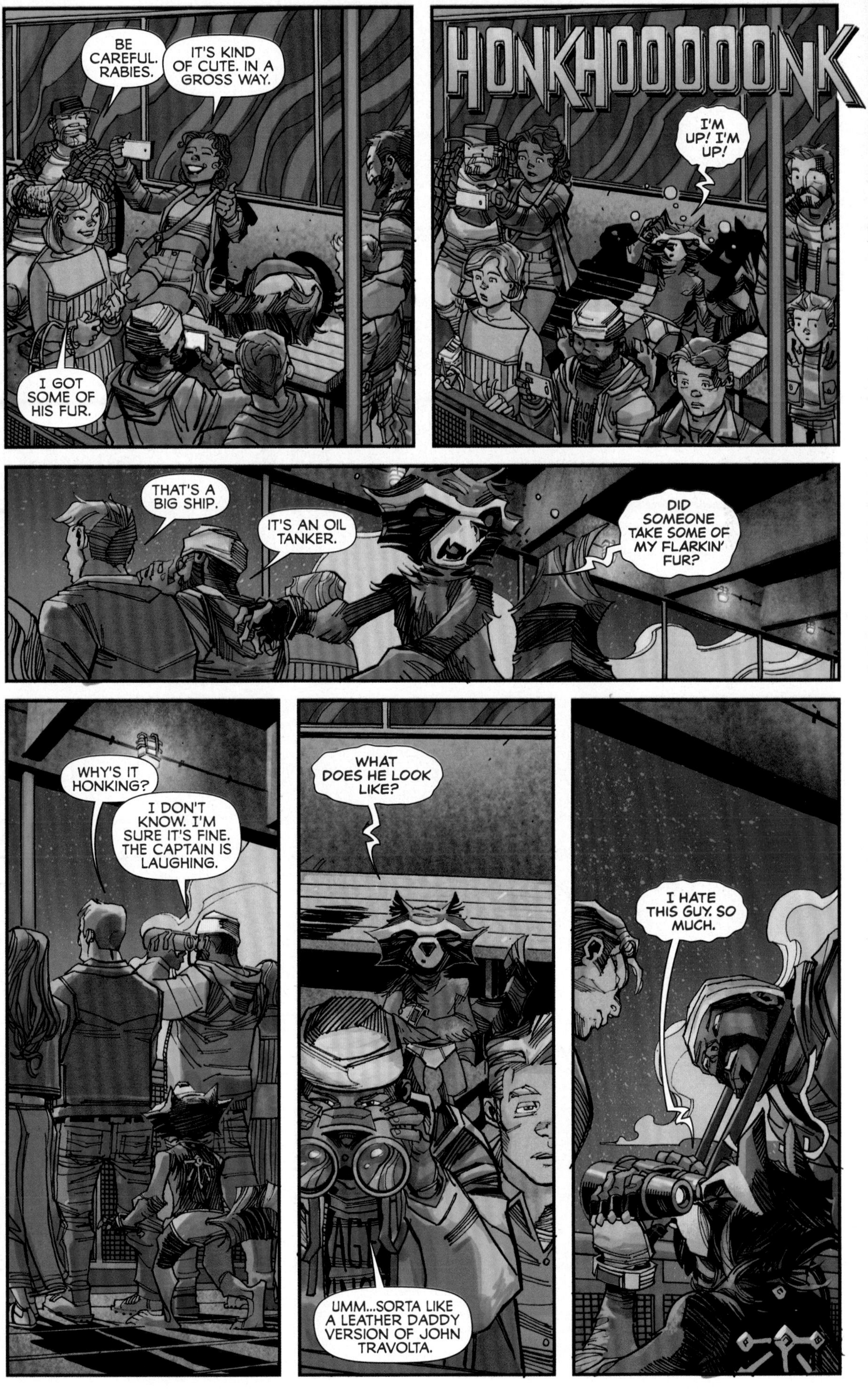
BE CAREFUL. RABIES.
IT'S KIND OF CUTE. IN A GROSS WAY.
I GOT SOME OF HIS FUR.
HONKHOOOOOONK
I'M UP! I'M UP!
THAT'S A BIG SHIP.
IT'S AN OIL TANKER.
DID SOMEONE TAKE SOME OF MY FLARKIN' FUR?
WHY'S IT HONKING?
I DON'T KNOW. I'M SURE IT'S FINE. THE CAPTAIN IS LAUGHING.
WHAT DOES HE LOOK LIKE?
UMM...SORTA LIKE A LEATHER DADDY VERSION OF JOHN TRAVOLTA.
I HATE THIS GUY. SO MUCH.

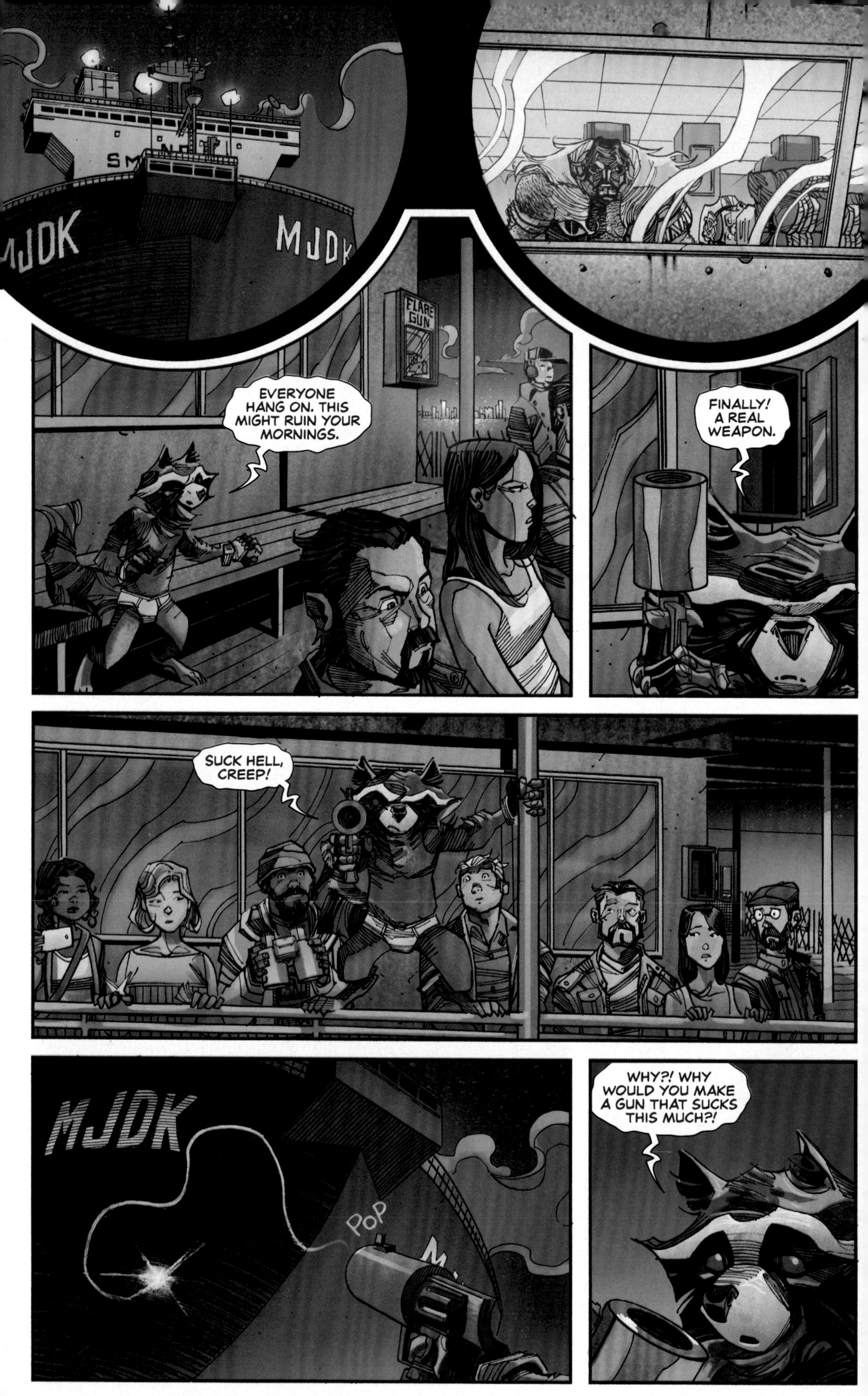
SM
MJDK
MJDK
FLARE GUN
EVERYONE HANG ON. THIS MIGHT RUIN YOUR MORNINGS.
FINALLY! A REAL WEAPON.
SUCK HELL, CREEP!
MJDK
POP
WHY?! WHY WOULD YOU MAKE A GUN THAT SUCKS THIS MUCH?!

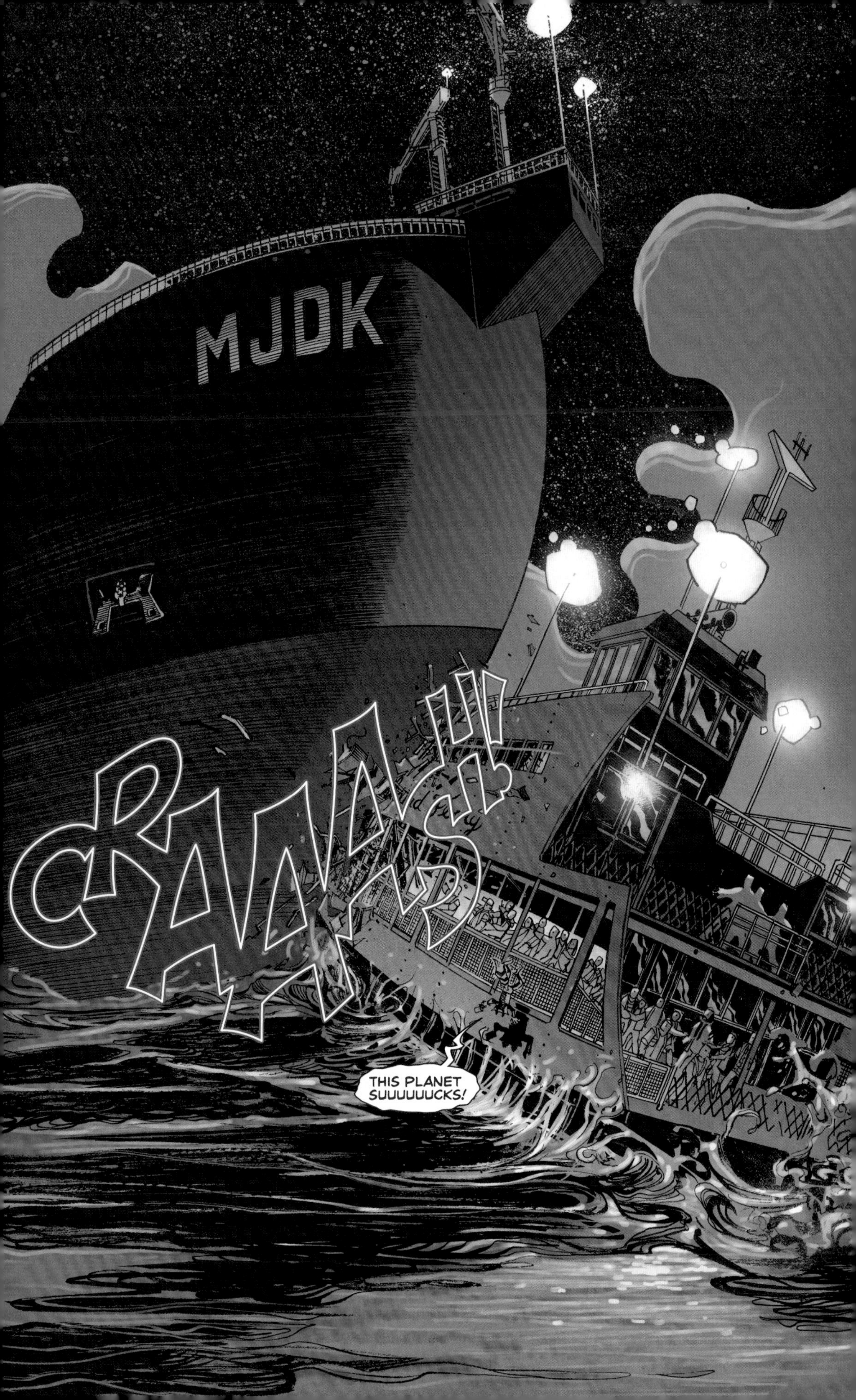
MJDK
CRAAASH!!
THIS PLANET SUUUUUUCKS!

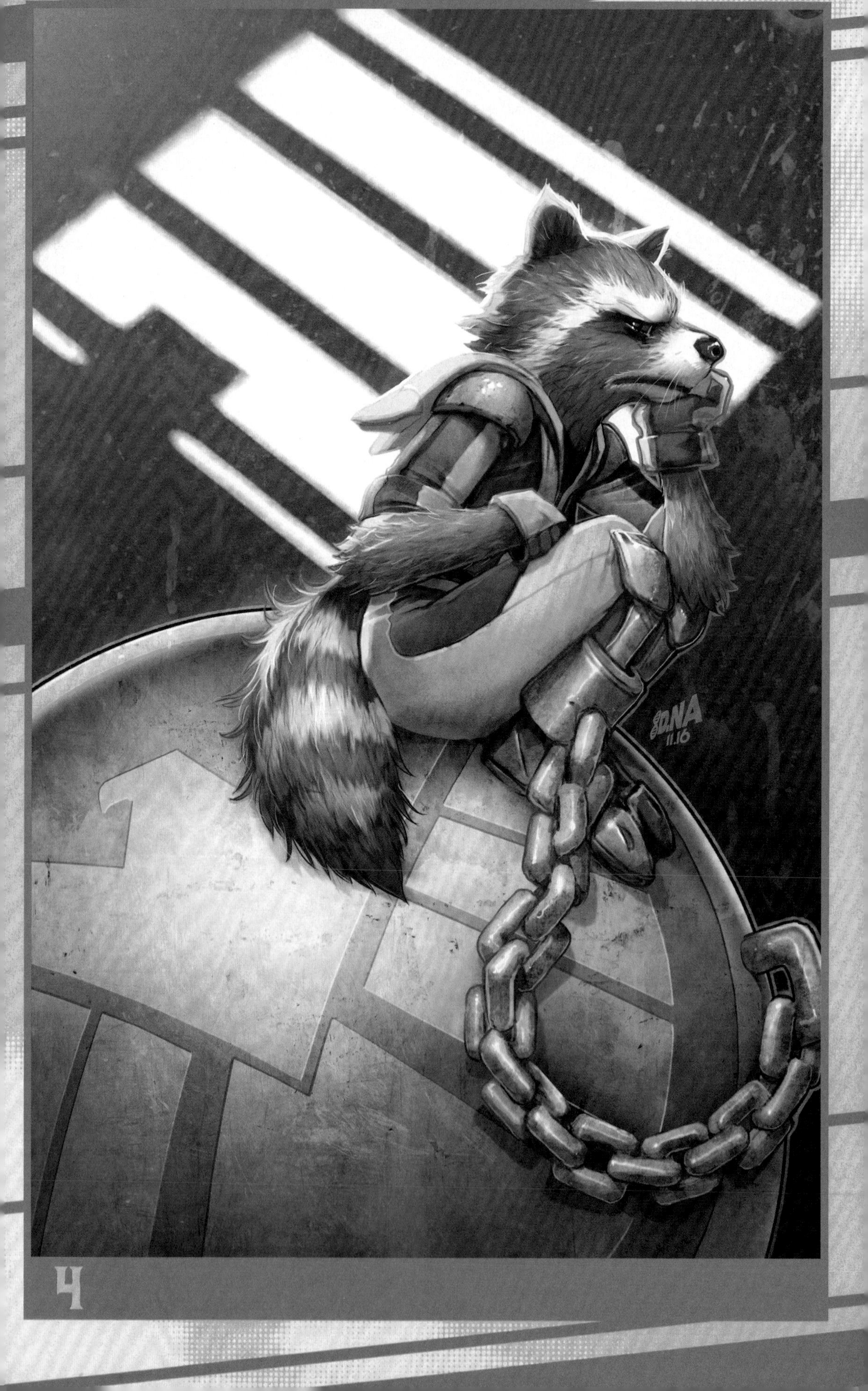

4

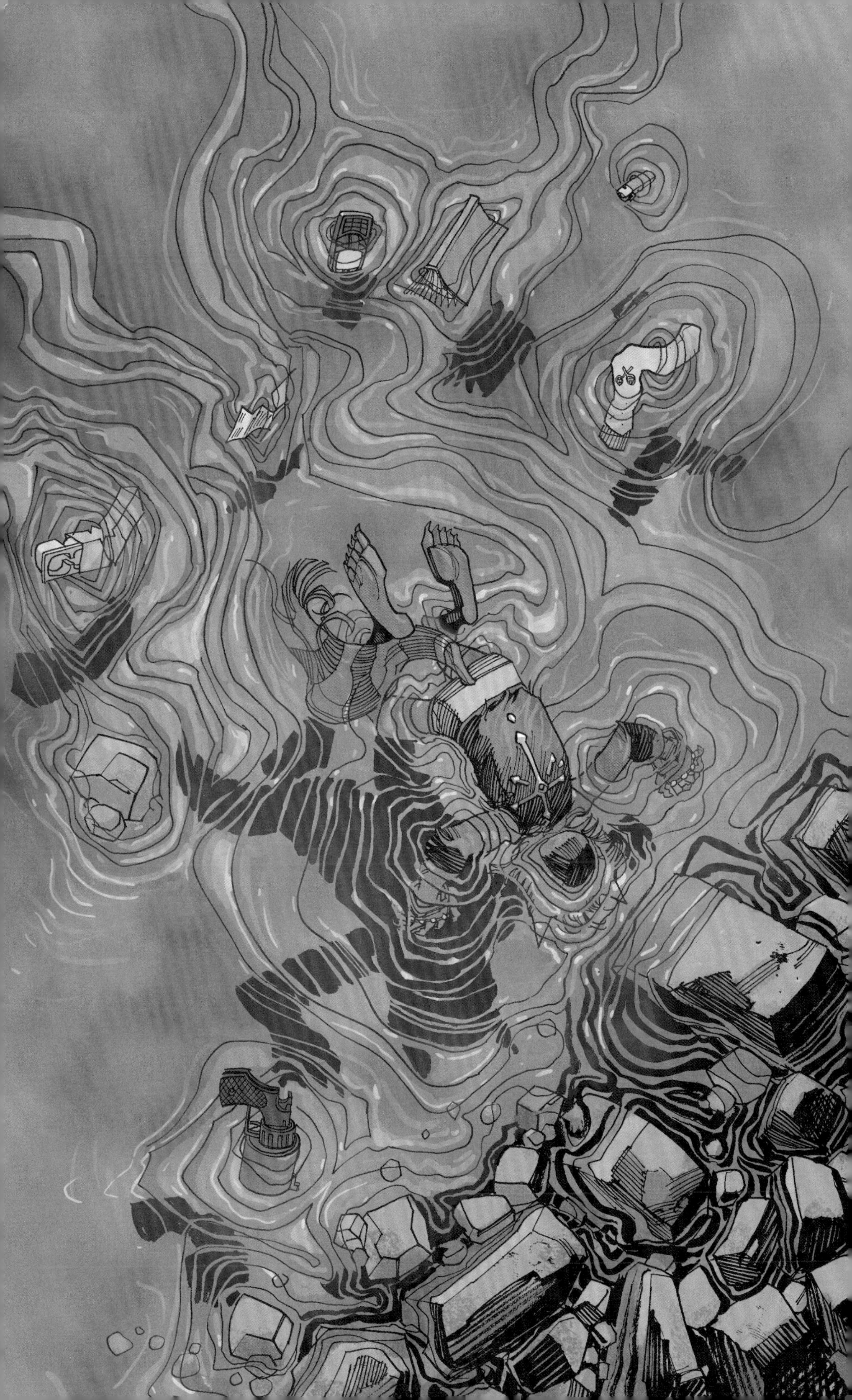

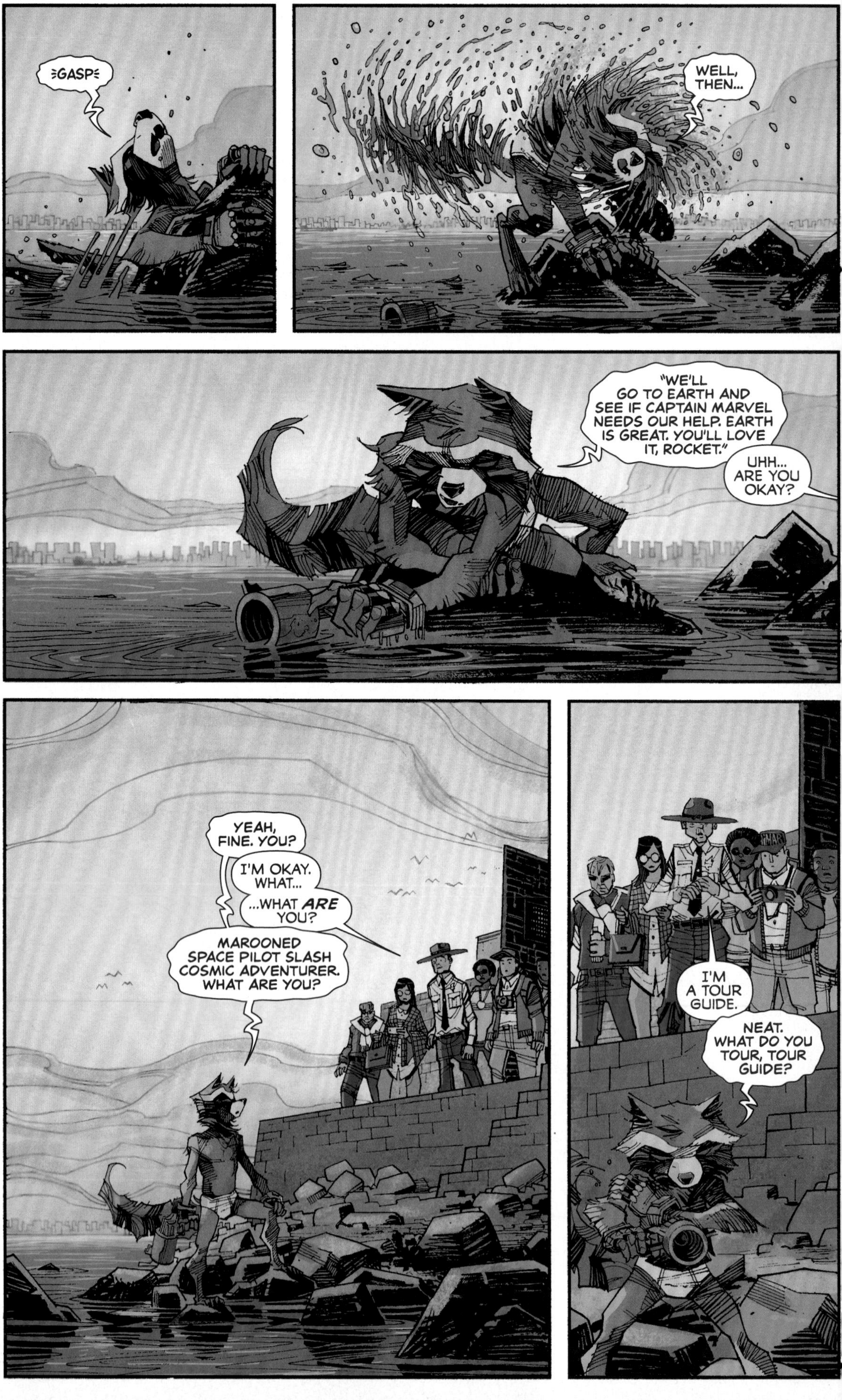

≡GASP≡
WELL, THEN...
"WE'LL GO TO EARTH AND SEE IF CAPTAIN MARVEL NEEDS OUR HELP. EARTH IS GREAT. YOU'LL LOVE IT, ROCKET."
UHH... ARE YOU OKAY?
YEAH, FINE. YOU?
I'M OKAY. WHAT...
...WHAT *ARE* YOU?
MAROONED SPACE PILOT SLASH COSMIC ADVENTURER. WHAT ARE YOU?
I'M A TOUR GUIDE.
NEAT. WHAT DO YOU TOUR, TOUR GUIDE?

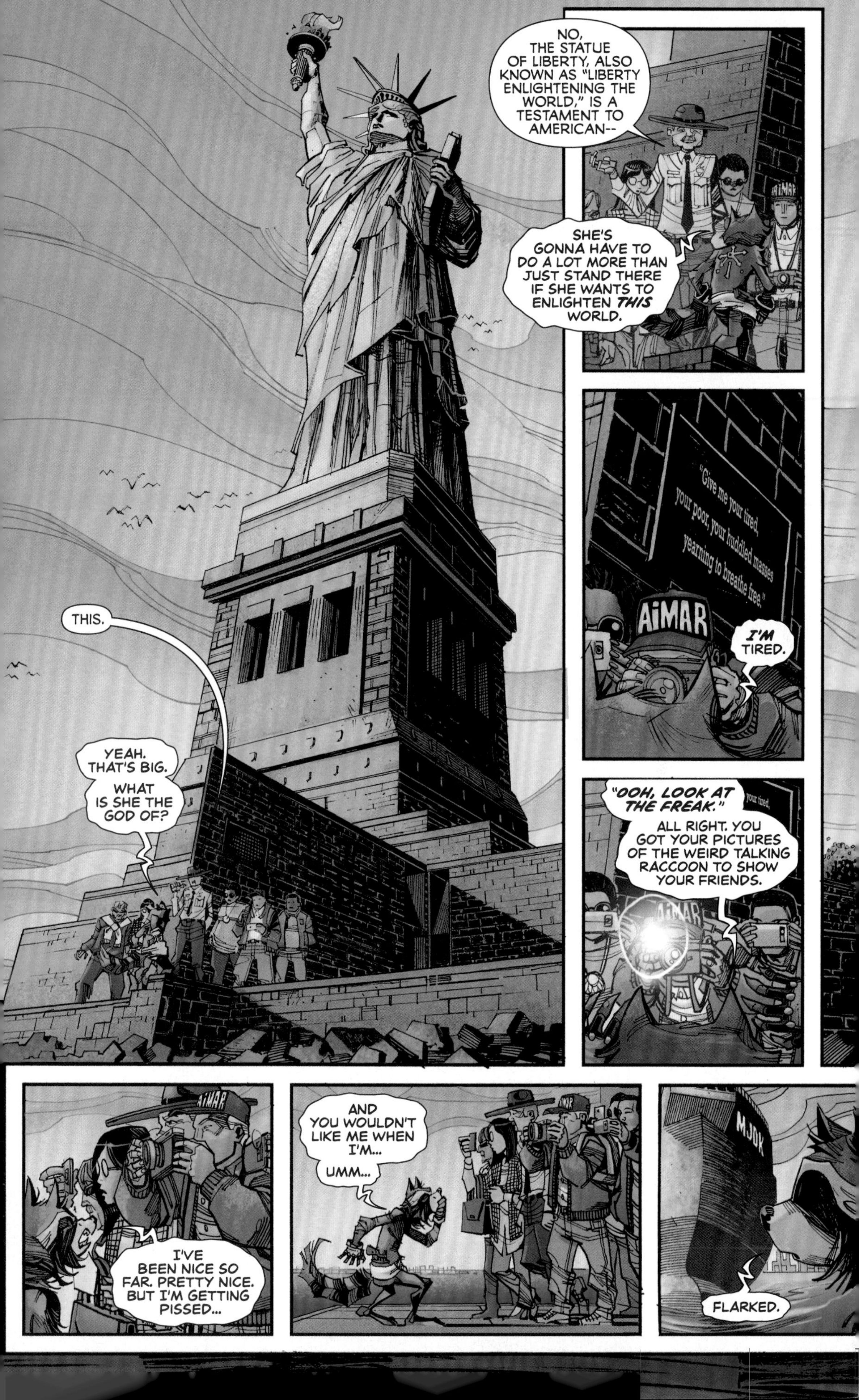
NO, THE STATUE OF LIBERTY, ALSO KNOWN AS "LIBERTY ENLIGHTENING THE WORLD," IS A TESTAMENT TO AMERICAN--
SHE'S GONNA HAVE TO DO A LOT MORE THAN JUST STAND THERE IF SHE WANTS TO ENLIGHTEN *THIS* WORLD.
THIS.
YEAH. THAT'S BIG.
WHAT IS SHE THE GOD OF?
"Give me your tired, your poor, your huddled masses yearning to breathe free."
AiMAR
I'M TIRED.
"OOH, LOOK AT THE FREAK."
ALL RIGHT. YOU GOT YOUR PICTURES OF THE WEIRD TALKING RACCOON TO SHOW YOUR FRIENDS.
I'VE BEEN NICE SO FAR. PRETTY NICE. BUT I'M GETTING PISSED...
AND YOU WOULDN'T LIKE ME WHEN I'M...
UMM...
MJOK
FLARKED.

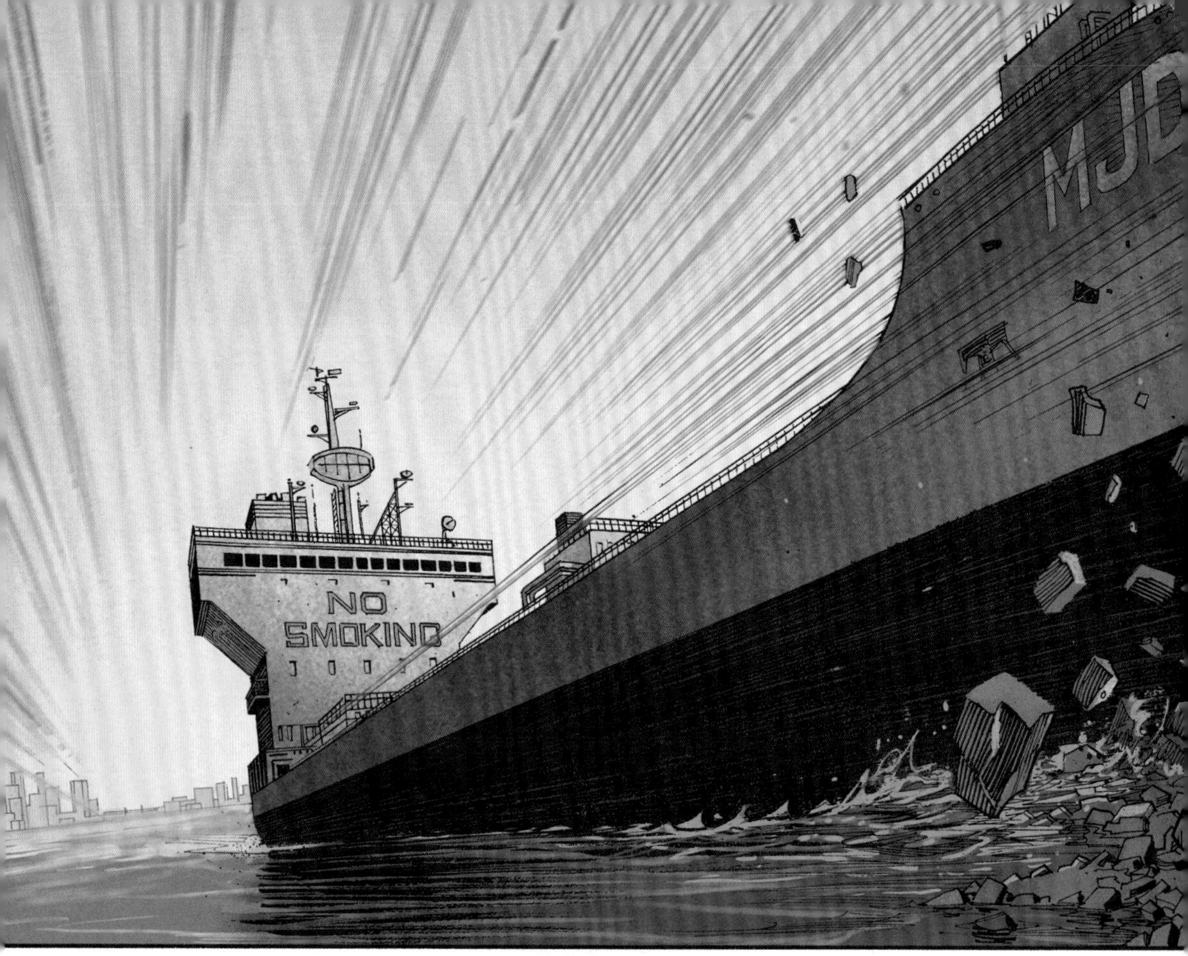
MJD
NO SMOKING

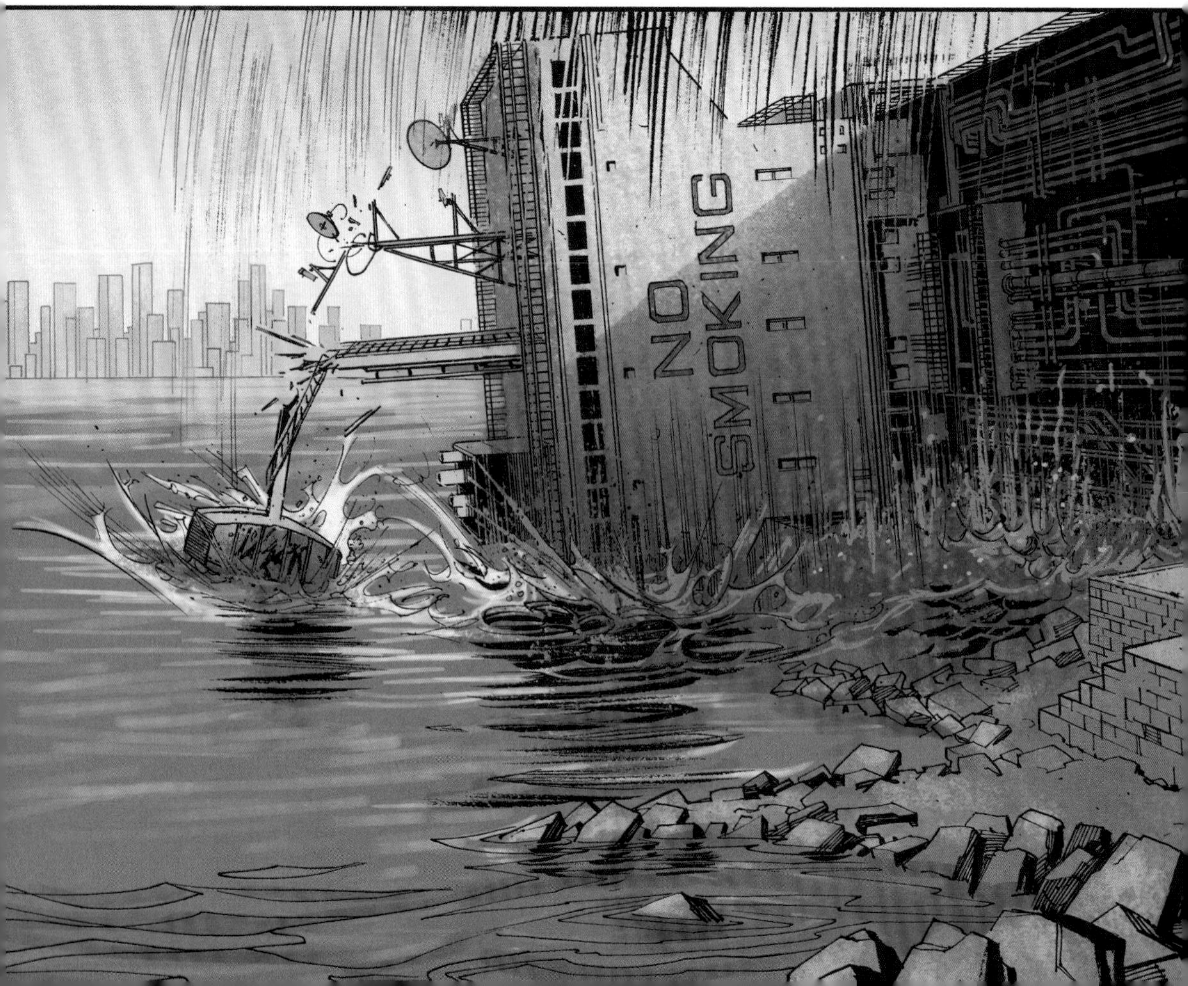
NO SMOKING

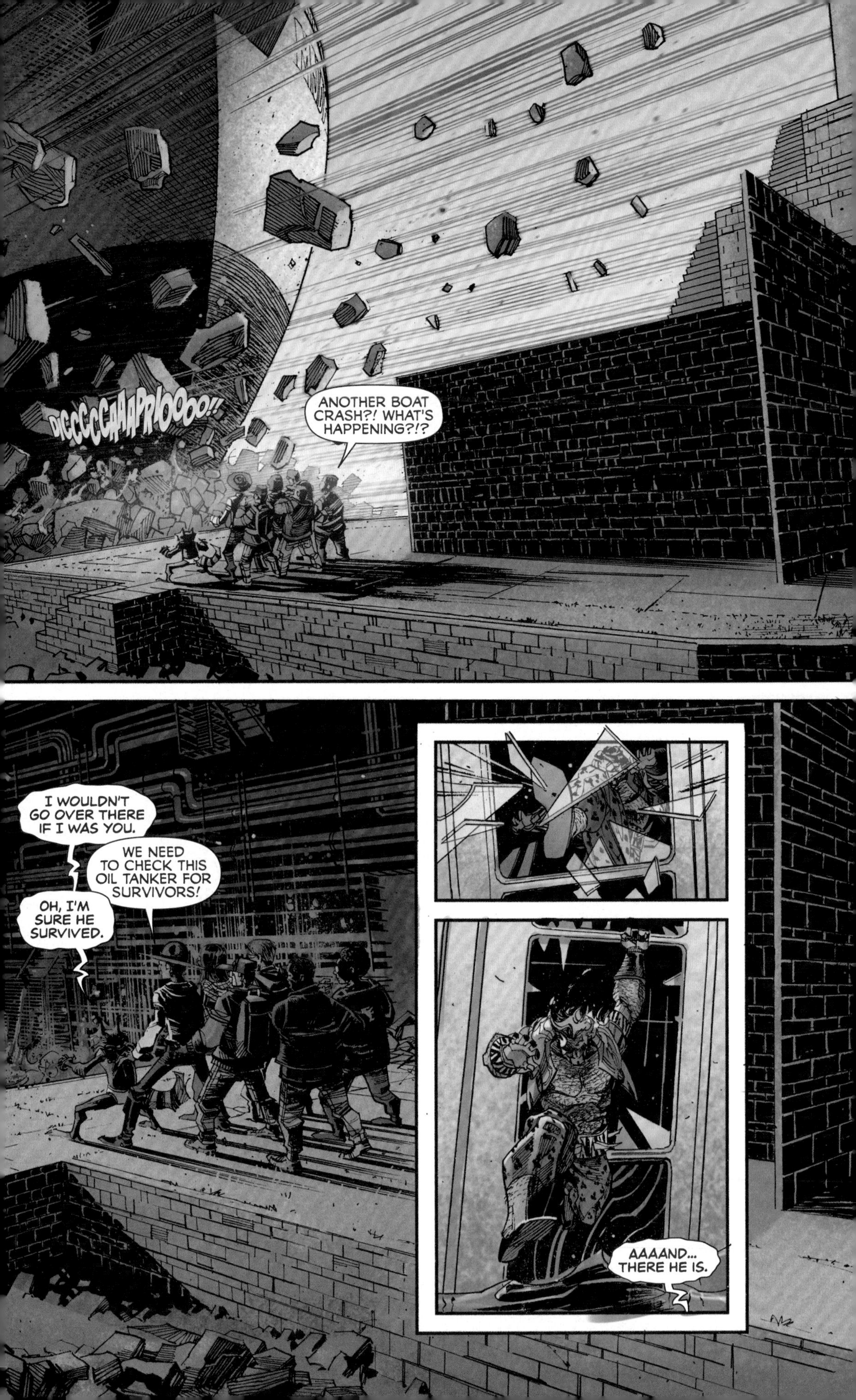
DICCCCCAAAPRIOOOOO!!
ANOTHER BOAT CRASH?! WHAT'S HAPPENING?!?
I WOULDN'T GO OVER THERE IF I WAS YOU.
WE NEED TO CHECK THIS OIL TANKER FOR SURVIVORS!
OH, I'M SURE HE SURVIVED.
AAAAND... THERE HE IS.

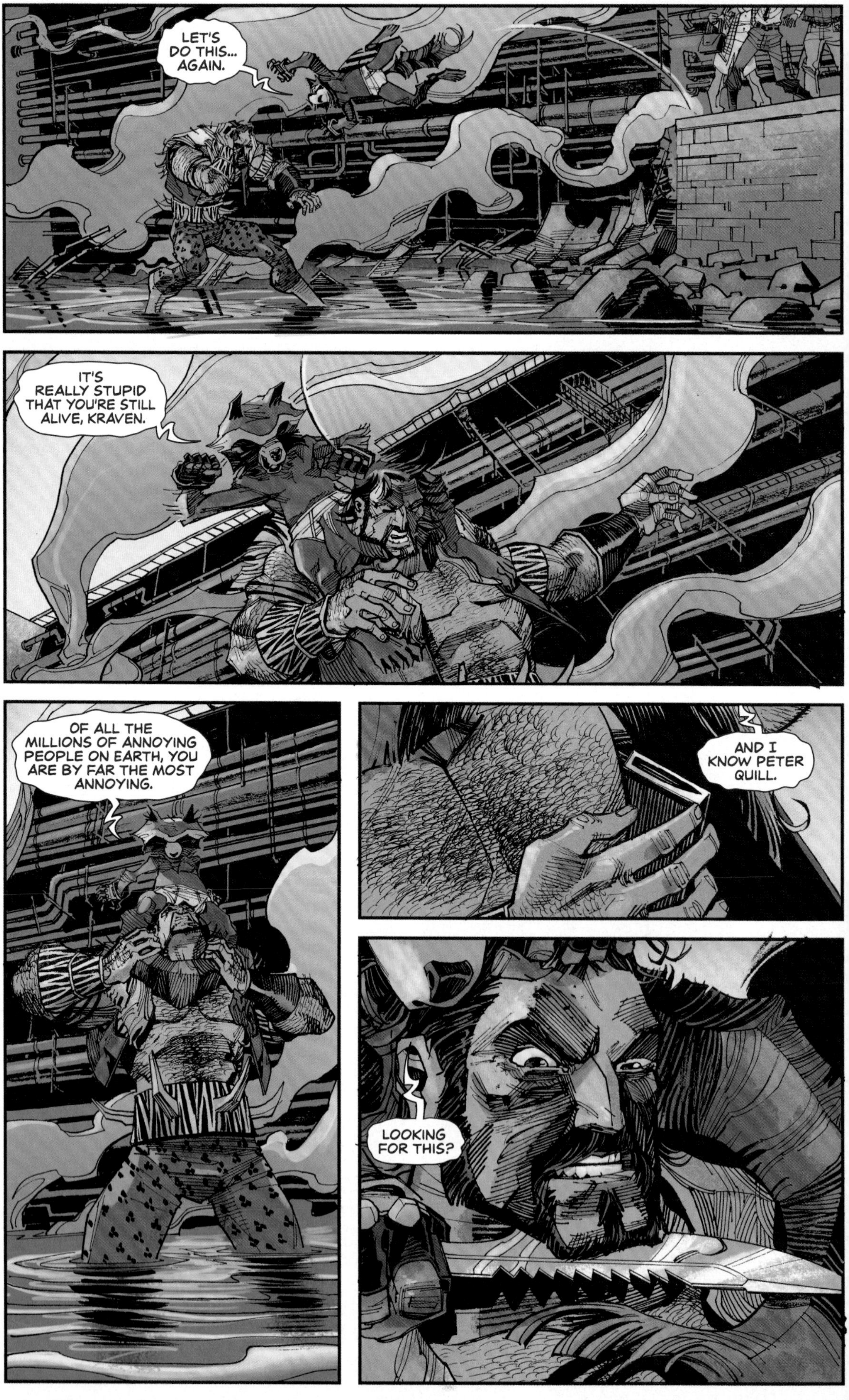
LET'S DO THIS... AGAIN.
IT'S REALLY STUPID THAT YOU'RE STILL ALIVE, KRAVEN.
OF ALL THE MILLIONS OF ANNOYING PEOPLE ON EARTH, YOU ARE BY FAR THE MOST ANNOYING.
AND I KNOW PETER QUILL.
LOOKING FOR THIS?

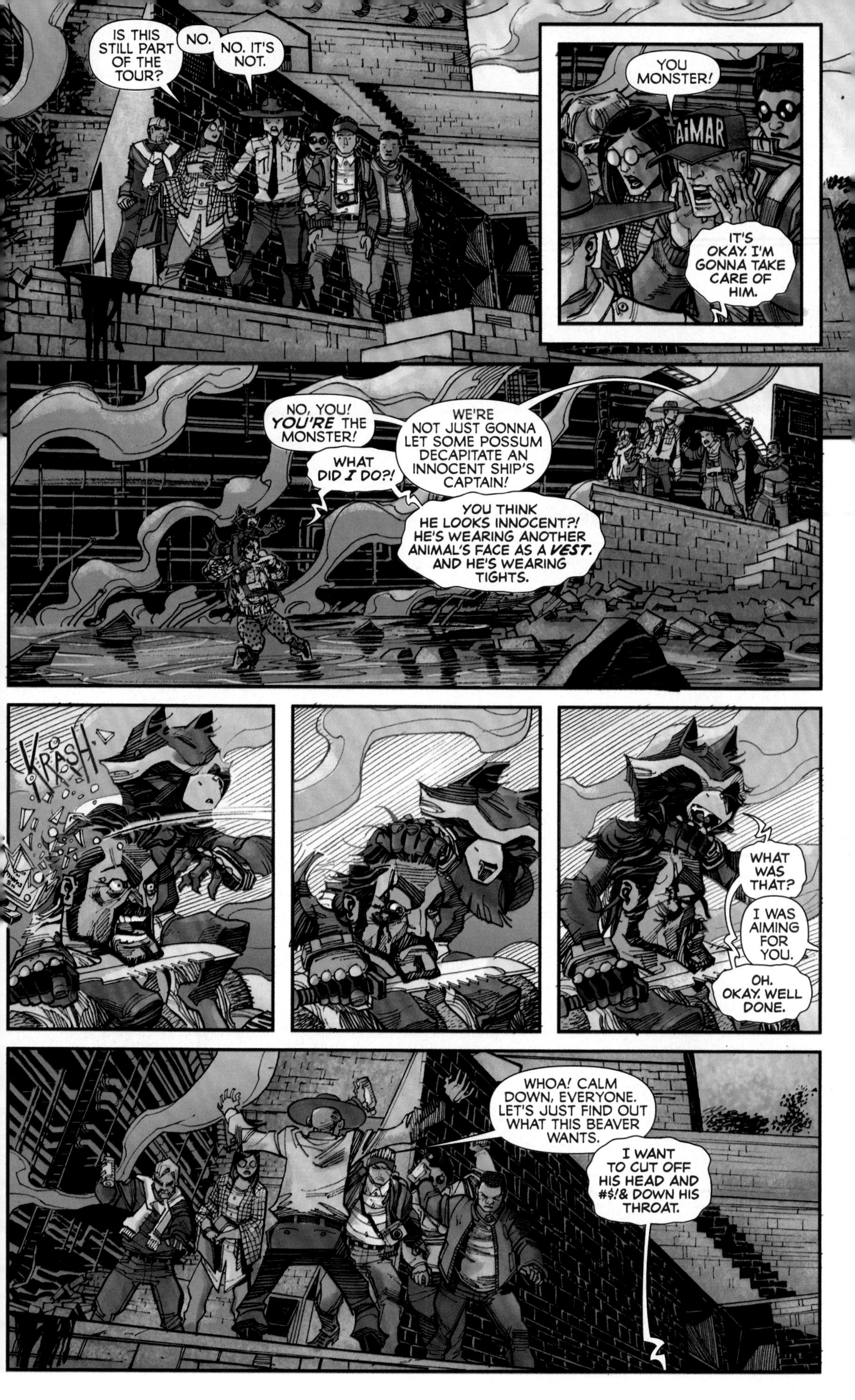
IS THIS STILL PART OF THE TOUR?
NO.
NO. IT'S NOT.
YOU MONSTER!
AiMAR
IT'S OKAY. I'M GONNA TAKE CARE OF HIM.
NO, YOU! YOU'RE THE MONSTER!
WE'RE NOT JUST GONNA LET SOME POSSUM DECAPITATE AN INNOCENT SHIP'S CAPTAIN!
WHAT DID I DO?!
YOU THINK HE LOOKS INNOCENT?! HE'S WEARING ANOTHER ANIMAL'S FACE AS A VEST. AND HE'S WEARING TIGHTS.
KRASH
WHAT WAS THAT?
I WAS AIMING FOR YOU.
OH. OKAY. WELL DONE.
WHOA! CALM DOWN, EVERYONE. LET'S JUST FIND OUT WHAT THIS BEAVER WANTS.
I WANT TO CUT OFF HIS HEAD AND #$!& DOWN HIS THROAT.

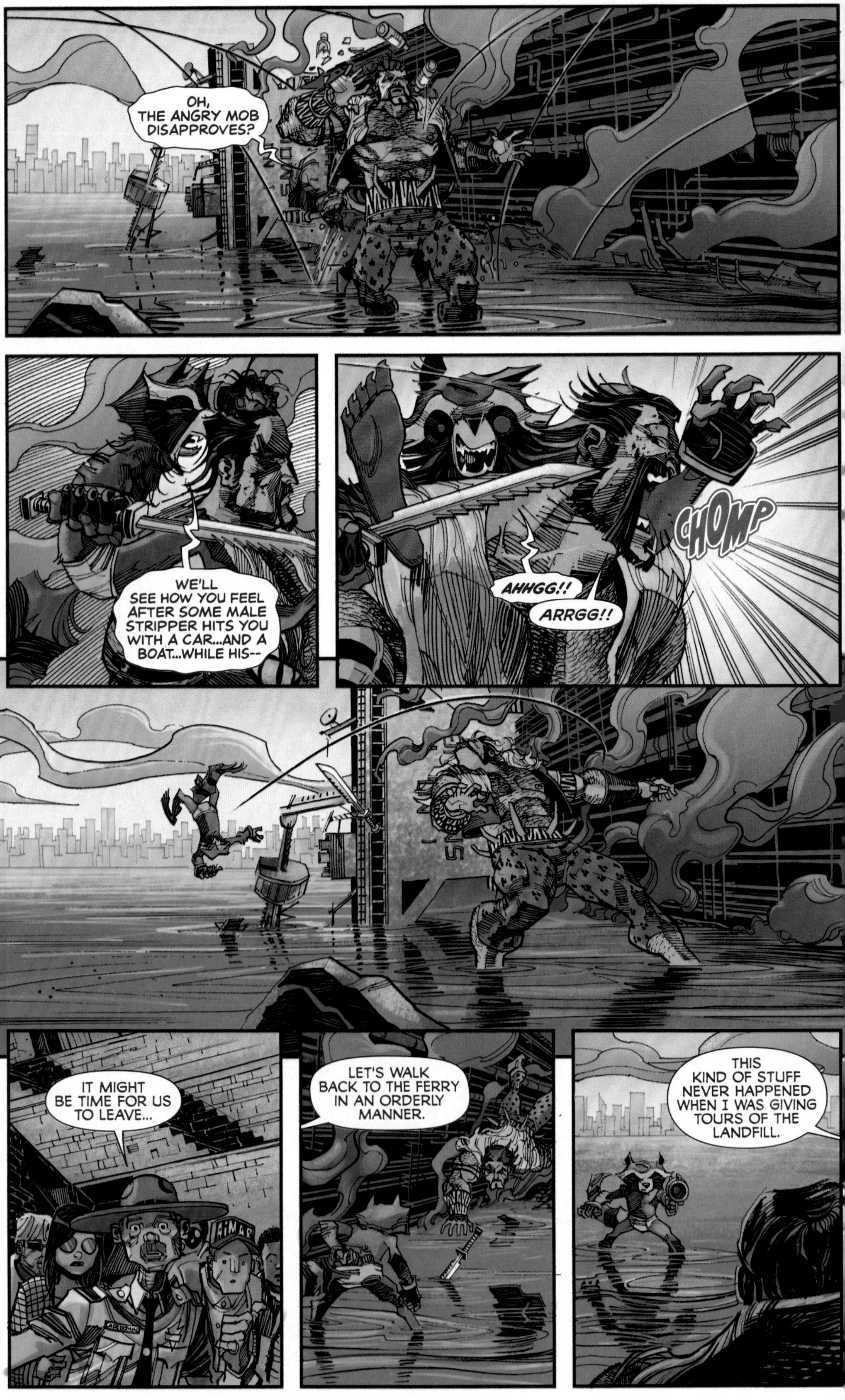
OH, THE ANGRY MOB DISAPPROVES?
WE'LL SEE HOW YOU FEEL AFTER SOME MALE STRIPPER HITS YOU WITH A CAR...AND A BOAT...WHILE HIS--
CHOMP
AHHGG!!
ARRGG!!
IT MIGHT BE TIME FOR US TO LEAVE...
LET'S WALK BACK TO THE FERRY IN AN ORDERLY MANNER.
THIS KIND OF STUFF NEVER HAPPENED WHEN I WAS GIVING TOURS OF THE LANDFILL.

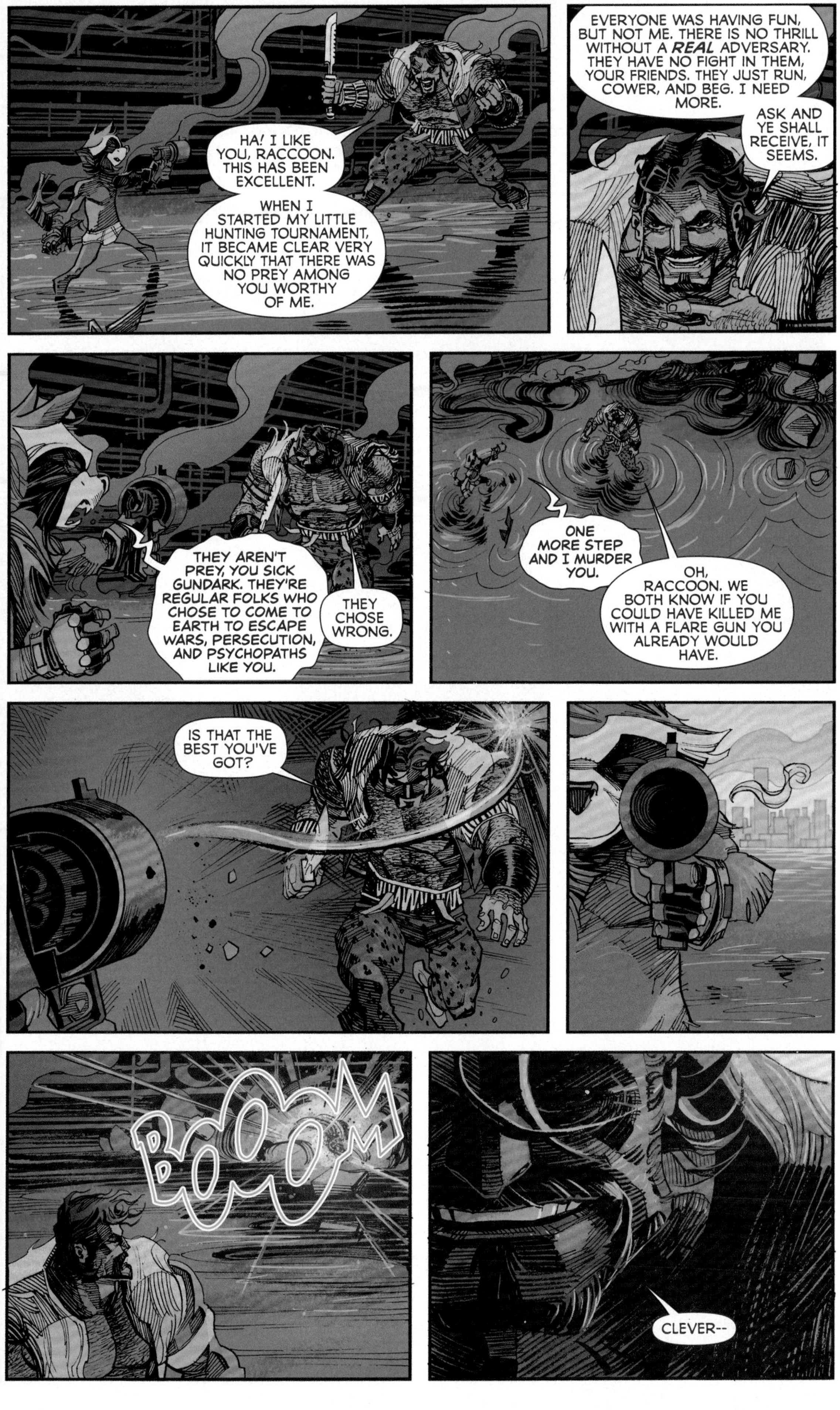
HA! I LIKE YOU, RACCOON. THIS HAS BEEN EXCELLENT.
WHEN I STARTED MY LITTLE HUNTING TOURNAMENT, IT BECAME CLEAR VERY QUICKLY THAT THERE WAS NO PREY AMONG YOU WORTHY OF ME.
EVERYONE WAS HAVING FUN, BUT NOT ME. THERE IS NO THRILL WITHOUT A *REAL* ADVERSARY. THEY HAVE NO FIGHT IN THEM, YOUR FRIENDS. THEY JUST RUN, COWER, AND BEG. I NEED MORE.
ASK AND YE SHALL RECEIVE, IT SEEMS.
THEY AREN'T PREY, YOU SICK GUNDARK. THEY'RE REGULAR FOLKS WHO CHOSE TO COME TO EARTH TO ESCAPE WARS, PERSECUTION, AND PSYCHOPATHS LIKE YOU.
THEY CHOSE WRONG.
ONE MORE STEP AND I MURDER YOU.
OH, RACCOON. WE BOTH KNOW IF YOU COULD HAVE KILLED ME WITH A FLARE GUN YOU ALREADY WOULD HAVE.
IS THAT THE BEST YOU'VE GOT?
BOOOOM
CLEVER--

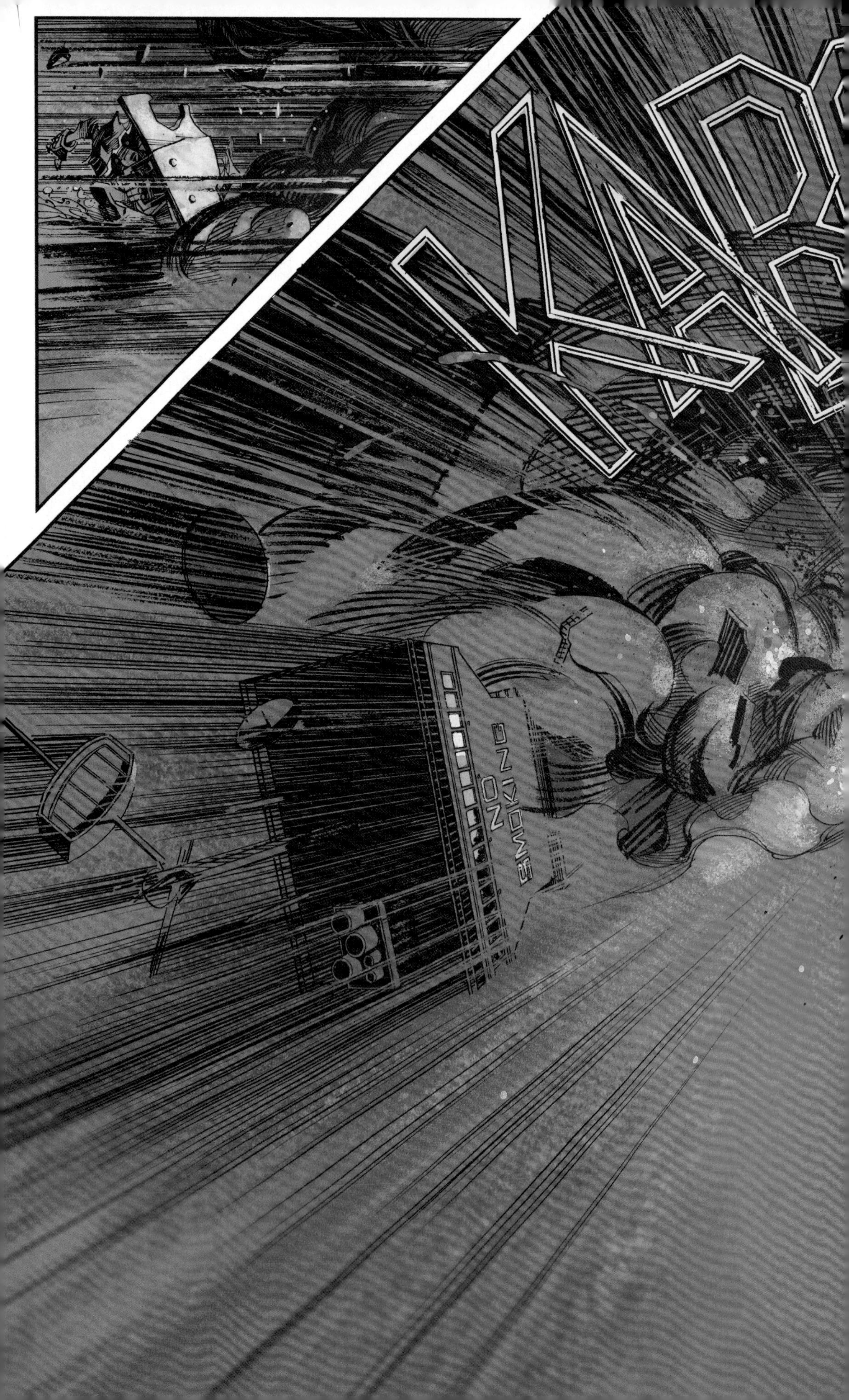
NO SMOKING

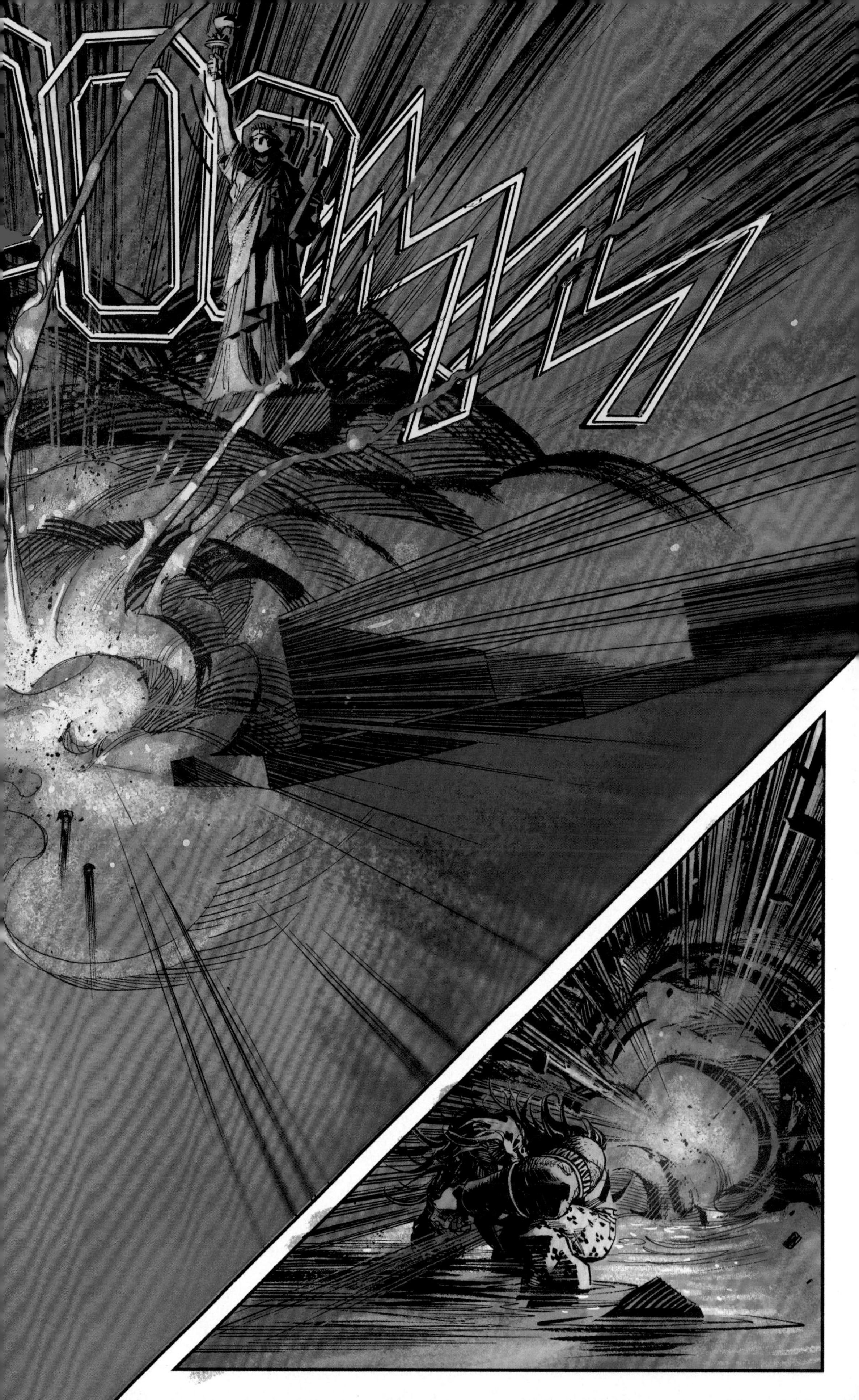

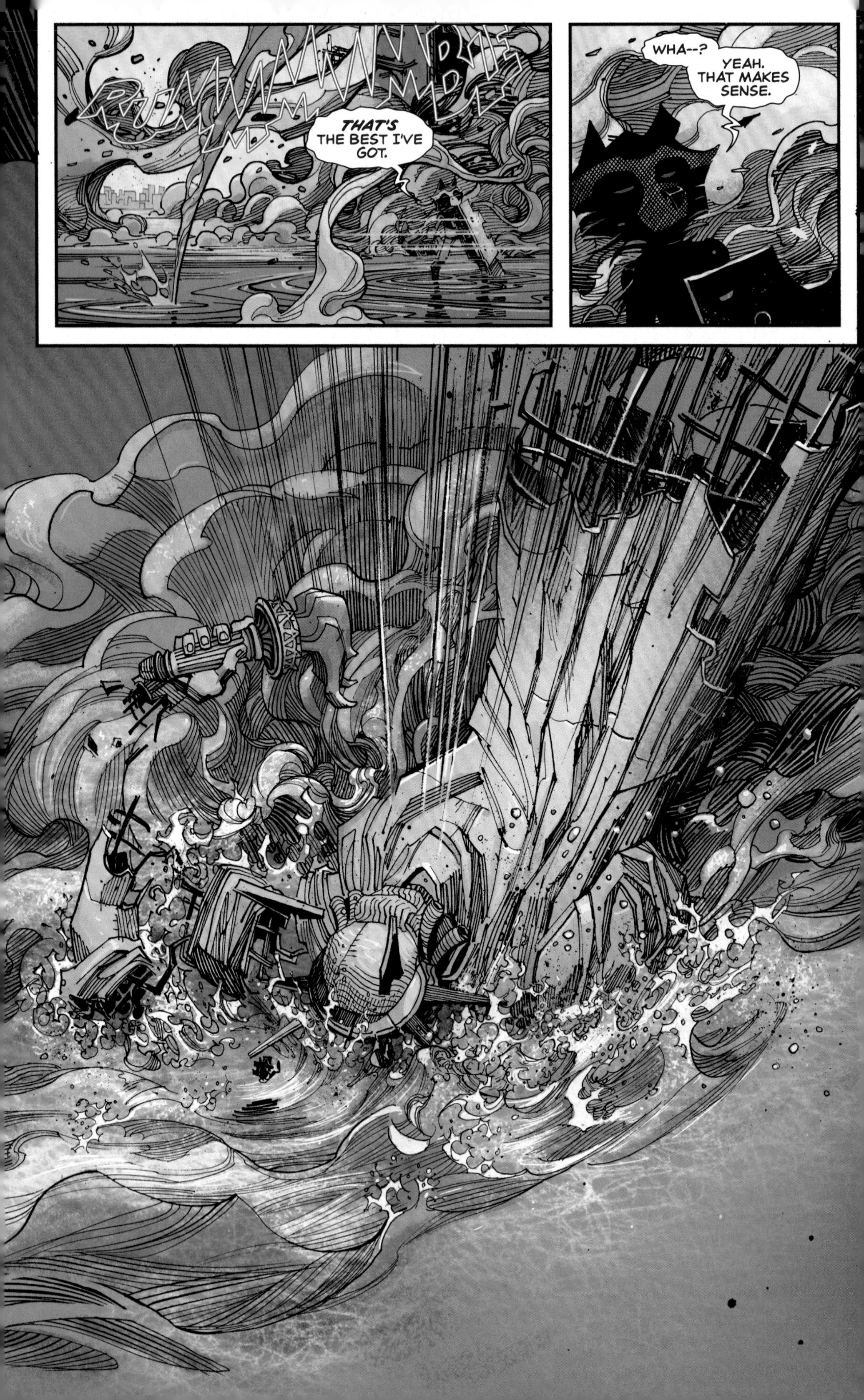
THAT'S THE BEST I'VE GOT.
WHA--?
YEAH. THAT MAKES SENSE.

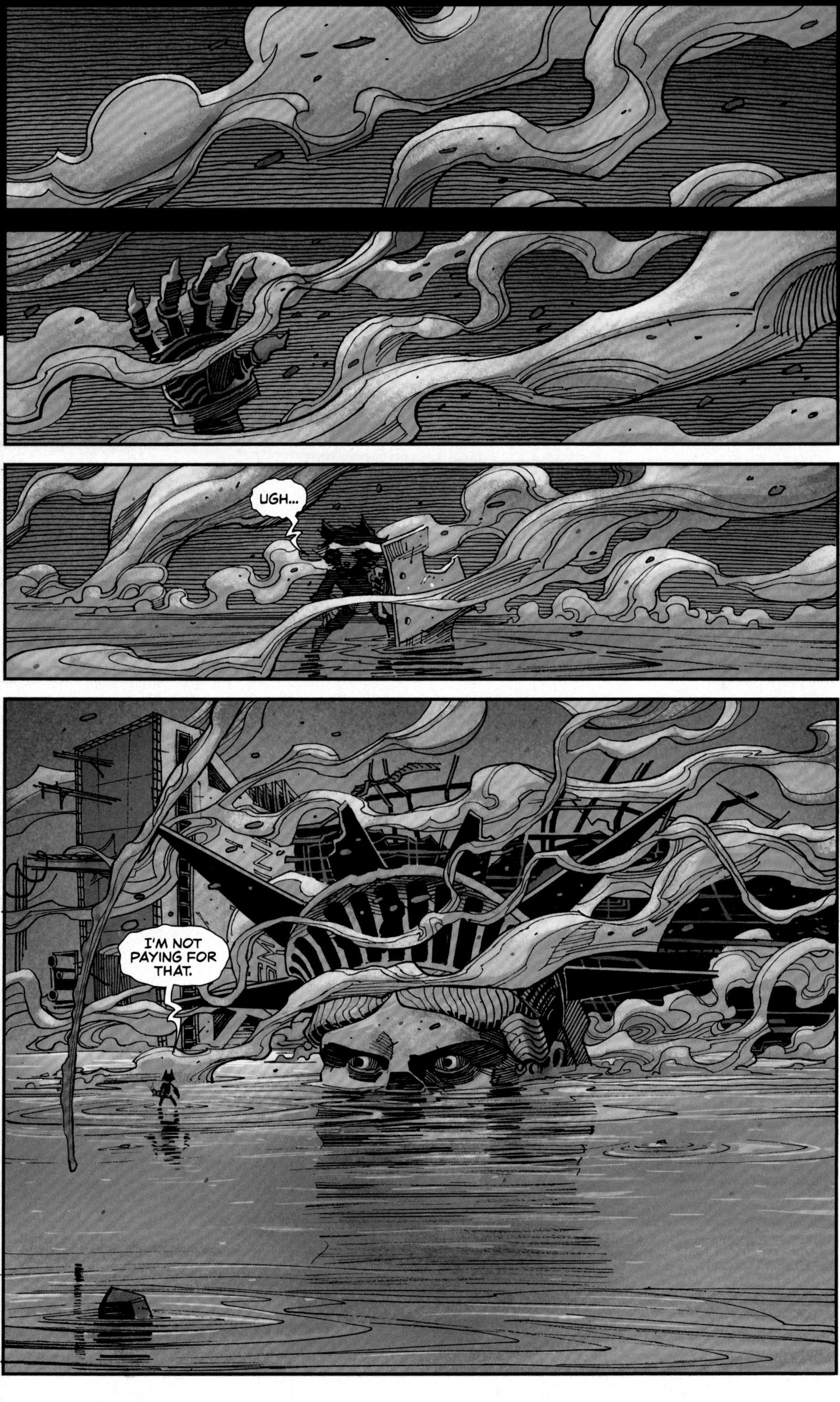
UGH...
I'M NOT PAYING FOR THAT.

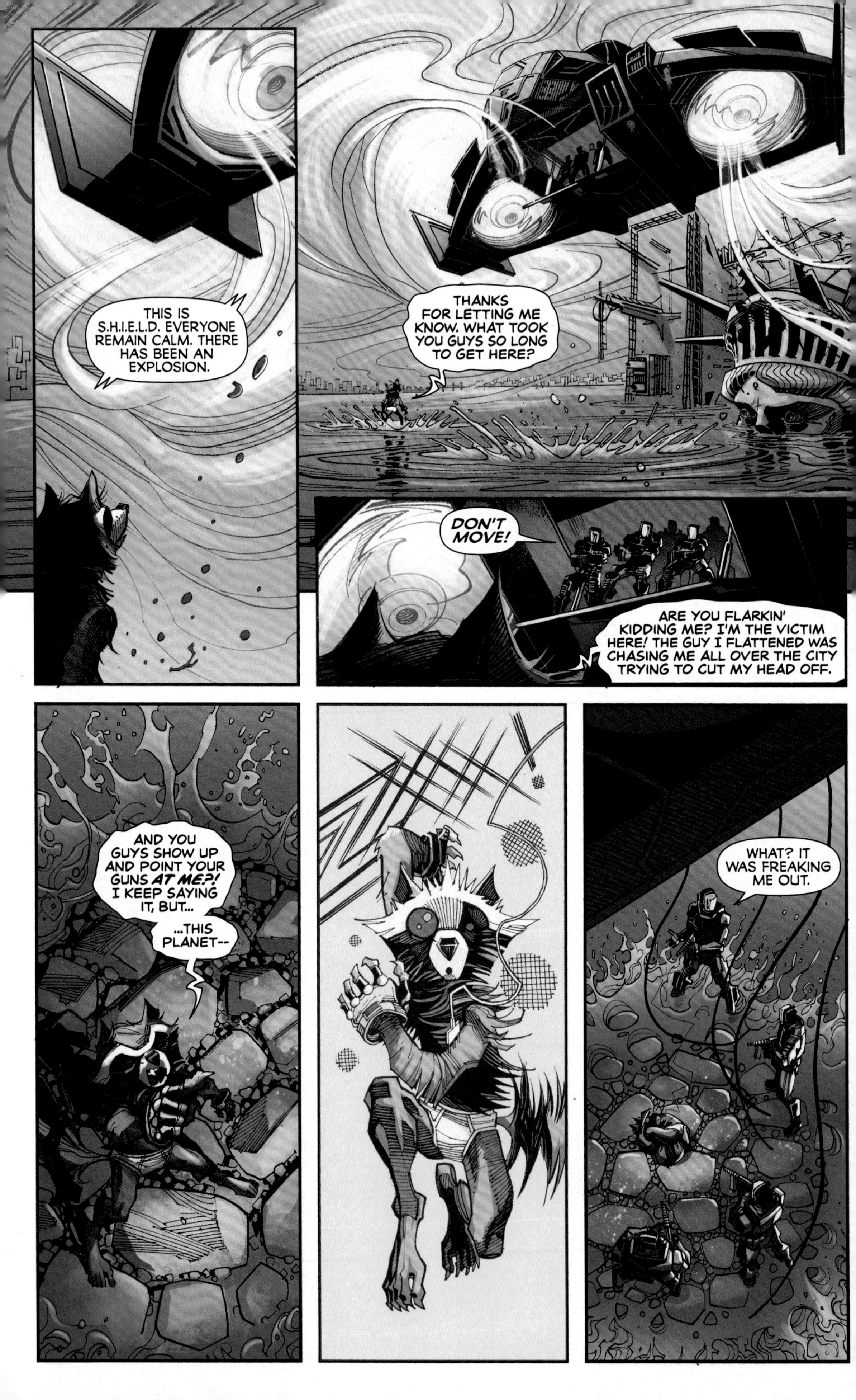
THIS IS S.H.I.E.L.D. EVERYONE REMAIN CALM. THERE HAS BEEN AN EXPLOSION.
THANKS FOR LETTING ME KNOW. WHAT TOOK YOU GUYS SO LONG TO GET HERE?
DON'T MOVE!
ARE YOU FLARKIN' KIDDING ME? I'M THE VICTIM HERE! THE GUY I FLATTENED WAS CHASING ME ALL OVER THE CITY TRYING TO CUT MY HEAD OFF.
AND YOU GUYS SHOW UP AND POINT YOUR GUNS AT ME?! I KEEP SAYING IT, BUT...
...THIS PLANET--
WHAT? IT WAS FREAKING ME OUT.

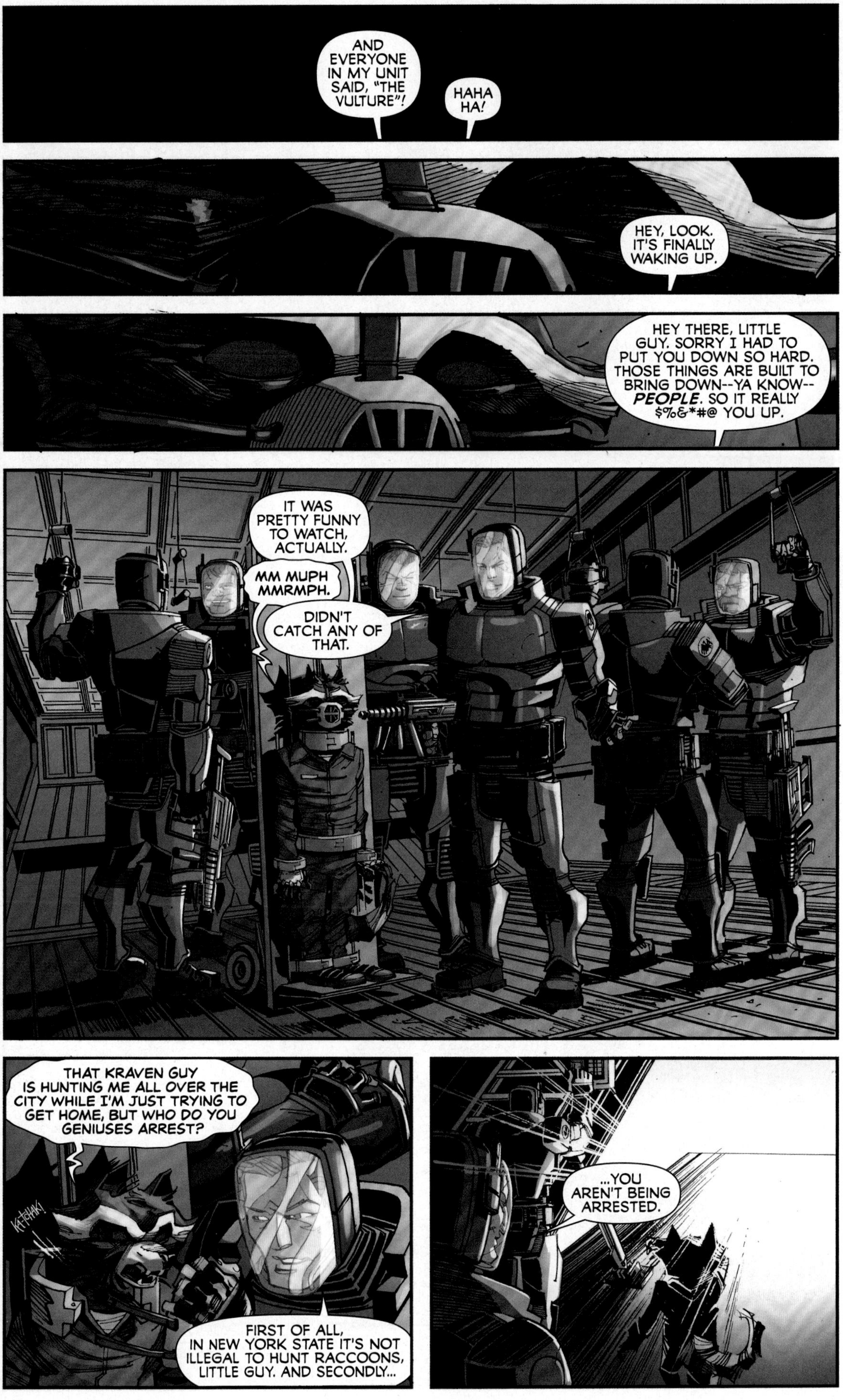
AND EVERYONE IN MY UNIT SAID, "THE VULTURE"!
HAHA HA!
HEY, LOOK. IT'S FINALLY WAKING UP.
HEY THERE, LITTLE GUY. SORRY I HAD TO PUT YOU DOWN SO HARD. THOSE THINGS ARE BUILT TO BRING DOWN--YA KNOW--*PEOPLE*. SO IT REALLY $%&*#@ YOU UP.
IT WAS PRETTY FUNNY TO WATCH, ACTUALLY.
MM MUPH MMRMPH.
DIDN'T CATCH ANY OF THAT.
THAT KRAVEN GUY IS HUNTING ME ALL OVER THE CITY WHILE I'M JUST TRYING TO GET HOME, BUT WHO DO YOU GENIUSES ARREST?
KA-TCHAK!
FIRST OF ALL, IN NEW YORK STATE IT'S NOT ILLEGAL TO HUNT RACCOONS, LITTLE GUY. AND SECONDLY...
...YOU AREN'T BEING ARRESTED.

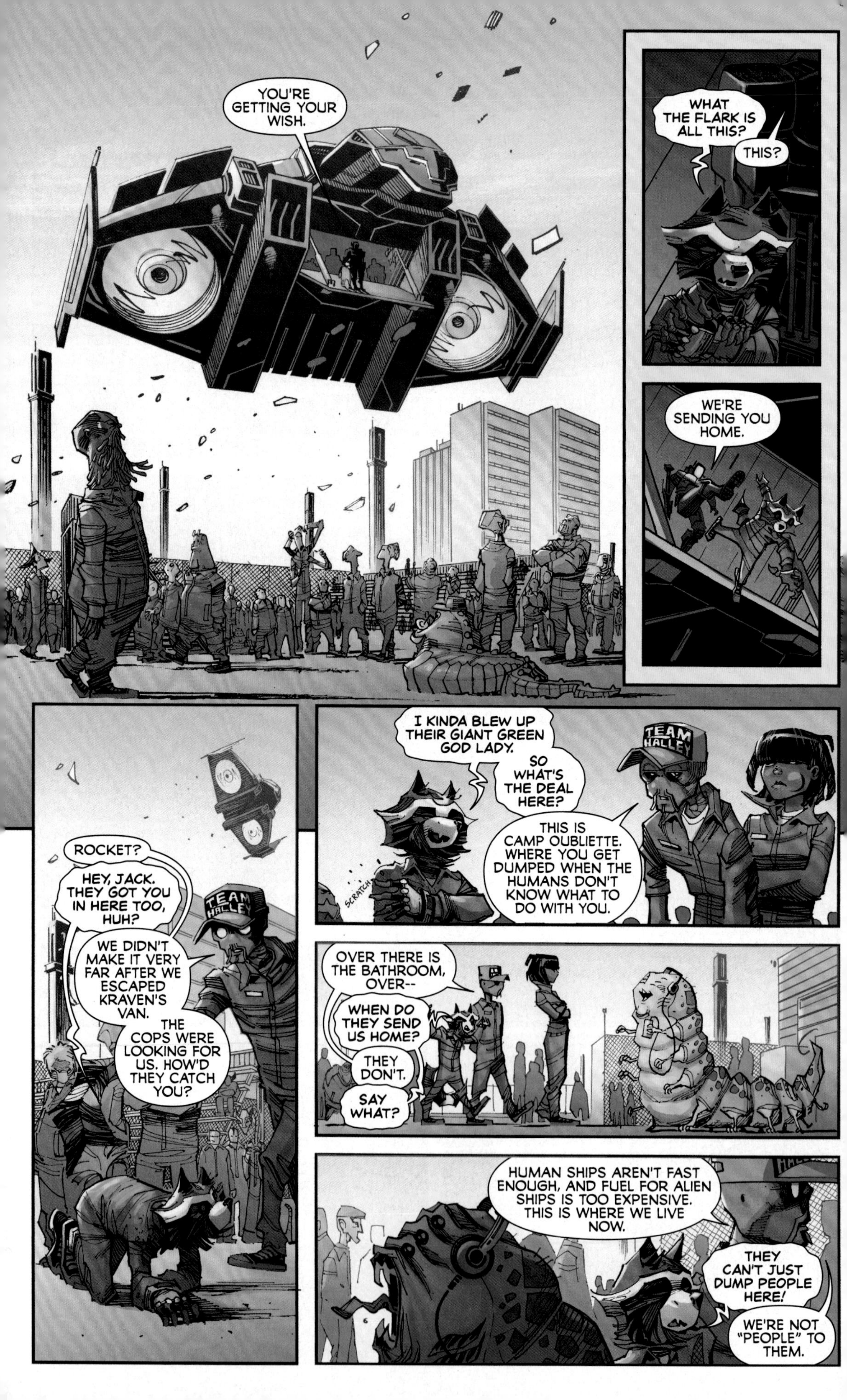
YOU'RE GETTING YOUR WISH.
WHAT THE FLARK IS ALL THIS?
THIS?
WE'RE SENDING YOU HOME.
ROCKET?
HEY, JACK. THEY GOT YOU IN HERE TOO, HUH?
WE DIDN'T MAKE IT VERY FAR AFTER WE ESCAPED KRAVEN'S VAN.
THE COPS WERE LOOKING FOR US. HOW'D THEY CATCH YOU?
I KINDA BLEW UP THEIR GIANT GREEN GOD LADY.
SO WHAT'S THE DEAL HERE?
SCRATCH
THIS IS CAMP OUBLIETTE. WHERE YOU GET DUMPED WHEN THE HUMANS DON'T KNOW WHAT TO DO WITH YOU.
OVER THERE IS THE BATHROOM, OVER--
WHEN DO THEY SEND US HOME?
THEY DON'T.
SAY WHAT?
HUMAN SHIPS AREN'T FAST ENOUGH, AND FUEL FOR ALIEN SHIPS IS TOO EXPENSIVE. THIS IS WHERE WE LIVE NOW.
THEY CAN'T JUST DUMP PEOPLE HERE!
WE'RE NOT "PEOPLE" TO THEM.

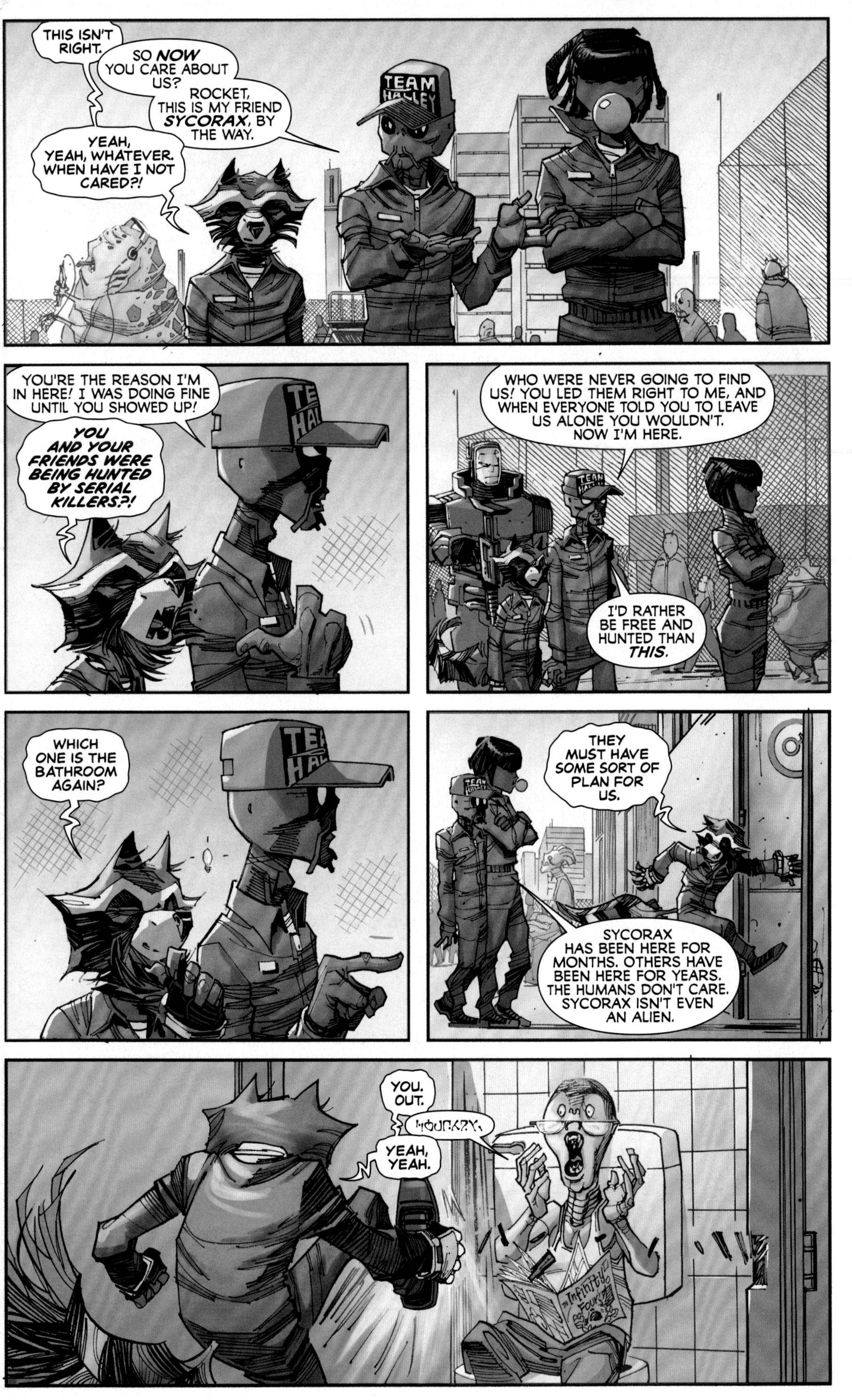
THIS ISN'T RIGHT.
SO *NOW* YOU CARE ABOUT US?
ROCKET, THIS IS MY FRIEND ***SYCORAX***, BY THE WAY.
YEAH, YEAH, WHATEVER. WHEN HAVE I NOT CARED?!
YOU'RE THE REASON I'M IN HERE! I WAS DOING FINE UNTIL YOU SHOWED UP!
YOU AND YOUR FRIENDS WERE BEING HUNTED BY SERIAL KILLERS?!
WHO WERE NEVER GOING TO FIND US! YOU LED THEM RIGHT TO ME, AND WHEN EVERYONE TOLD YOU TO LEAVE US ALONE YOU WOULDN'T. NOW I'M HERE.
I'D RATHER BE FREE AND HUNTED THAN ***THIS.***
WHICH ONE IS THE BATHROOM AGAIN?
THEY MUST HAVE SOME SORT OF PLAN FOR US.
SYCORAX HAS BEEN HERE FOR MONTHS. OTHERS HAVE BEEN HERE FOR YEARS. THE HUMANS DON'T CARE. SYCORAX ISN'T EVEN AN ALIEN.
YOU. OUT.
YEAH, YEAH.
The Infinity Four

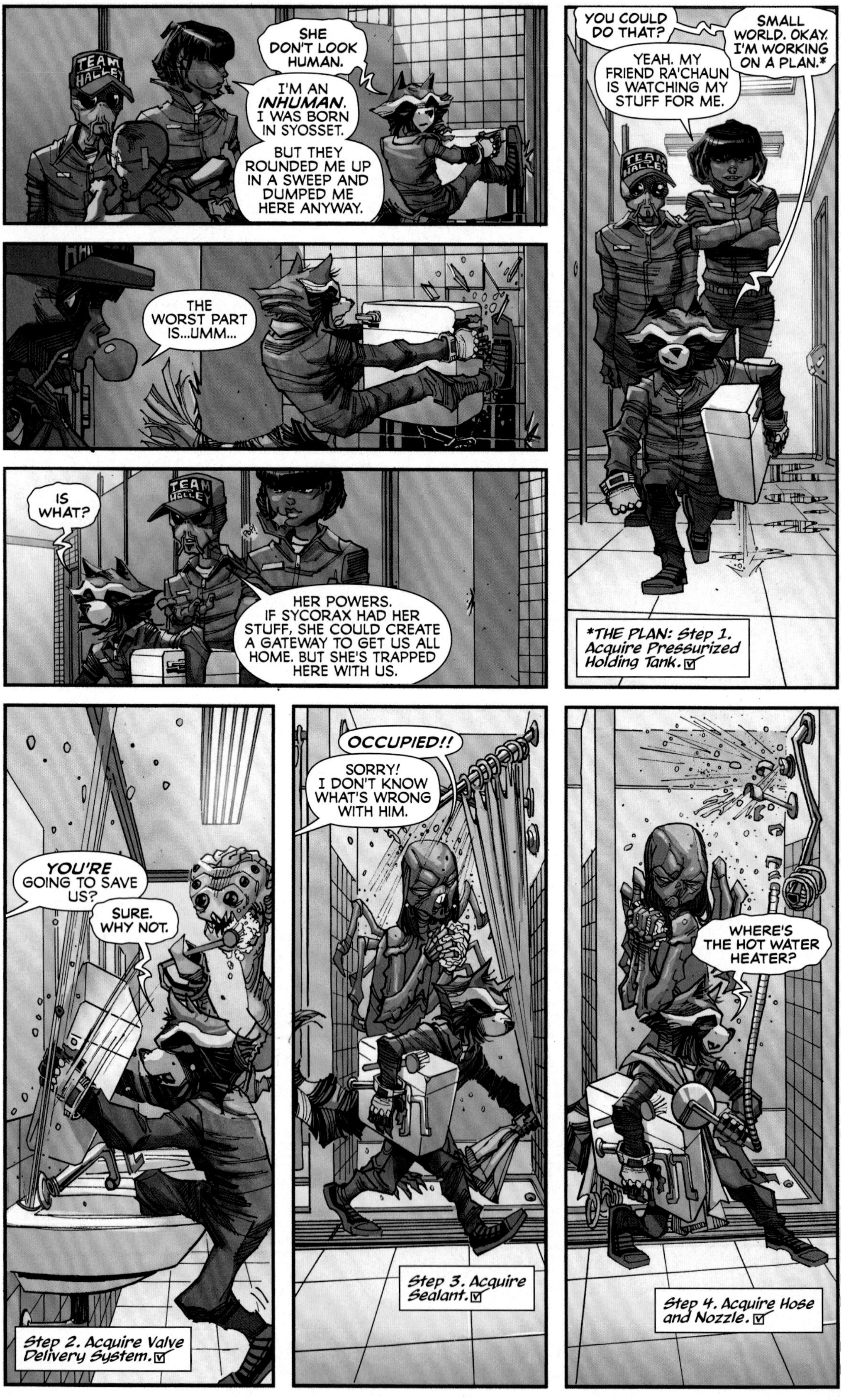
SHE DON'T LOOK HUMAN.
I'M AN *INHUMAN*. I WAS BORN IN SYOSSET.
BUT THEY ROUNDED ME UP IN A SWEEP AND DUMPED ME HERE ANYWAY.
TEAM HALLEY
THE WORST PART IS...UMM...
IS WHAT?
HER POWERS. IF SYCORAX HAD HER STUFF, SHE COULD CREATE A GATEWAY TO GET US ALL HOME. BUT SHE'S TRAPPED HERE WITH US.
YOU COULD DO THAT?
SMALL WORLD. OKAY. I'M WORKING ON A PLAN.*
YEAH. MY FRIEND RA'CHAUN IS WATCHING MY STUFF FOR ME.
*THE PLAN: Step 1. Acquire Pressurized Holding Tank. ☑
YOU'RE GOING TO SAVE US?
SURE. WHY NOT.
Step 2. Acquire Valve Delivery System. ☑
OCCUPIED!!
SORRY! I DON'T KNOW WHAT'S WRONG WITH HIM.
Step 3. Acquire Sealant. ☑
WHERE'S THE HOT WATER HEATER?
Step 4. Acquire Hose and Nozzle. ☑

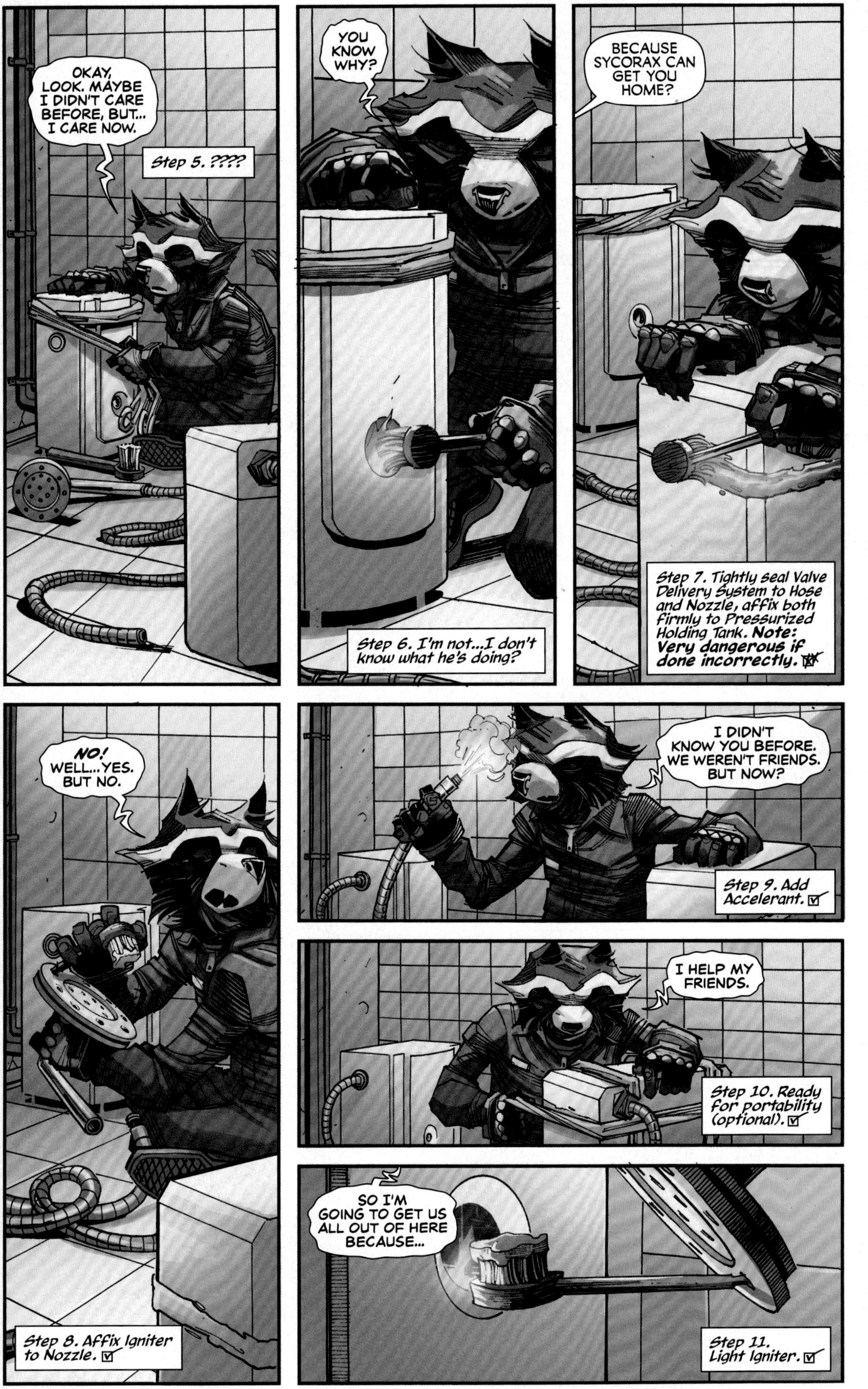
OKAY, LOOK. MAYBE I DIDN'T CARE BEFORE, BUT... I CARE NOW.
Step 5. ????
YOU KNOW WHY?
Step 6. I'm not...I don't know what he's doing?
BECAUSE SYCORAX CAN GET YOU HOME?
Step 7. Tightly seal Valve Delivery System to Hose and Nozzle, affix both firmly to Pressurized Holding Tank. Note: Very dangerous if done incorrectly.
NO! WELL...YES. BUT NO.
Step 8. Affix Igniter to Nozzle.
I DIDN'T KNOW YOU BEFORE. WE WEREN'T FRIENDS. BUT NOW?
Step 9. Add Accelerant.
I HELP MY FRIENDS.
Step 10. Ready for portability (optional).
SO I'M GOING TO GET US ALL OUT OF HERE BECAUSE...
Step 11. Light Igniter.

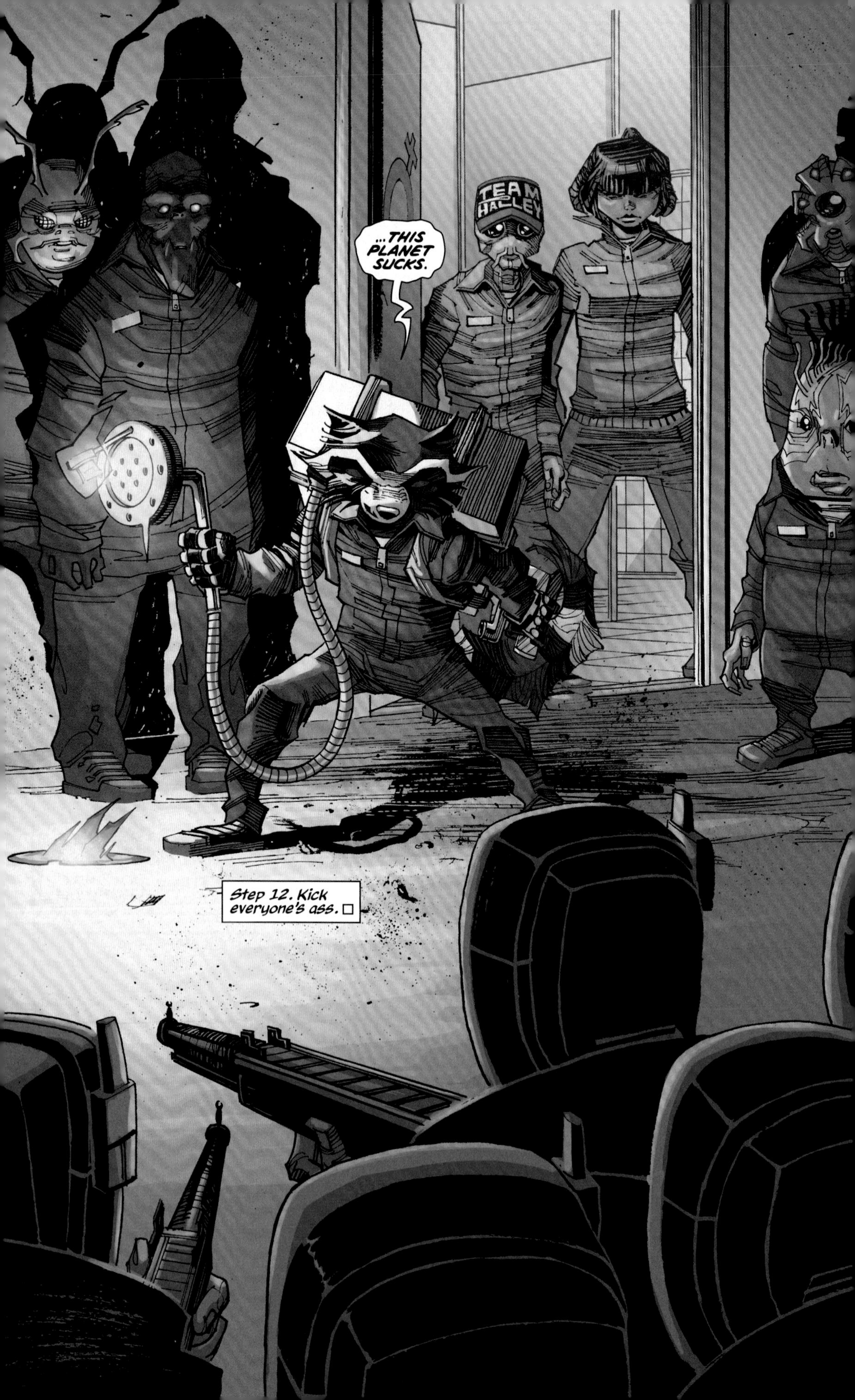
TEAM HALLEY
...THIS PLANET SUCKS.
Step 12. Kick everyone's ass.

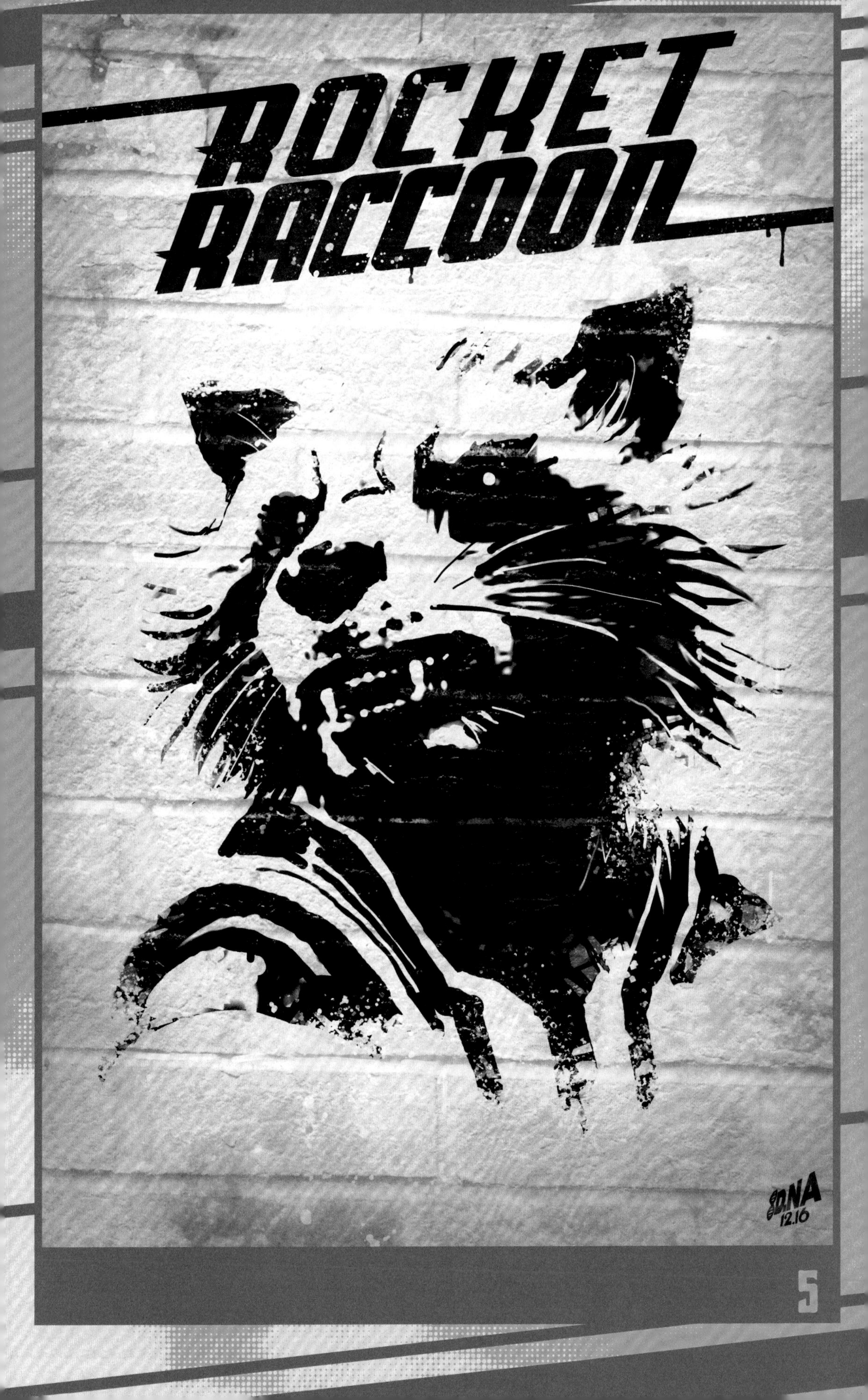
ROCKET
RACCOON
DNA
12.16

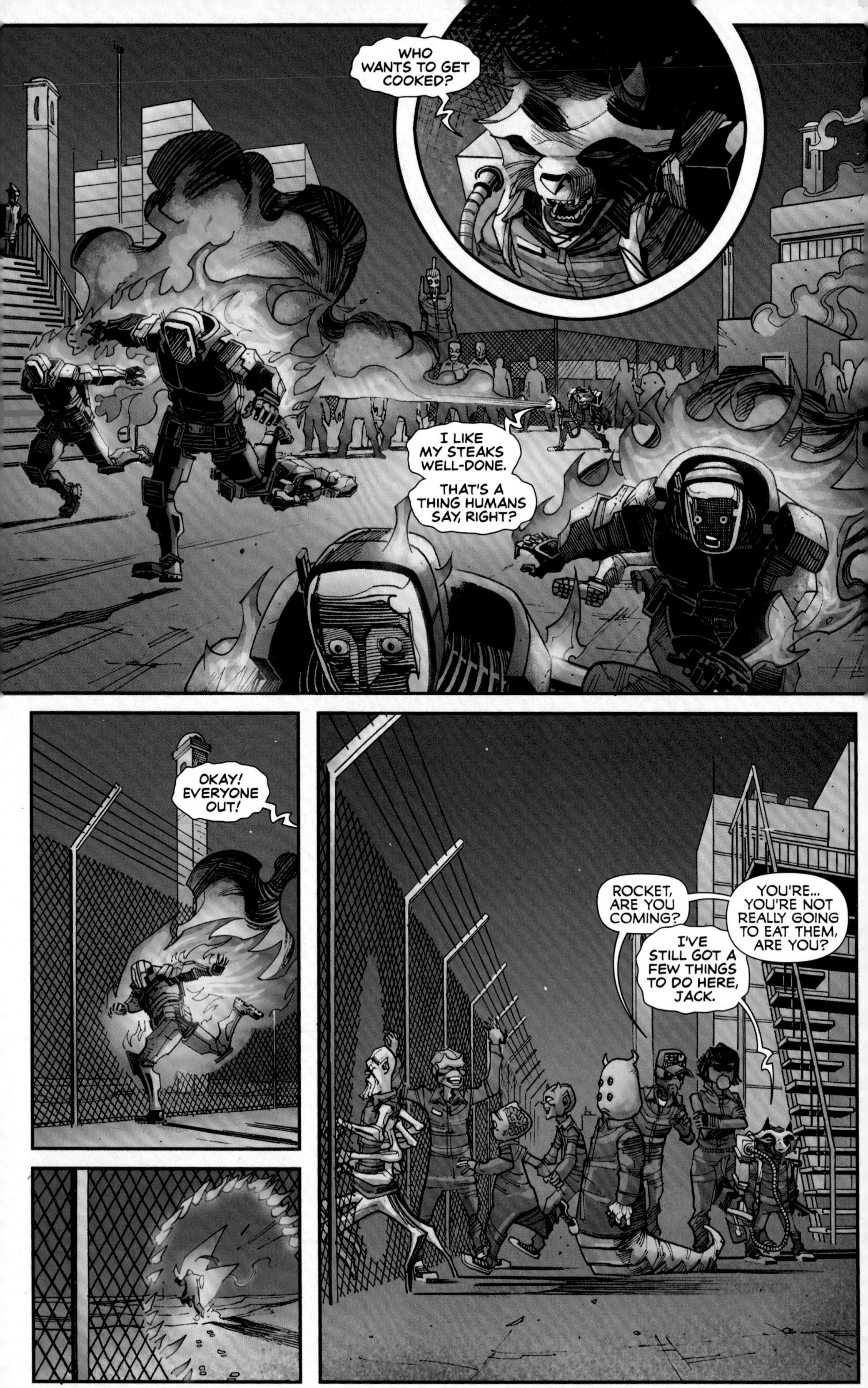
WHO WANTS TO GET COOKED?
I LIKE MY STEAKS WELL-DONE.
THAT'S A THING HUMANS SAY, RIGHT?
OKAY! EVERYONE OUT!
ROCKET, ARE YOU COMING?
I'VE STILL GOT A FEW THINGS TO DO HERE, JACK.
YOU'RE... YOU'RE NOT REALLY GOING TO EAT THEM, ARE YOU?

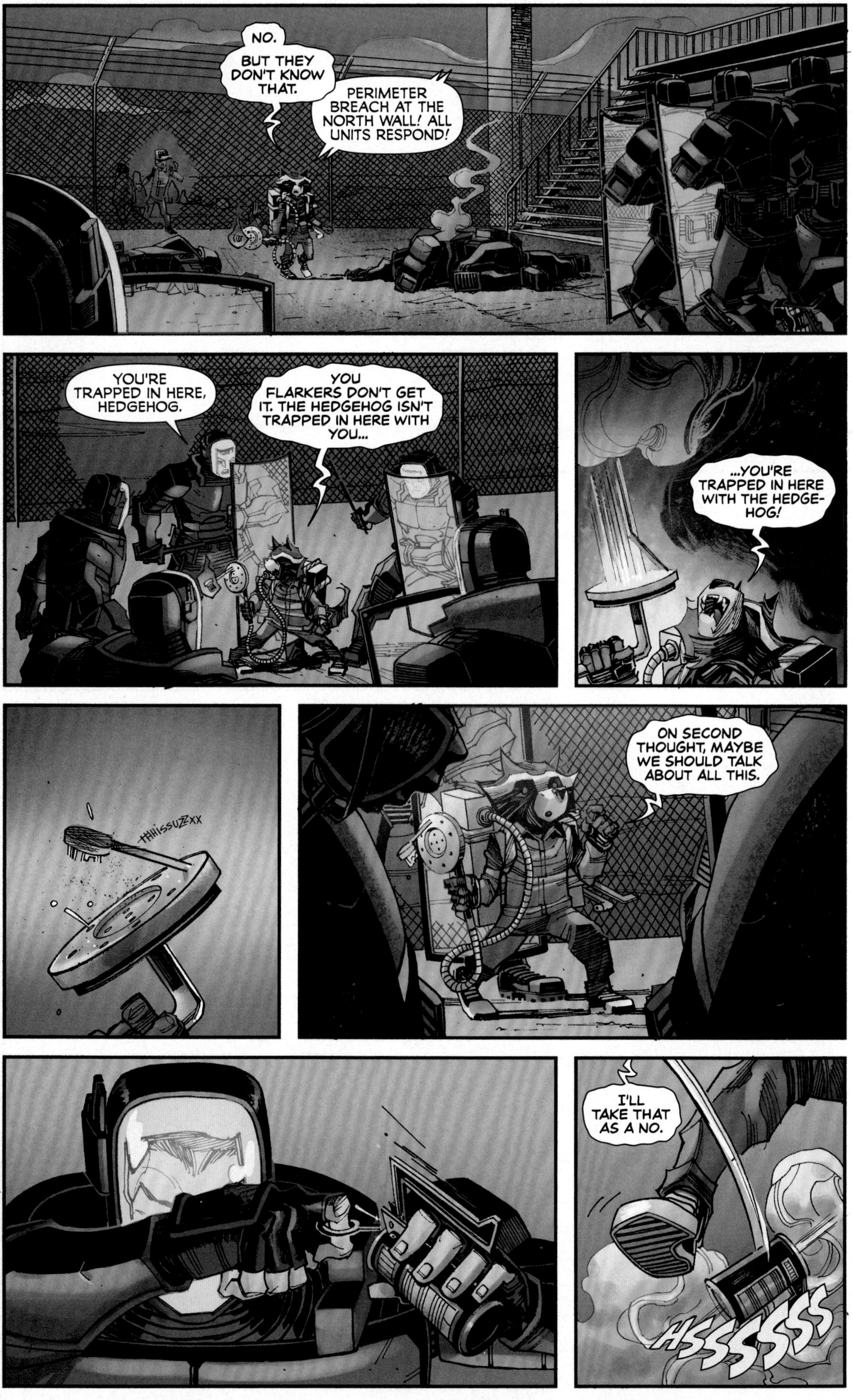
NO.
BUT THEY DON'T KNOW THAT.
PERIMETER BREACH AT THE NORTH WALL! ALL UNITS RESPOND!
YOU'RE TRAPPED IN HERE, HEDGEHOG.
YOU FLARKERS DON'T GET IT. THE HEDGEHOG ISN'T TRAPPED IN HERE WITH YOU...
...YOU'RE TRAPPED IN HERE WITH THE HEDGE-HOG!
THHISSUZZXX
ON SECOND THOUGHT, MAYBE WE SHOULD TALK ABOUT ALL THIS.
I'LL TAKE THAT AS A NO.
HSSSSSS

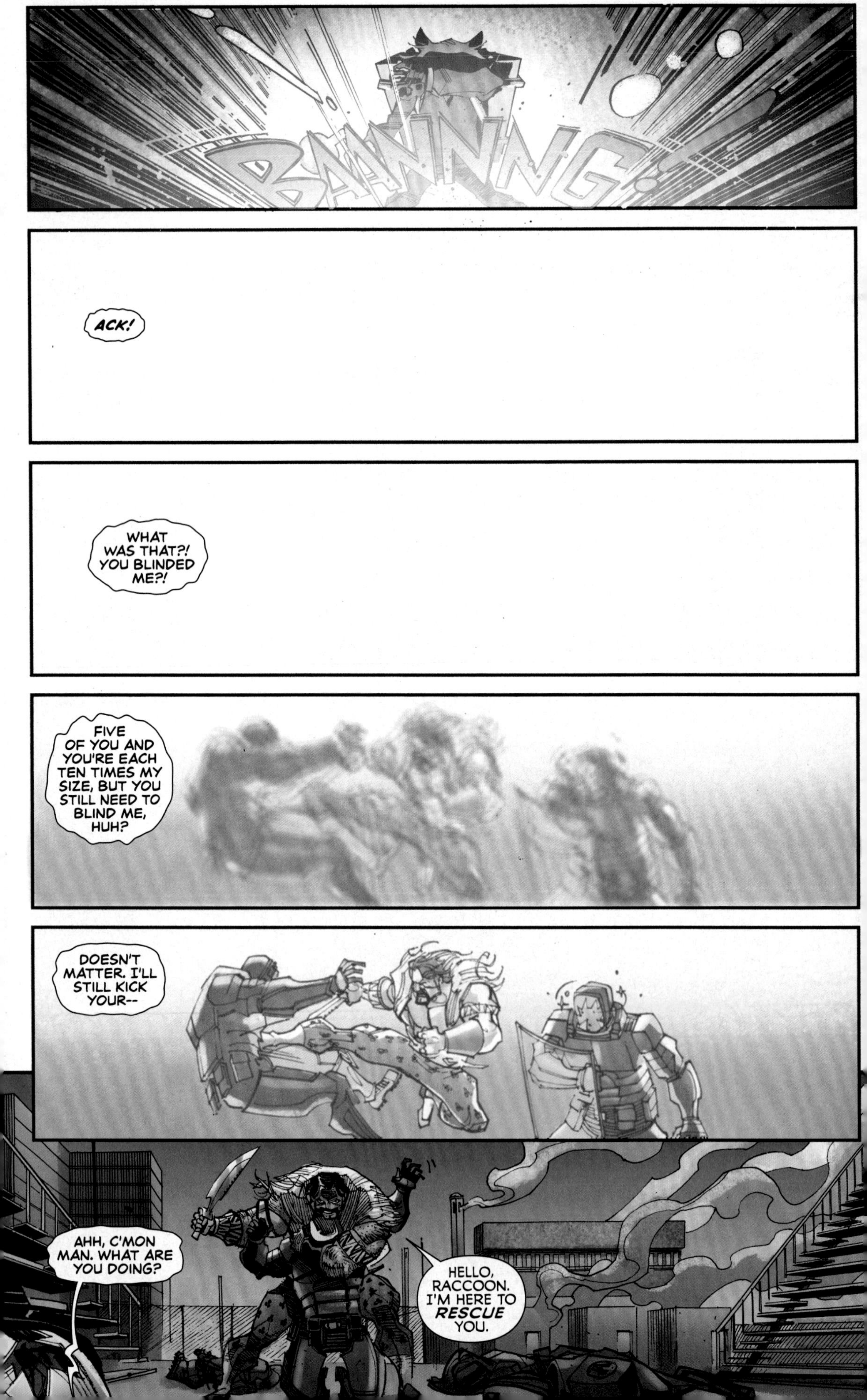
BAANNG!
ACK!
WHAT WAS THAT?! YOU BLINDED ME?!
FIVE OF YOU AND YOU'RE EACH TEN TIMES MY SIZE, BUT YOU STILL NEED TO BLIND ME, HUH?
DOESN'T MATTER. I'LL STILL KICK YOUR--
AHH, C'MON MAN. WHAT ARE YOU DOING?
HELLO, RACCOON. I'M HERE TO *RESCUE* YOU.

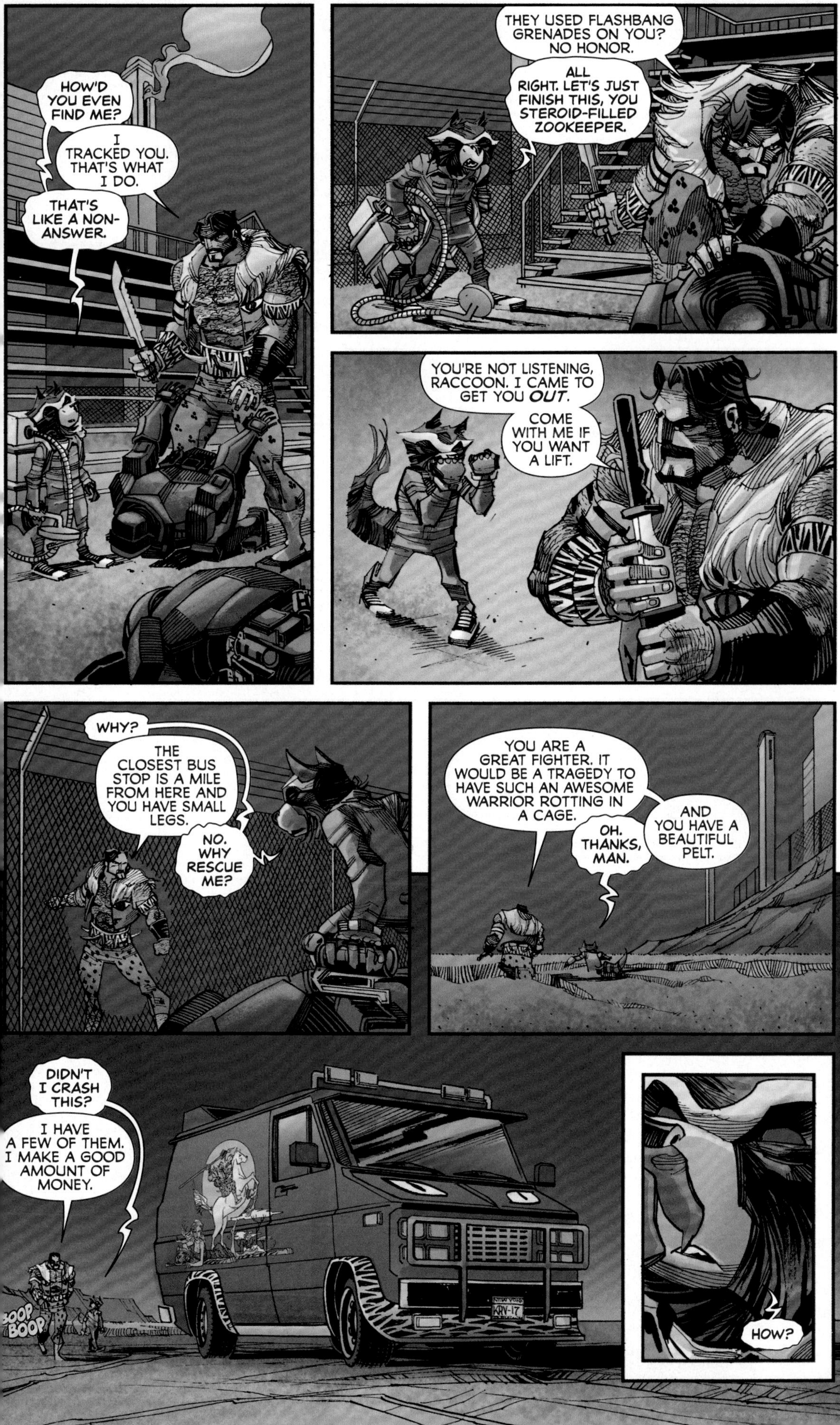
HOW'D YOU EVEN FIND ME?
I TRACKED YOU. THAT'S WHAT I DO.
THAT'S LIKE A NON-ANSWER.
THEY USED FLASHBANG GRENADES ON YOU? NO HONOR.
ALL RIGHT. LET'S JUST FINISH THIS, YOU STEROID-FILLED ZOOKEEPER.
YOU'RE NOT LISTENING, RACCOON. I CAME TO GET YOU *OUT*.
COME WITH ME IF YOU WANT A LIFT.
WHY?
THE CLOSEST BUS STOP IS A MILE FROM HERE AND YOU HAVE SMALL LEGS.
NO. WHY RESCUE ME?
YOU ARE A GREAT FIGHTER. IT WOULD BE A TRAGEDY TO HAVE SUCH AN AWESOME WARRIOR ROTTING IN A CAGE.
OH. THANKS, MAN.
AND YOU HAVE A BEAUTIFUL PELT.
DIDN'T I CRASH THIS?
I HAVE A FEW OF THEM. I MAKE A GOOD AMOUNT OF MONEY.
BOOP BOOP
NEW YORK KRV-17
HOW?

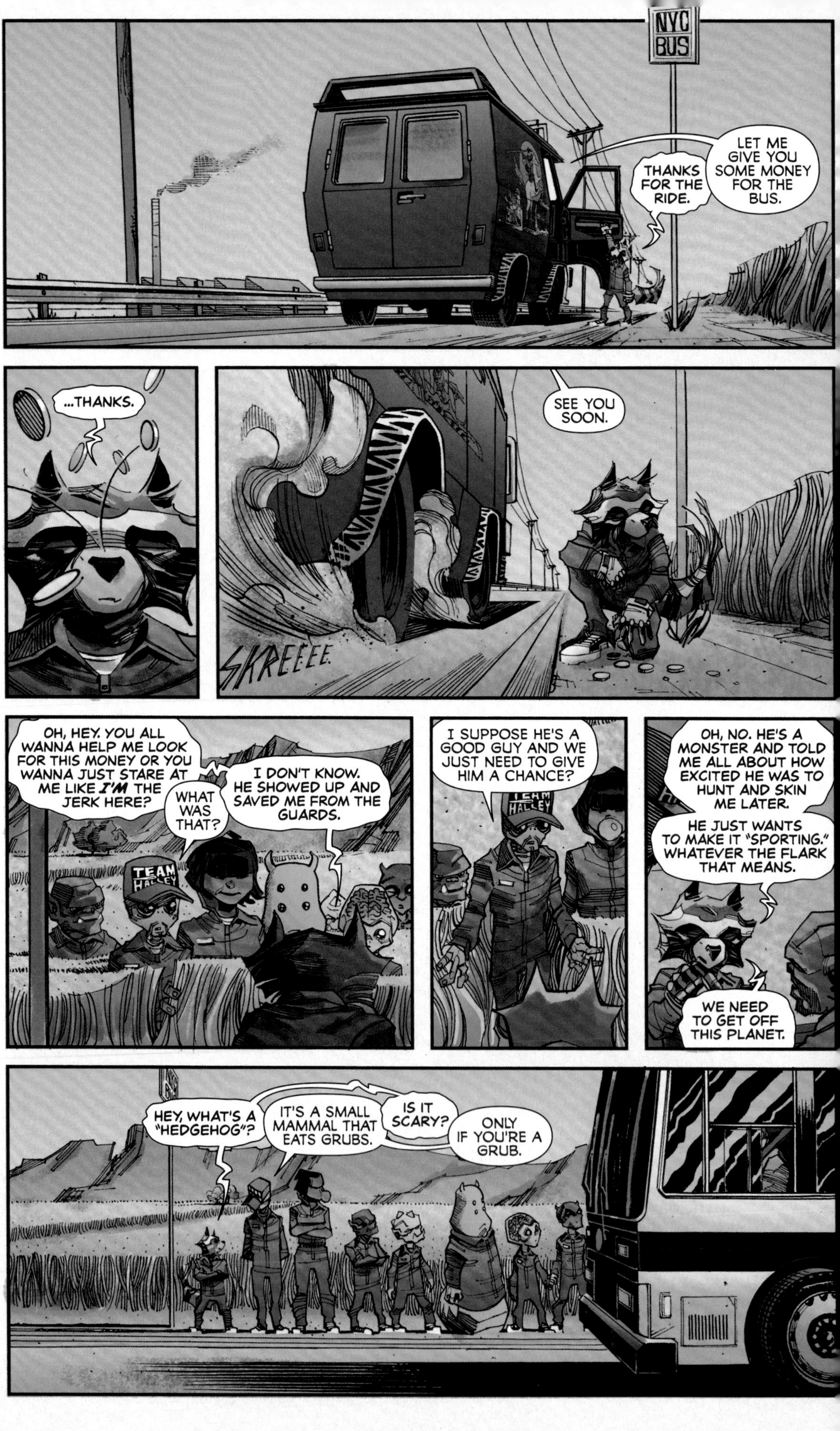
NYC BUS
THANKS FOR THE RIDE.
LET ME GIVE YOU SOME MONEY FOR THE BUS.
...THANKS.
SEE YOU SOON.
SKREEEE.
OH, HEY. YOU ALL WANNA HELP ME LOOK FOR THIS MONEY OR YOU WANNA JUST STARE AT ME LIKE *I'M* THE JERK HERE?
WHAT WAS THAT?
I DON'T KNOW. HE SHOWED UP AND SAVED ME FROM THE GUARDS.
TEAM HALLEY
I SUPPOSE HE'S A GOOD GUY AND WE JUST NEED TO GIVE HIM A CHANCE?
OH, NO. HE'S A MONSTER AND TOLD ME ALL ABOUT HOW EXCITED HE WAS TO HUNT AND SKIN ME LATER.
HE JUST WANTS TO MAKE IT "SPORTING." WHATEVER THE FLARK THAT MEANS.
WE NEED TO GET OFF THIS PLANET.
HEY, WHAT'S A "HEDGEHOG"?
IT'S A SMALL MAMMAL THAT EATS GRUBS.
IS IT SCARY?
ONLY IF YOU'RE A GRUB.

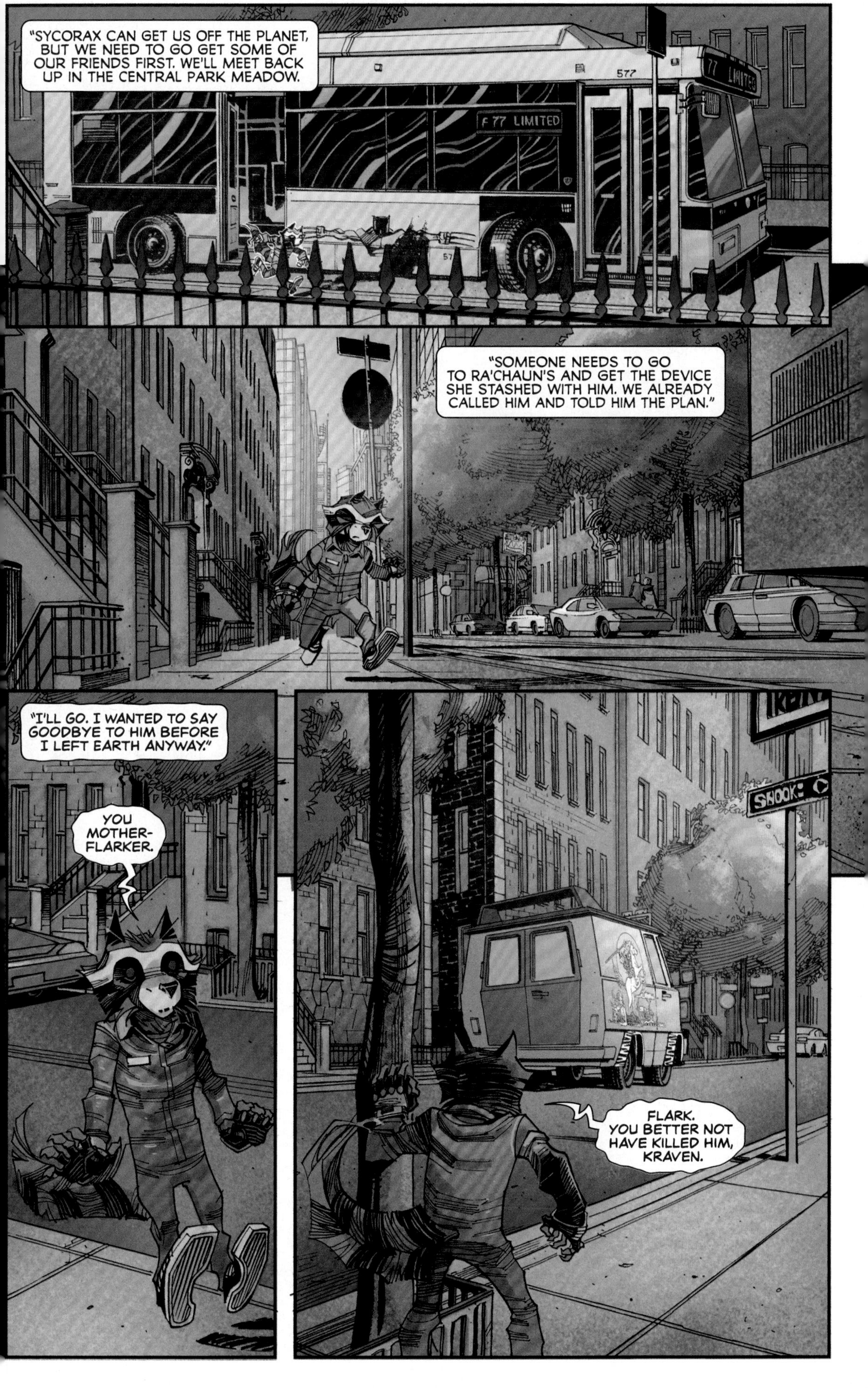

"SYCORAX CAN GET US OFF THE PLANET, BUT WE NEED TO GO GET SOME OF OUR FRIENDS FIRST. WE'LL MEET BACK UP IN THE CENTRAL PARK MEADOW.
577
77 LIMITED
F 77 LIMITED
"SOMEONE NEEDS TO GO TO RA'CHAUN'S AND GET THE DEVICE SHE STASHED WITH HIM. WE ALREADY CALLED HIM AND TOLD HIM THE PLAN."
"I'LL GO. I WANTED TO SAY GOODBYE TO HIM BEFORE I LEFT EARTH ANYWAY."
YOU MOTHER-FLARKER.
SHOOK
FLARK. YOU BETTER NOT HAVE KILLED HIM, KRAVEN.

FLARK.

FLARK.

FLARK.

FLARK.

WHAT THE FLARK?

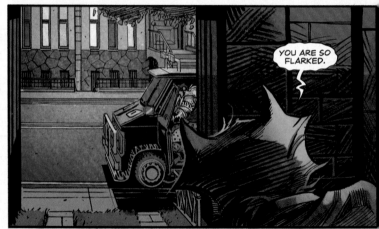

YOU ARE SO FLARKED.

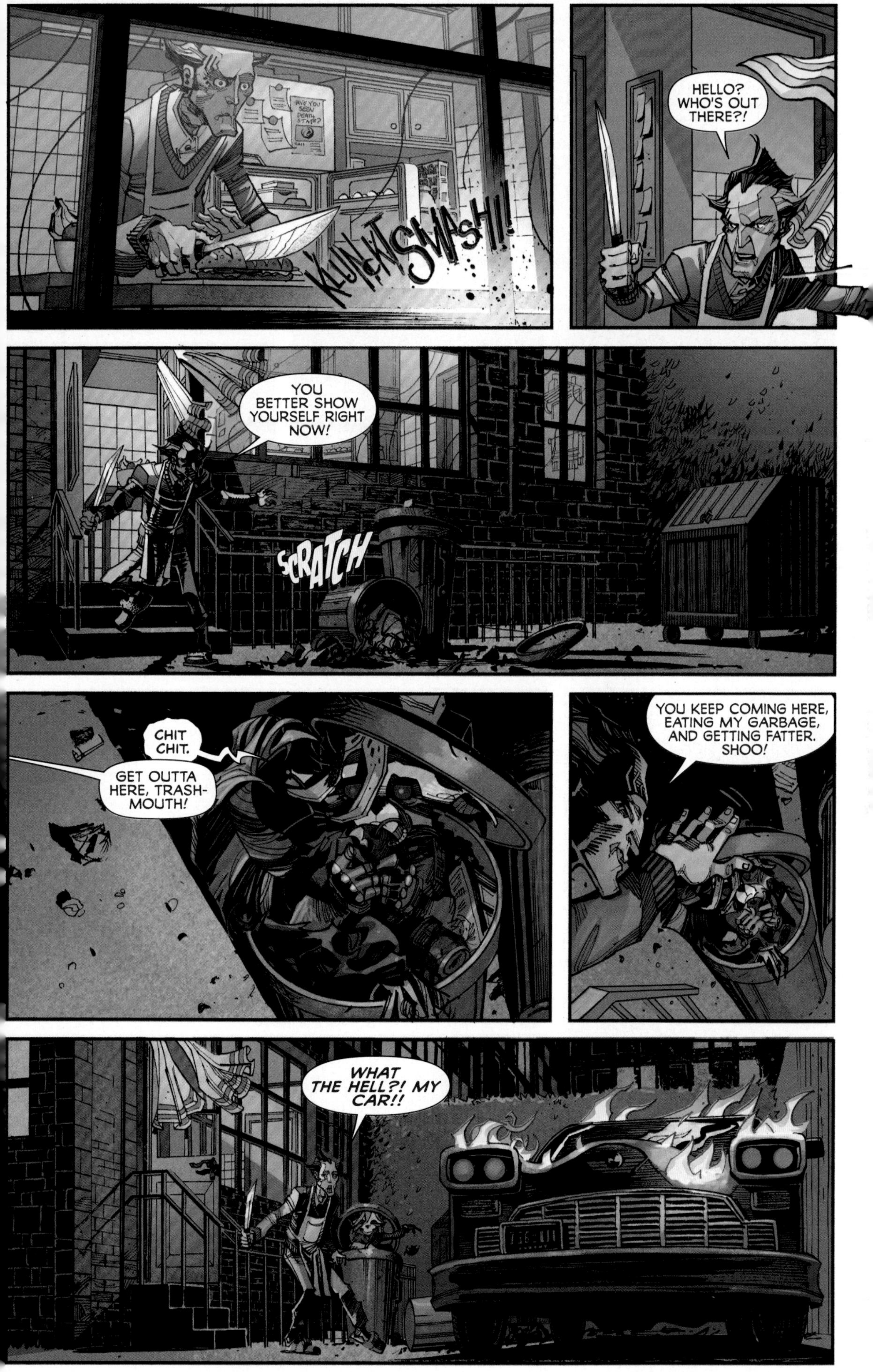
KLUNCHSMASH!!
HELLO? WHO'S OUT THERE?!
YOU BETTER SHOW YOURSELF RIGHT NOW!
SCRATCH
CHIT CHIT.
GET OUTTA HERE, TRASH-MOUTH!
YOU KEEP COMING HERE, EATING MY GARBAGE, AND GETTING FATTER. SHOO!
WHAT THE HELL?! MY CAR!!

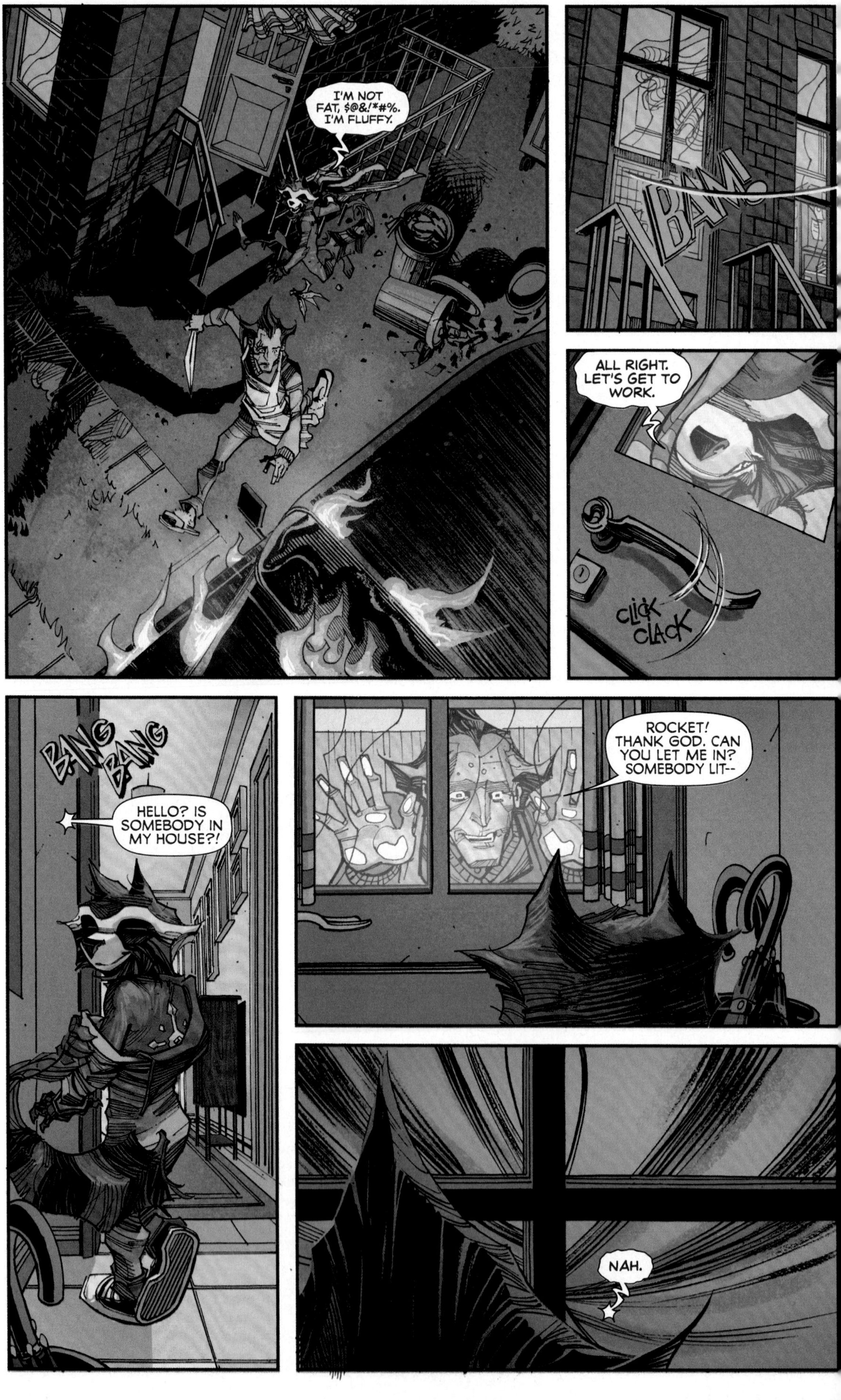
I'M NOT FAT, $@&!*#%. I'M FLUFFY.
BAM!
ALL RIGHT. LET'S GET TO WORK.
CLICK CLACK
BANG BANG
HELLO? IS SOMEBODY IN MY HOUSE?!
ROCKET! THANK GOD. CAN YOU LET ME IN? SOMEBODY LIT--
NAH.

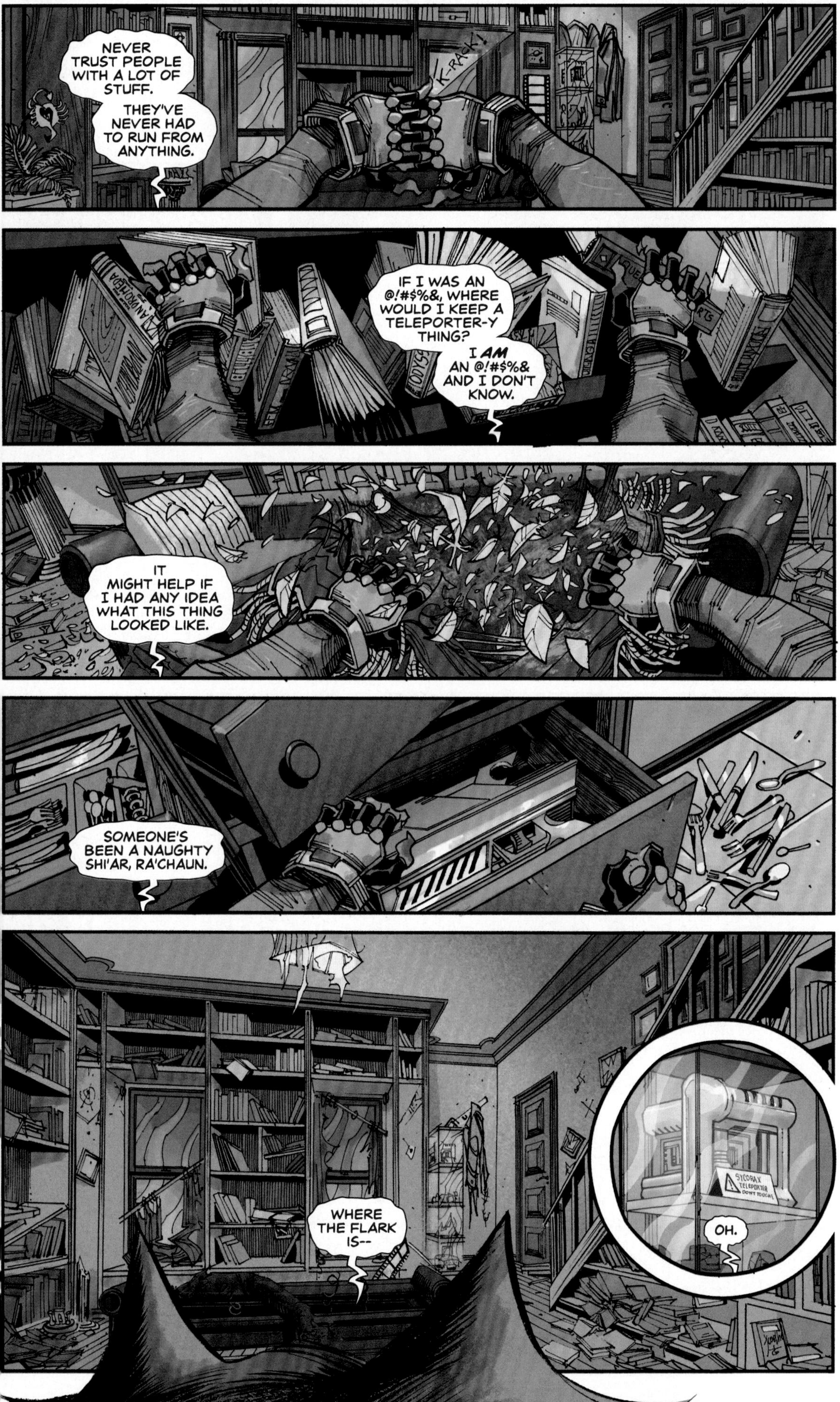
NEVER TRUST PEOPLE WITH A LOT OF STUFF.
THEY'VE NEVER HAD TO RUN FROM ANYTHING.
K-RACK!
IF I WAS AN @!#$%&, WHERE WOULD I KEEP A TELEPORTER-Y THING?
I *AM* AN @!#$%& AND I DON'T KNOW.
IT MIGHT HELP IF I HAD ANY IDEA WHAT THIS THING LOOKED LIKE.
SOMEONE'S BEEN A NAUGHTY SHI'AR, RA'CHAUN.
WHERE THE FLARK IS--
SYCORAX TELEPORTER DON'T TOUCH!
OH.

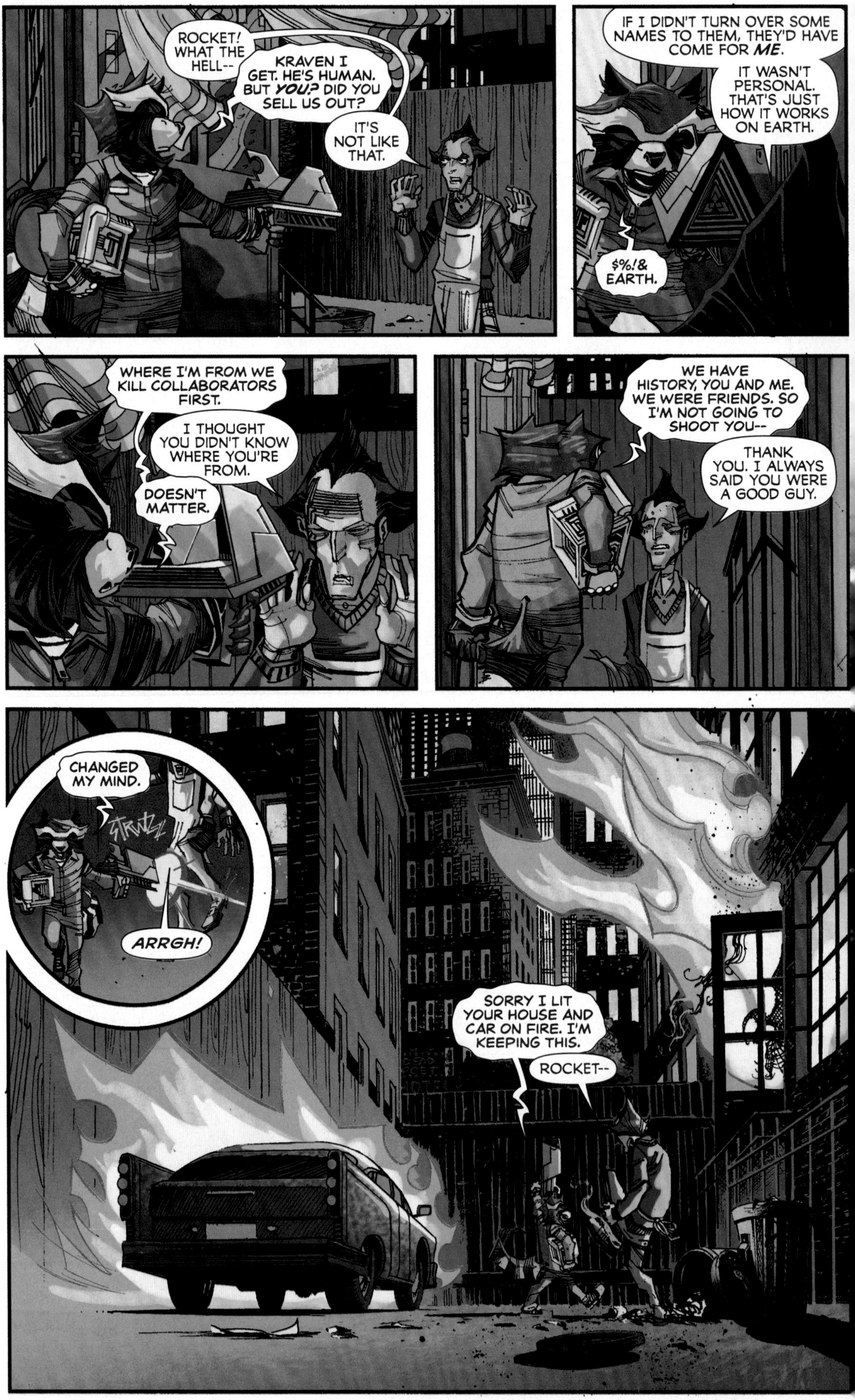
ROCKET! WHAT THE HELL--
KRAVEN I GET. HE'S HUMAN. BUT *YOU?* DID YOU SELL US OUT?
IT'S NOT LIKE THAT.
IF I DIDN'T TURN OVER SOME NAMES TO THEM, THEY'D HAVE COME FOR *ME*.
IT WASN'T PERSONAL. THAT'S JUST HOW IT WORKS ON EARTH.
$%!& EARTH.
WHERE I'M FROM WE KILL COLLABORATORS FIRST.
I THOUGHT YOU DIDN'T KNOW WHERE YOU'RE FROM.
DOESN'T MATTER.
WE HAVE HISTORY, YOU AND ME. WE WERE FRIENDS. SO I'M NOT GOING TO SHOOT YOU--
THANK YOU. I ALWAYS SAID YOU WERE A GOOD GUY.
CHANGED MY MIND.
STRVTZZ
ARRGH!
SORRY I LIT YOUR HOUSE AND CAR ON FIRE. I'M KEEPING THIS.
ROCKET--

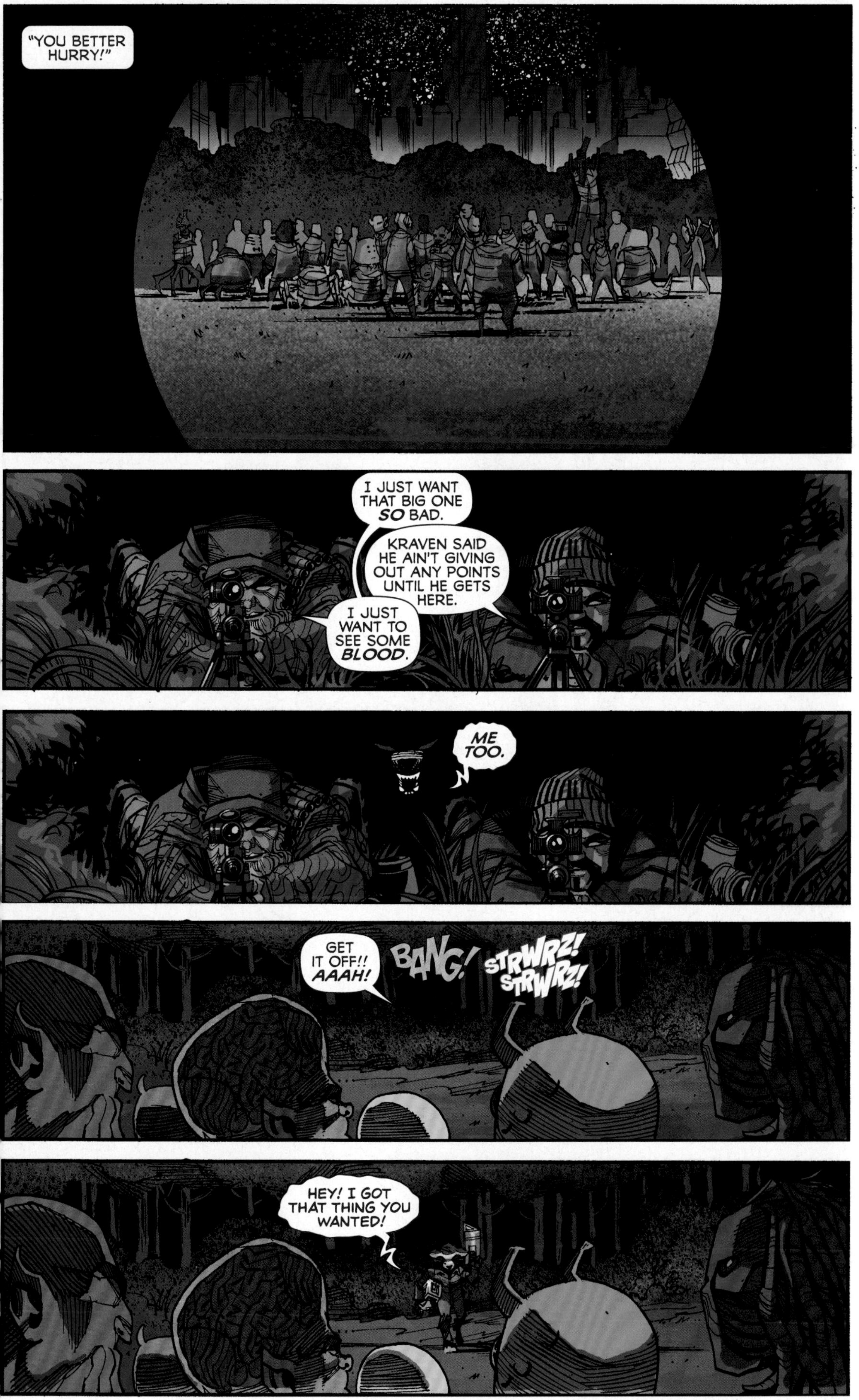
"YOU BETTER HURRY!"
I JUST WANT THAT BIG ONE SO BAD.
KRAVEN SAID HE AIN'T GIVING OUT ANY POINTS UNTIL HE GETS HERE.
I JUST WANT TO SEE SOME BLOOD.
ME TOO.
GET IT OFF!! AAAH!
BANG!
STRWRZ! STRWRZ!
HEY! I GOT THAT THING YOU WANTED!

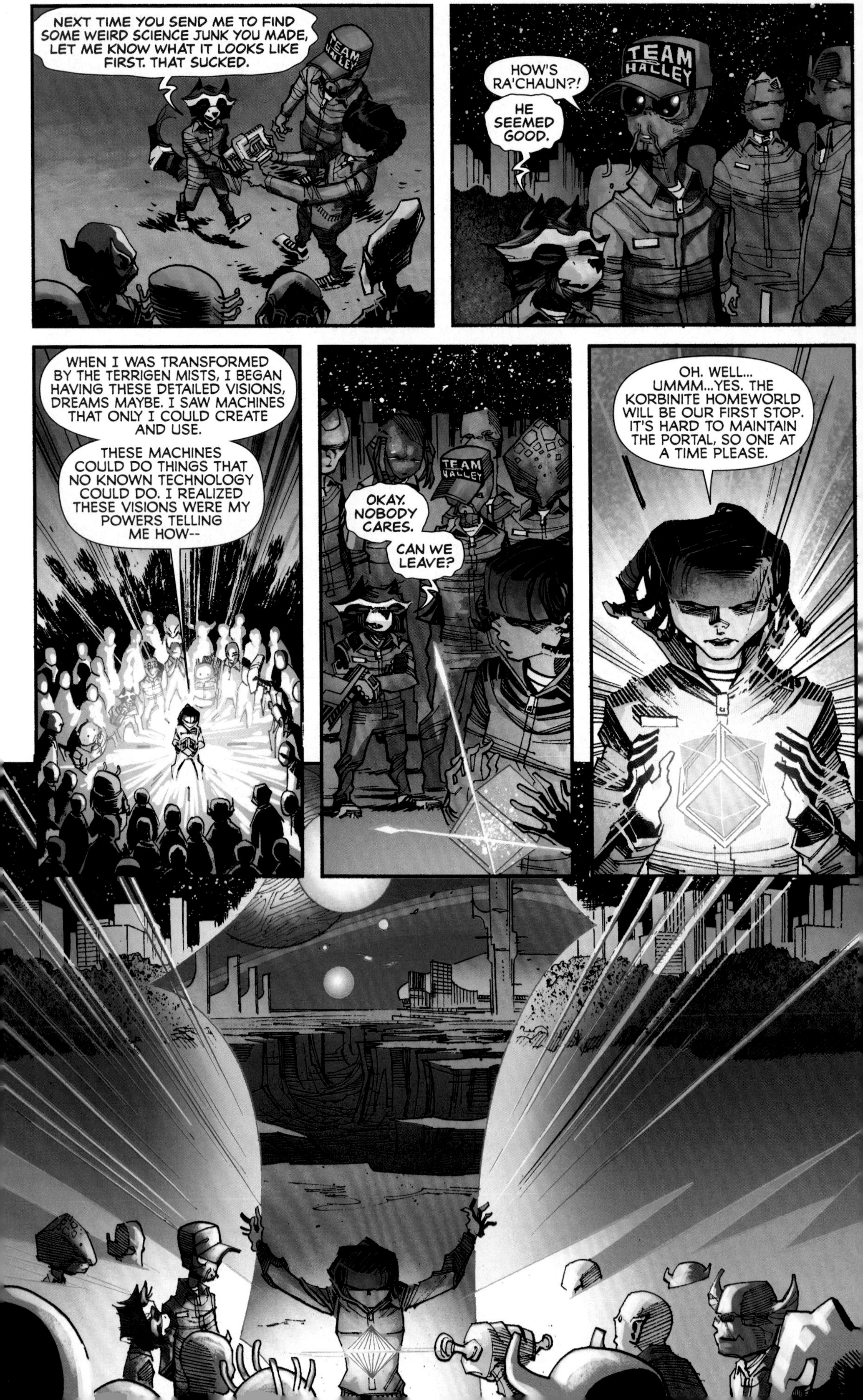
NEXT TIME YOU SEND ME TO FIND SOME WEIRD SCIENCE JUNK YOU MADE, LET ME KNOW WHAT IT LOOKS LIKE FIRST. THAT SUCKED.
TEAM HALLEY
TEAM HALLEY
HOW'S RA'CHAUN?!
HE SEEMED GOOD.
WHEN I WAS TRANSFORMED BY THE TERRIGEN MISTS, I BEGAN HAVING THESE DETAILED VISIONS, DREAMS MAYBE. I SAW MACHINES THAT ONLY I COULD CREATE AND USE.
THESE MACHINES COULD DO THINGS THAT NO KNOWN TECHNOLOGY COULD DO. I REALIZED THESE VISIONS WERE MY POWERS TELLING ME HOW--
TEAM HALLEY
OKAY. NOBODY CARES.
CAN WE LEAVE?
OH. WELL... UMMM...YES. THE KORBINITE HOMEWORLD WILL BE OUR FIRST STOP. IT'S HARD TO MAINTAIN THE PORTAL, SO ONE AT A TIME PLEASE.

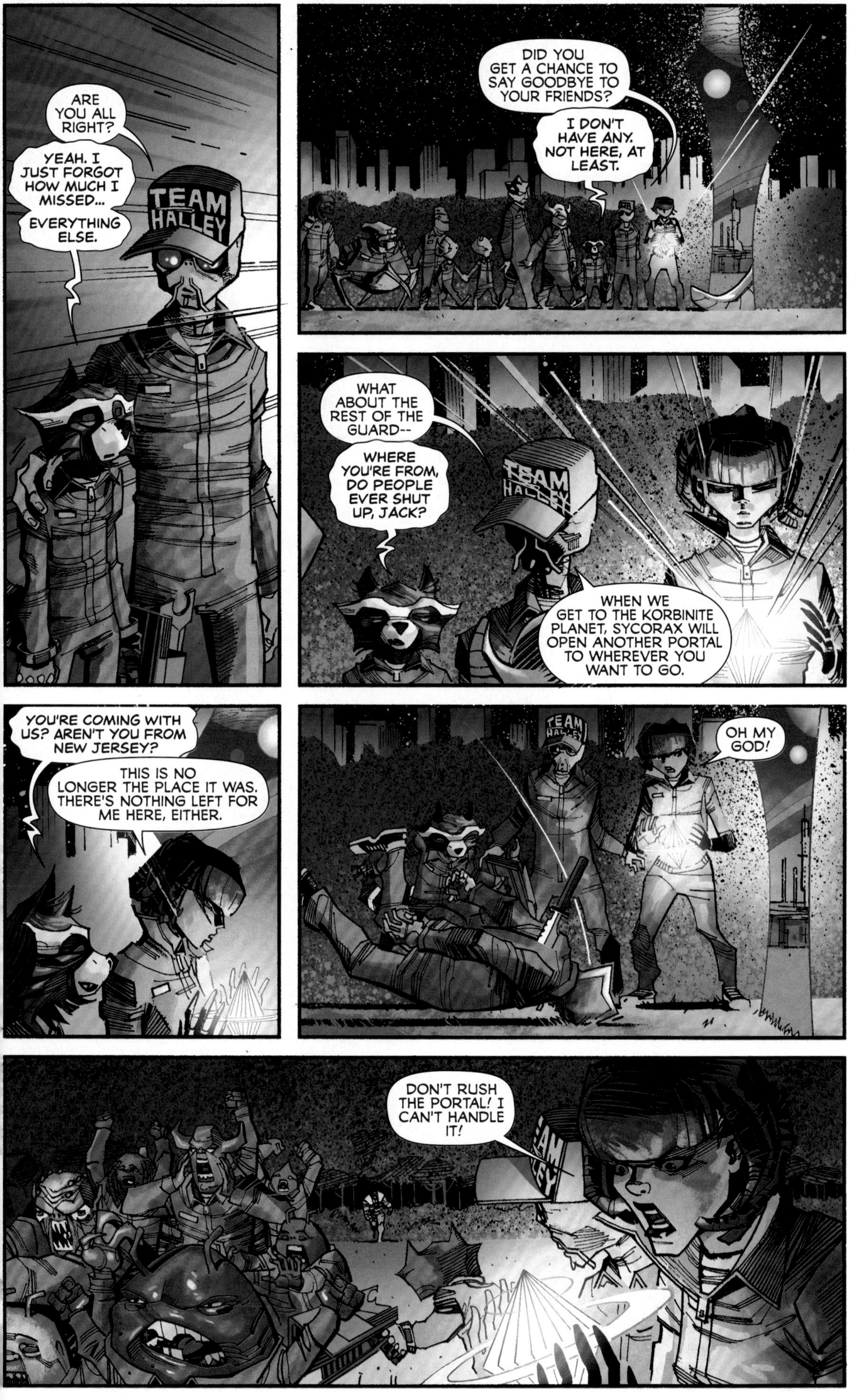
ARE YOU ALL RIGHT?
YEAH. I JUST FORGOT HOW MUCH I MISSED...
EVERYTHING ELSE.
TEAM HALLEY
DID YOU GET A CHANCE TO SAY GOODBYE TO YOUR FRIENDS?
I DON'T HAVE ANY. NOT HERE, AT LEAST.
WHAT ABOUT THE REST OF THE GUARD--
WHERE YOU'RE FROM, DO PEOPLE EVER SHUT UP, JACK?
TEAM HALLEY
WHEN WE GET TO THE KORBINITE PLANET, SYCORAX WILL OPEN ANOTHER PORTAL TO WHEREVER YOU WANT TO GO.
YOU'RE COMING WITH US? AREN'T YOU FROM NEW JERSEY?
THIS IS NO LONGER THE PLACE IT WAS. THERE'S NOTHING LEFT FOR ME HERE, EITHER.
TEAM HALLEY
OH MY GOD!
DON'T RUSH THE PORTAL! I CAN'T HANDLE IT!

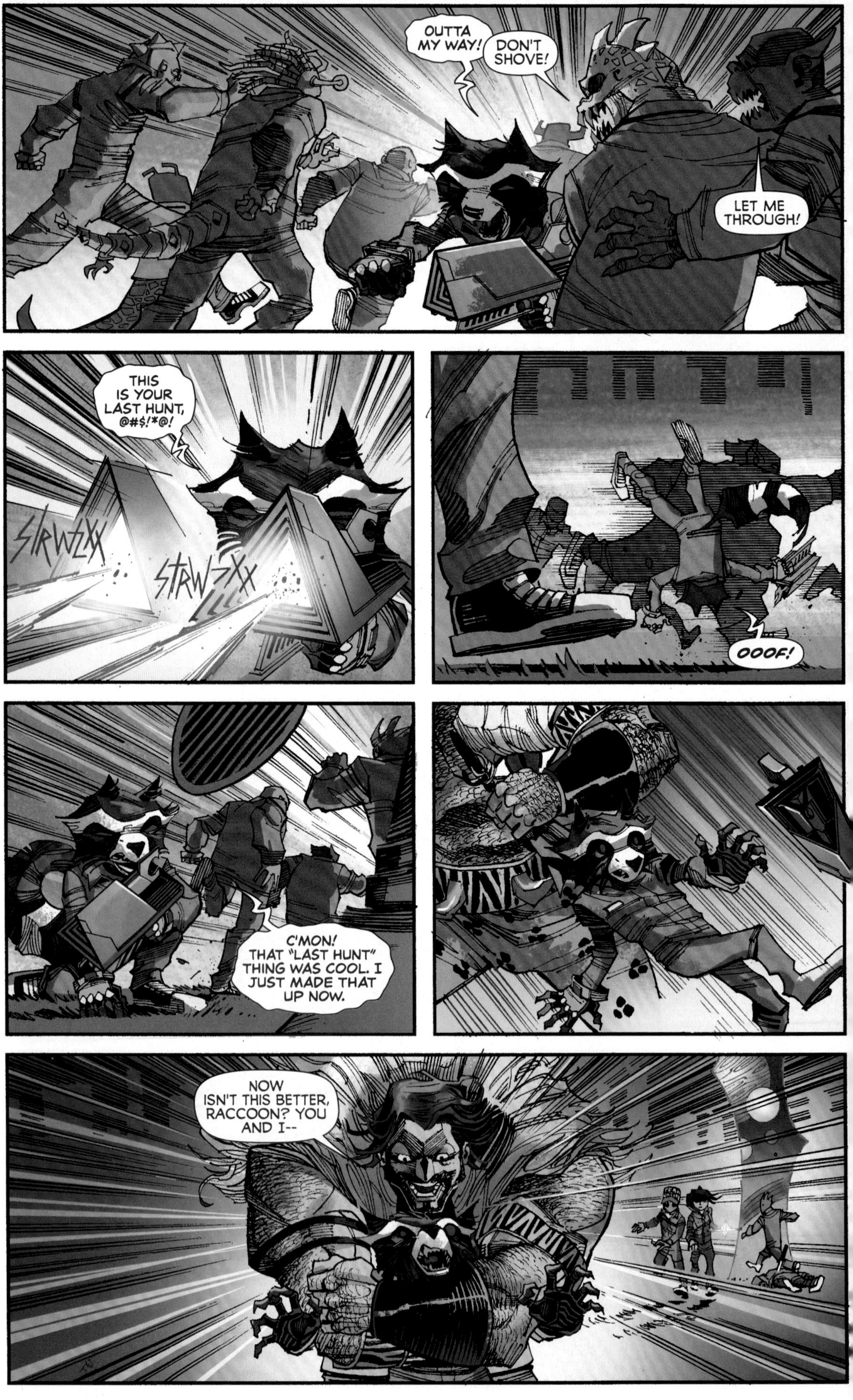

OUTTA MY WAY!
DON'T SHOVE!
LET ME THROUGH!
THIS IS YOUR LAST HUNT, @#$!*@!
STRWZXX
STRWZXX
OOOF!
C'MON! THAT "LAST HUNT" THING WAS COOL. I JUST MADE THAT UP NOW.
NOW ISN'T THIS BETTER, RACCOON? YOU AND I--

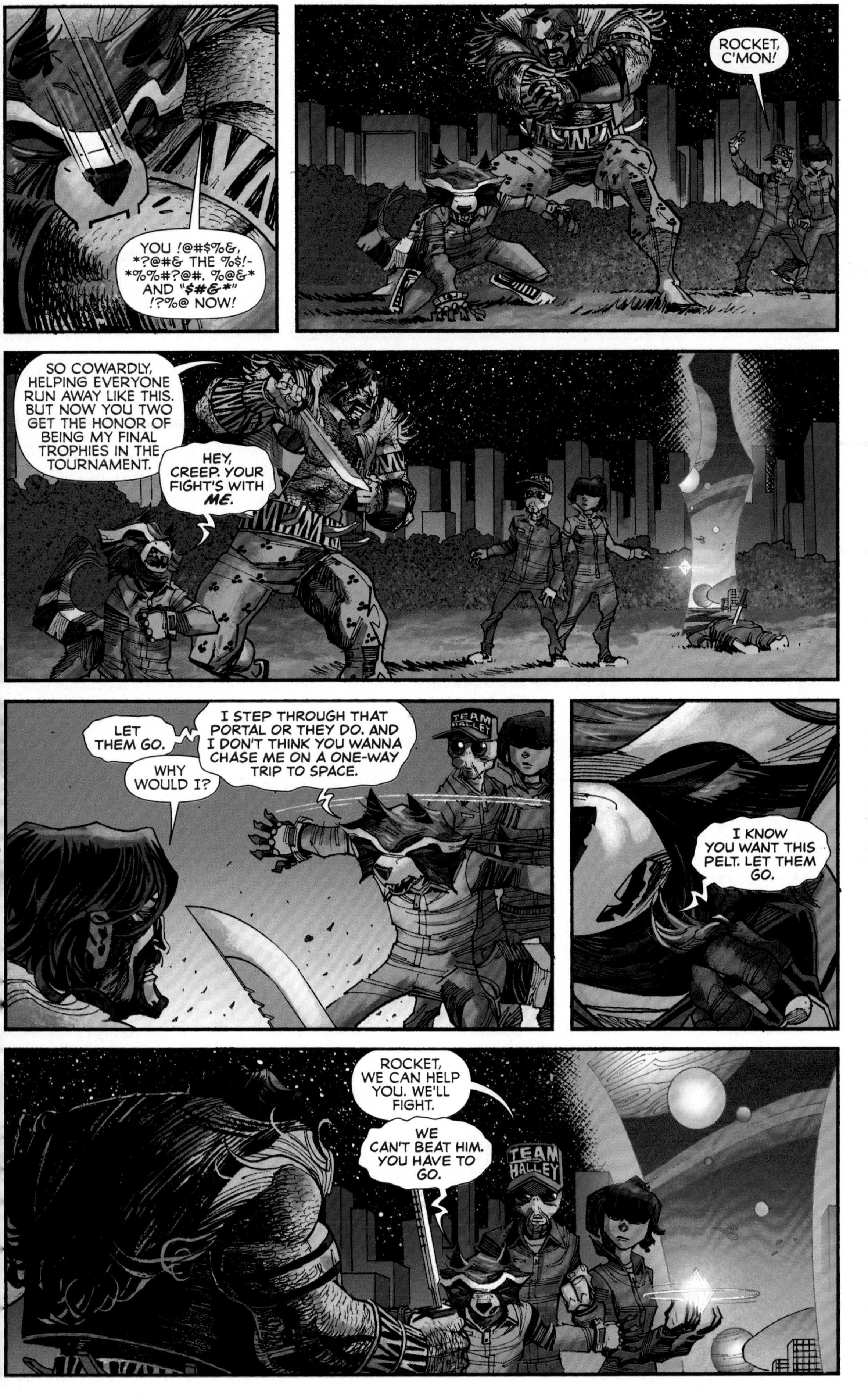

YOU !@#$%&, *?@#& THE %$!- *%%#?@#. %@&* AND "$#&*" !?%@ NOW!
ROCKET, C'MON!
SO COWARDLY, HELPING EVERYONE RUN AWAY LIKE THIS. BUT NOW YOU TWO GET THE HONOR OF BEING MY FINAL TROPHIES IN THE TOURNAMENT.
HEY, CREEP. YOUR FIGHT'S WITH ME.
LET THEM GO.
WHY WOULD I?
I STEP THROUGH THAT PORTAL OR THEY DO. AND I DON'T THINK YOU WANNA CHASE ME ON A ONE-WAY TRIP TO SPACE.
TEAM HALLEY
I KNOW YOU WANT THIS PELT. LET THEM GO.
ROCKET, WE CAN HELP YOU. WE'LL FIGHT.
WE CAN'T BEAT HIM. YOU HAVE TO GO.
TEAM HALLEY

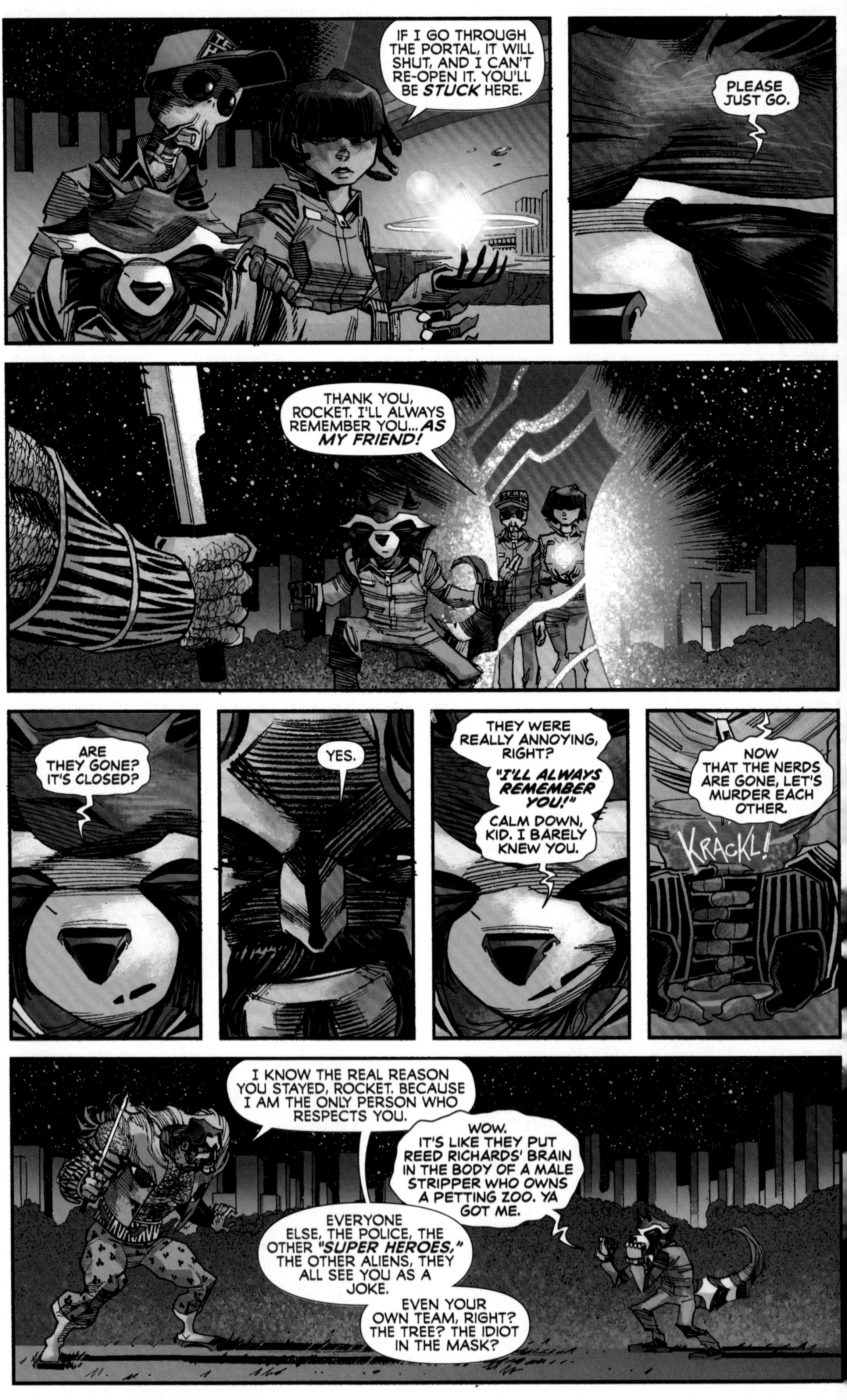
IF I GO THROUGH THE PORTAL, IT WILL SHUT, AND I CAN'T RE-OPEN IT. YOU'LL BE *STUCK* HERE.
PLEASE JUST GO.
THANK YOU, ROCKET. I'LL ALWAYS REMEMBER YOU... *AS MY FRIEND!*
ARE THEY GONE? IT'S CLOSED?
YES.
THEY WERE REALLY ANNOYING, RIGHT?
"I'LL ALWAYS REMEMBER YOU!"
CALM DOWN, KID. I BARELY KNEW YOU.
NOW THAT THE NERDS ARE GONE, LET'S MURDER EACH OTHER.
KRACKL!
I KNOW THE REAL REASON YOU STAYED, ROCKET. BECAUSE I AM THE ONLY PERSON WHO RESPECTS YOU.
WOW. IT'S LIKE THEY PUT REED RICHARDS' BRAIN IN THE BODY OF A MALE STRIPPER WHO OWNS A PETTING ZOO. YA GOT ME.
EVERYONE ELSE, THE POLICE, THE OTHER *"SUPER HEROES,"* THE OTHER ALIENS, THEY ALL SEE YOU AS A JOKE.
EVEN YOUR OWN TEAM, RIGHT? THE TREE? THE IDIOT IN THE MASK?

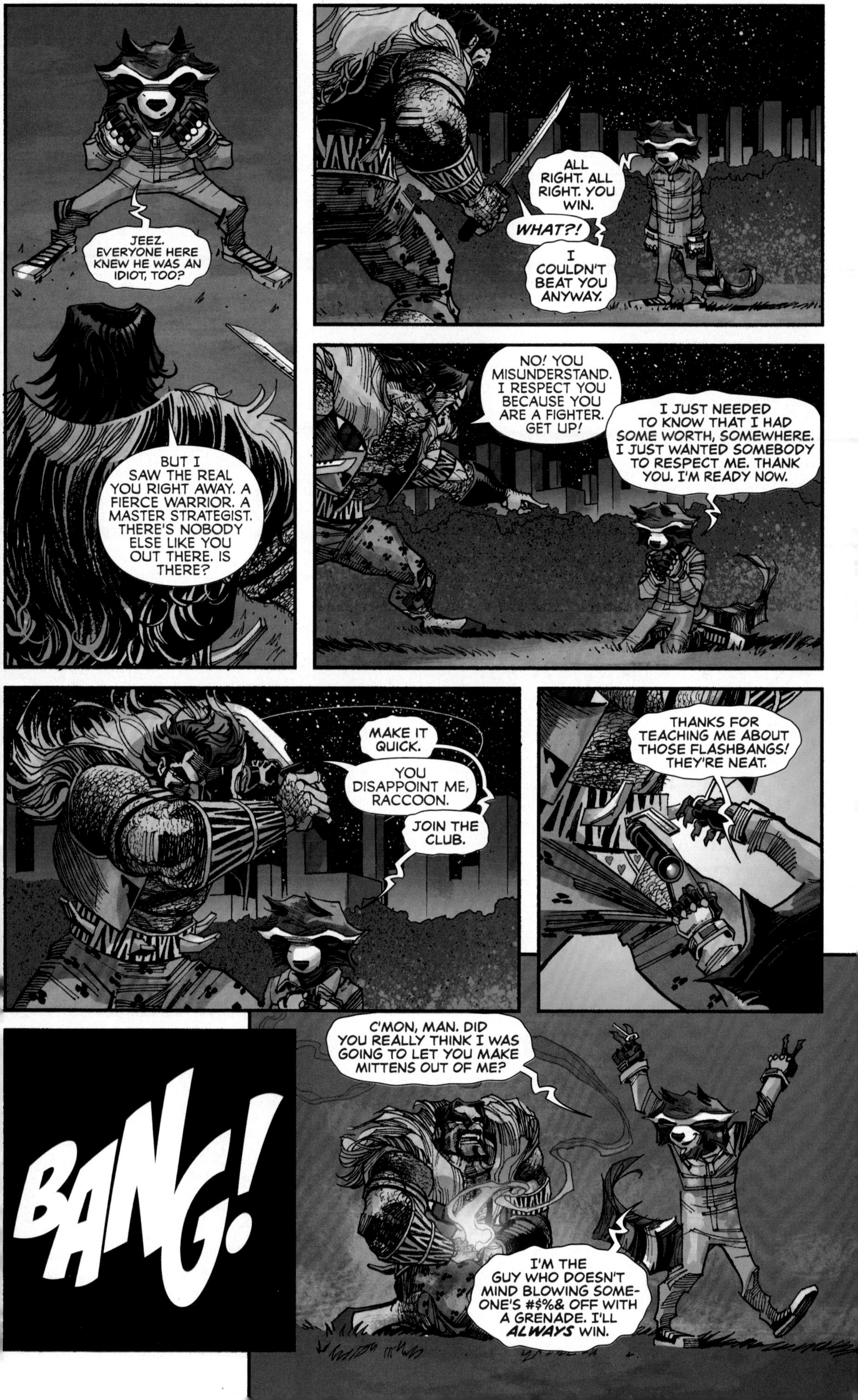
JEEZ. EVERYONE HERE KNEW HE WAS AN IDIOT, TOO?
BUT I SAW THE REAL YOU RIGHT AWAY. A FIERCE WARRIOR. A MASTER STRATEGIST. THERE'S NOBODY ELSE LIKE YOU OUT THERE. IS THERE?
ALL RIGHT. ALL RIGHT. YOU WIN.
WHAT?!
I COULDN'T BEAT YOU ANYWAY.
NO! YOU MISUNDERSTAND. I RESPECT YOU BECAUSE YOU ARE A FIGHTER. GET UP!
I JUST NEEDED TO KNOW THAT I HAD SOME WORTH, SOMEWHERE. I JUST WANTED SOMEBODY TO RESPECT ME. THANK YOU. I'M READY NOW.
MAKE IT QUICK.
YOU DISAPPOINT ME, RACCOON.
JOIN THE CLUB.
THANKS FOR TEACHING ME ABOUT THOSE FLASHBANGS! THEY'RE NEAT.
BANG!
C'MON, MAN. DID YOU REALLY THINK I WAS GOING TO LET YOU MAKE MITTENS OUT OF ME?
I'M THE GUY WHO DOESN'T MIND BLOWING SOME-ONE'S #$%& OFF WITH A GRENADE. I'LL ALWAYS WIN.

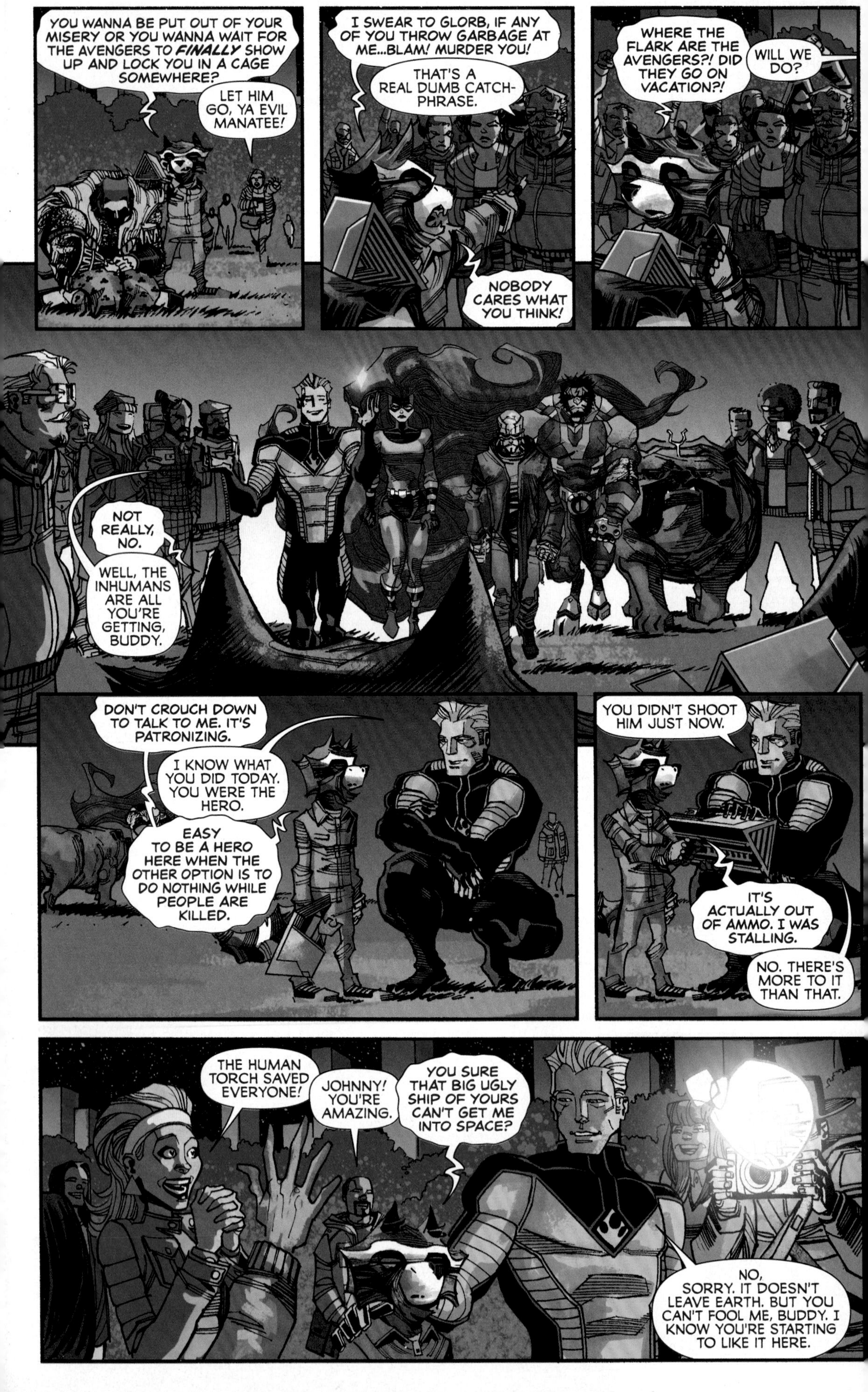
YOU WANNA BE PUT OUT OF YOUR MISERY OR YOU WANNA WAIT FOR THE AVENGERS TO *FINALLY* SHOW UP AND LOCK YOU IN A CAGE SOMEWHERE?
LET HIM GO, YA EVIL MANATEE!
I SWEAR TO GLORB, IF ANY OF YOU THROW GARBAGE AT ME...BLAM! MURDER YOU!
THAT'S A REAL DUMB CATCH-PHRASE.
NOBODY CARES WHAT YOU THINK!
WHERE THE FLARK ARE THE AVENGERS?! DID THEY GO ON VACATION?!
WILL WE DO?
NOT REALLY, NO.
WELL, THE INHUMANS ARE ALL YOU'RE GETTING, BUDDY.
DON'T CROUCH DOWN TO TALK TO ME. IT'S PATRONIZING.
I KNOW WHAT YOU DID TODAY. YOU WERE THE HERO.
EASY TO BE A HERO HERE WHEN THE OTHER OPTION IS TO DO NOTHING WHILE PEOPLE ARE KILLED.
YOU DIDN'T SHOOT HIM JUST NOW.
IT'S ACTUALLY OUT OF AMMO. I WAS STALLING.
NO. THERE'S MORE TO IT THAN THAT.
THE HUMAN TORCH SAVED EVERYONE!
JOHNNY! YOU'RE AMAZING.
YOU SURE THAT BIG UGLY SHIP OF YOURS CAN'T GET ME INTO SPACE?
NO, SORRY. IT DOESN'T LEAVE EARTH. BUT YOU CAN'T FOOL ME, BUDDY. I KNOW YOU'RE STARTING TO LIKE IT HERE.

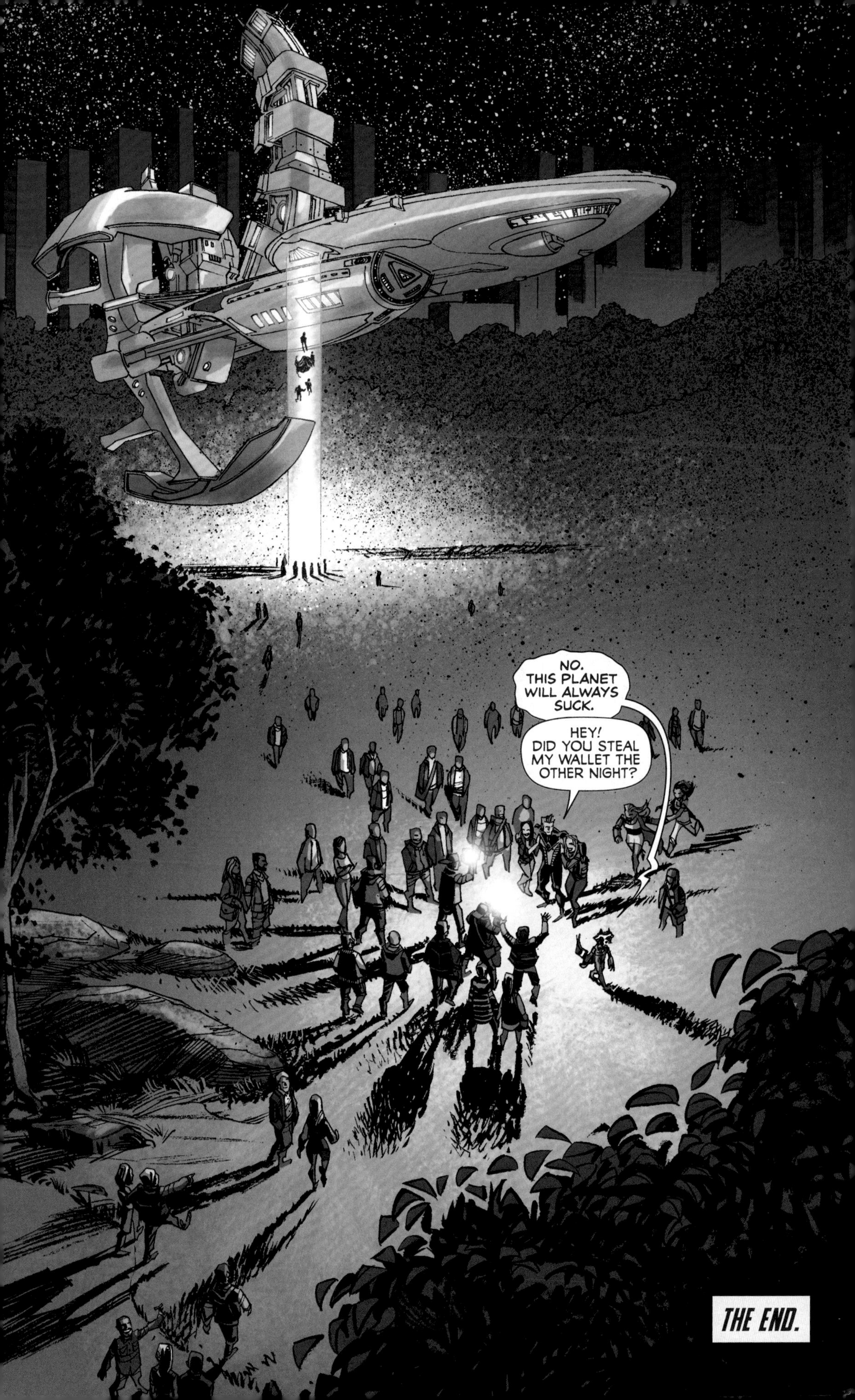
NO. THIS PLANET WILL ALWAYS SUCK.
HEY! DID YOU STEAL MY WALLET THE OTHER NIGHT?
THE END.

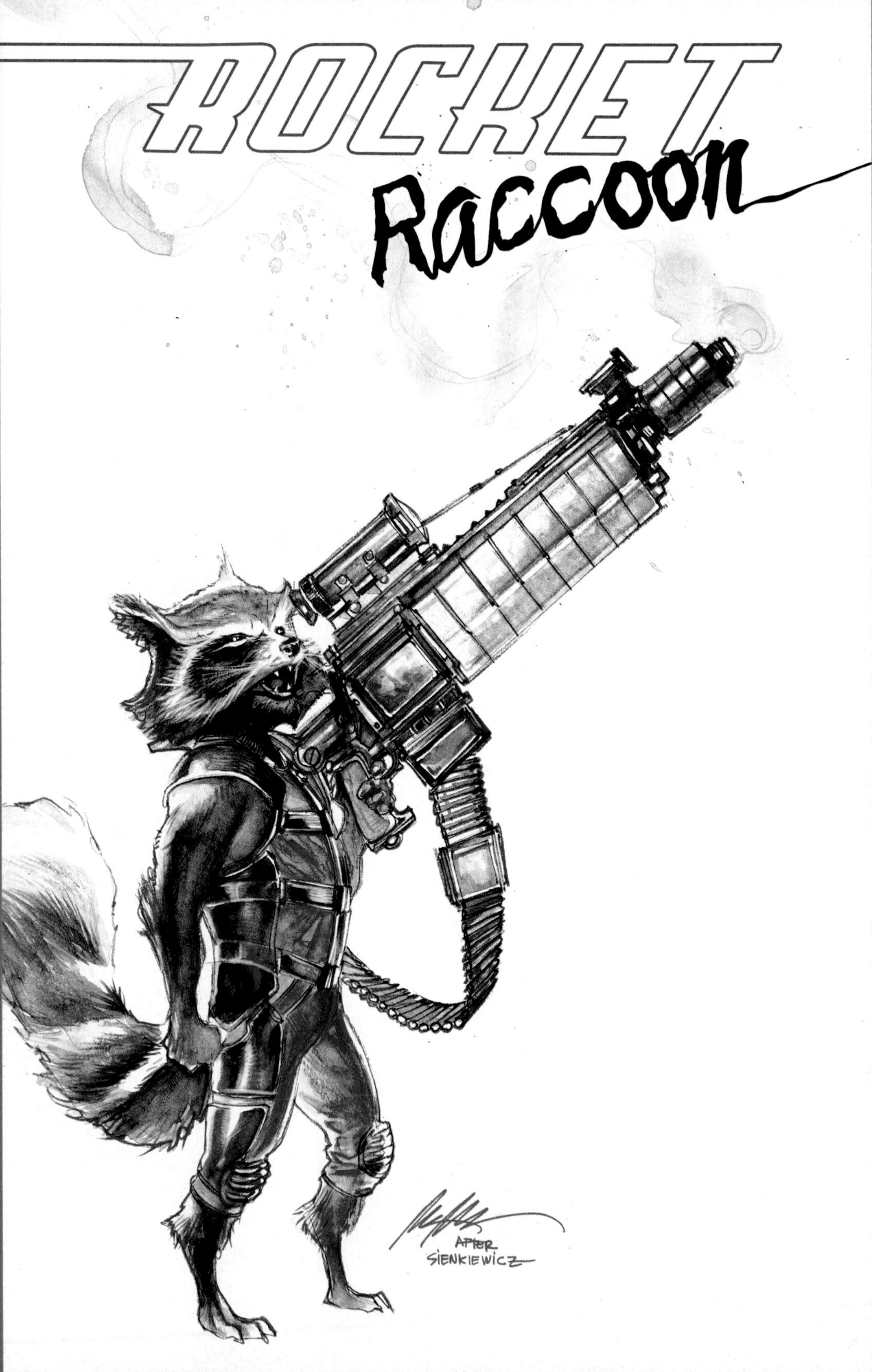
ROCKET
Raccoon
AFTER
SIENKIEWICZ

#1 VARIANT BY RAFAEL ALBUQUERQUE

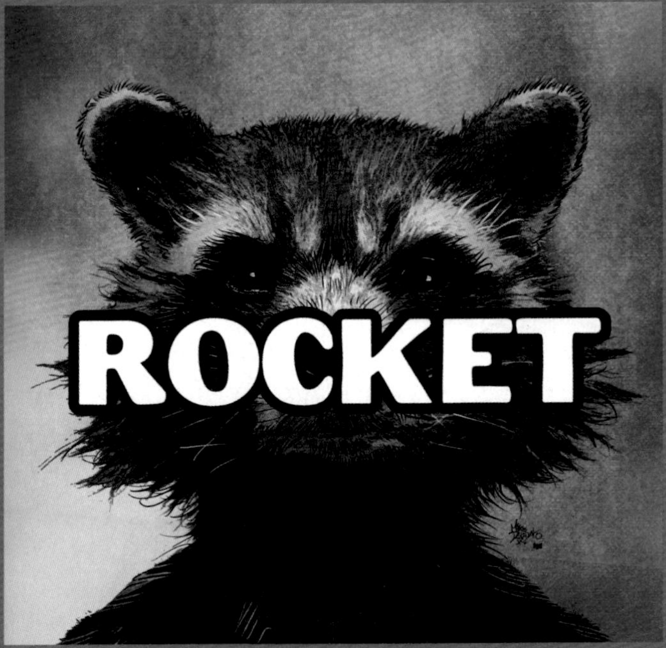
ROCKET

#1 HIP-HOP VARIANT BY
MIKE DEODATO JR.
& FRANK D'ARMATA

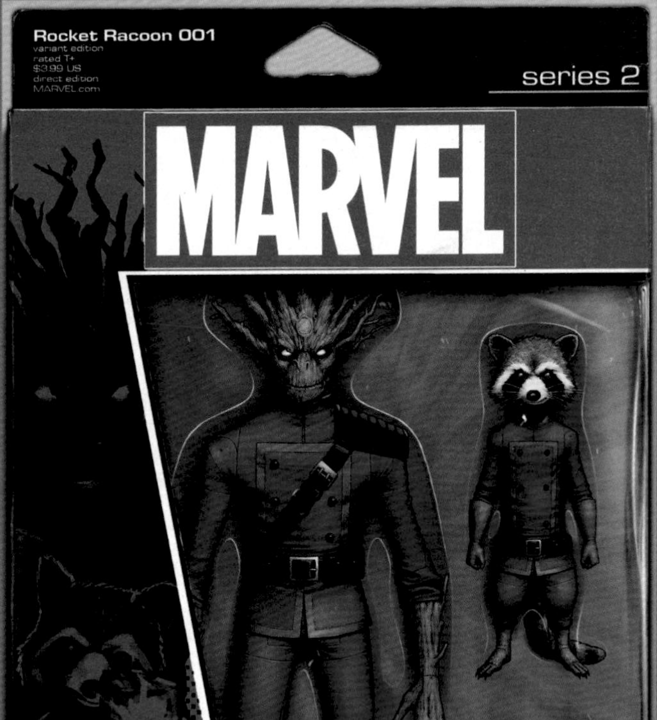
Rocket Racoon 001
variant edition
rated T+
$3.99 US
direct edition
MARVEL.com
series 2
MARVEL
ROCKET RACCOON
ROCKET & GROOT
classic

#1 ACTION FIGURE VARIANT BY
JOHN TYLER CHRISTOPHER

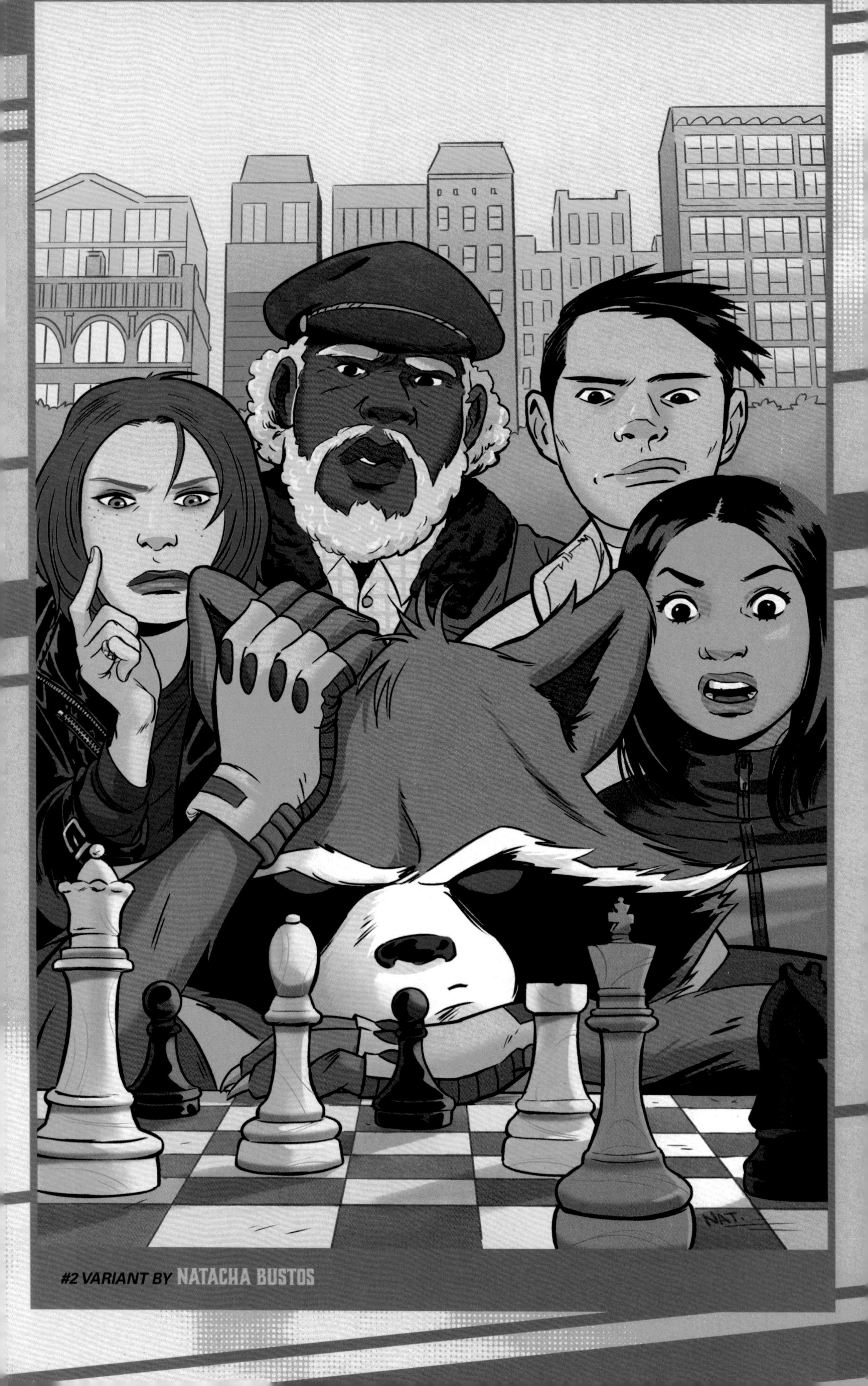
NAT.

#2 VARIANT BY NATACHA BUSTOS